Revise BTEC National Business Revision
ISBN 9781292150123
IMPORTANT ASSESSMENT UPDA

As a result of feedback from the Department for Education, there have been some updates to the Set Tasks for **Units 2, 6 and 7 of BTEC Nationals in Business**.

These updates mean there are now some changes required to this book. You need to be aware of these when using this book for revision.

PLEASE DO NOT USE PAGES 34–45 (Unit 2 skills), PAGES 119–127 (Unit 6 skills), OR PAGES 162–173 (Unit 7 skills) OF THIS BOOK

We have provided updated versions of these pages for Units 2, 6 and 7, along with updated answers, on the following website: www.pearsonfe.co.uk/BTECchanges

Changes to assessment of Unit 2: Developing a Marketing Campaign
You will now be given additional task information in **Part B** rather than Part A.
Your Part A notes to take into Part B (your supervised assessment period):   • **should** include facts and figures relating to organisations, such as the products they offer and the ways they use the marketing mix in their promotional campaigns   • should **not** include any analysis, evaluation or promotional plans.
You must complete your Part B (supervised assessment) task on the computer.
Changes to assessment of Unit 6: Principles of Management
You will now have a period of **1 week** (rather than 2 weeks) in which to complete the six hours allocated to Part A, in advance of Part B (your supervised assessment period).
You are **not** allowed to take any notes into Part B (your supervised assessment period).
Change to assessment of Unit 7: Business Decision Making
You will be asked to produce responses using appropriate business formats, as listed in H2 of the essential content in the Specification.

endorsed for
BTEC

REVISE BTEC NATIONAL
Business

REVISION GUIDE

Series Consultant: Harry Smith

Authors: Steve Jakubowski, Jon Sutherland and Diane Sutherland

A note from the publisher

In order to ensure that this resource offers high-quality support for the associated Pearson qualification, it has been through a review process by the awarding body. This process confirms that this resource fully covers the teaching and learning content of the specification or part of a specification at which it is aimed. It also confirms that it demonstrates an appropriate balance between the development of subject skills, knowledge and understanding, in addition to preparation for assessment.

Endorsement does not cover any guidance on assessment activities or processes (e.g. practice questions or advice on how to answer assessment questions), included in the resource nor does it prescribe any particular approach to the teaching or delivery of a related course.

While the publishers have made every attempt to ensure that advice on the qualification and its assessment

is accurate, the official specification and associated assessment guidance materials are the only authoritative source of information and should always be referred to for definitive guidance.

Pearson examiners have not contributed to any sections in this resource relevant to examination papers for which they had prior responsibility.

Examiners will not use endorsed resources as a source of material for any assessment set by Pearson.

Endorsement of a resource does not mean that the resource is required to achieve this Pearson qualification, nor does it mean that it is the only suitable material available to support the qualification, and any resource lists produced by the awarding body shall include this and other appropriate resources.

For the full range of Pearson revision titles across KS2, KS3, GCSE, Functional Skills, AS/A Level and BTEC visit:
www.pearsonschools.co.uk/revise

Pearson

Published by Pearson Education Limited, 80 Strand, London, WC2R 0RL.

www.pearsonschoolsandfecolleges.co.uk

Copies of official specifications for all Edexcel qualifications may be found on the website: www.edexcel.com

Text © Pearson Education Limited 2016
Typeset and illustrated by Kamae Design
Produced by Out of House Publishing
Cover illustration by Miriam Sturdee

The rights of Steve Jakubowski, Jon Sutherland and Diane Sutherland to be identified as authors of this work have been asserted by them in accordance with the Copyright, Designs and Patents Act 1988.
First published 2016

19 18 17
10 9 8 7 6 5 4 3 2

British Library Cataloguing in Publication Data
A catalogue record for this book is available from the British Library

ISBN 978 1 292 15012 3

Acknowledgements

We are grateful to the following for permission to reproduce copyright material:

Figures

Figure on page 71 from Jon and Diane Sutherland

Logos

Logo on page 115 from https://www.investorsinpeople.com/; Logo on page 115 from http://www.iso.org/; Logo on page 115 from http://www.bsigroup.com/, Permission to reproduce extracts from British Standards is granted by BSI Standards Limited (BSI). No other use of this material is permitted. British Standards can be obtained in PDF or hard copy formats from the BSI online shop: www.bsigroup.com/Shop

Tables

Table on page 58 adapted from http://www.financialombudsman.org.uk/publications/ar15/about.html#a3

Text

Extract on page 42 adapted from http://www.britishsoftdrinks.com/; Text on page 115 from http://www.bsigroup.com/, Permission to reproduce extracts from British Standards is granted by BSI Standards Limited (BSI). No other use of this material is permitted. British Standards can be obtained in PDF or hard copy formats from the BSI online shop: www.bsigroup.com/Shop; Text on page 115 adapted from https://www.investorsinpeople.com/; Text on page 115, page 145 adapted from http://www.iso.org/; Extract on page 129 from http://www.nisaretail.com/

The publisher would like to thank the following for their kind permission to reproduce their photographs:

(Key: b-bottom; c-centre; l-left; r-right; t-top)

Alamy Images: Art Directors & Trip 1, Chris Dorney 6l, david hancock 7, Hero Images Inc 46, Ian Dagnall Commercial Collection 20b, macana 59, Peter Alvey 4t, Peter Scholey 57, Simon Rawles 33, YAY Media AS 3; **BSI:** 115t; **Courtesy of Nestle Waters:** 6b; **Dulux:** 6r; **Fotolia.com:** 3d_generator 29, baranq 27t, gemenacom 143, Olly 20t, ty 27b; **Getty Images:** Bloomberg 2, macrovector 32, Patrick Eagar / Popperfoto 23, Tim Whitby / Stringer 24r, ulsteinbild 106, Zero Creatives 24l; **Investors in People:** 115b; **ISO:** 115c; **Nisa Retail Limited:** 129; **Reproduced with kind permission of Unilever PLC and group companies:** 31; **Shutterstock.com:** gcpics 4b, guruXOX 47, Oleksiy Mark 82, Paul Prescott 8r, Thomas Koch 8l, Wavebreakmedia 13, 112; **Tesco Stores Ltd:** 9, 11; **William Reed Business Media Ltd:** 12

All other images © Pearson Education

Introduction

Which units should you revise?

This Revision Guide has been designed to support you in preparing for the externally assessed units of your course. Remember that you won't necessarily be studying all the units included here – it will depend on the qualification you are taking.

BTEC National Qualification	Externally assessed units
Certificate	Unit 2 Developing a Marketing Campaign
Extended Certificate Foundation Diploma	Unit 2 Developing a Marketing Campaign Unit 3 Personal and Business Finance
Diploma	Unit 2 Developing a Marketing Campaign Unit 3 Personal and Business Finance Unit 6 Principles of Management
Extended Diploma	Unit 2 Developing a Marketing Campaign Unit 3 Personal and Business Finance Unit 6 Principles of Management Unit 7 Business Decision Making

Your Revision Guide

Each unit in this Revision Guide contains two types of pages, shown below.

Content pages help you revise the essential content you need to know for each unit.

Skills pages help you prepare for your exam or assessed task. Skills pages have a coloured edge and are shaded in the table of contents.

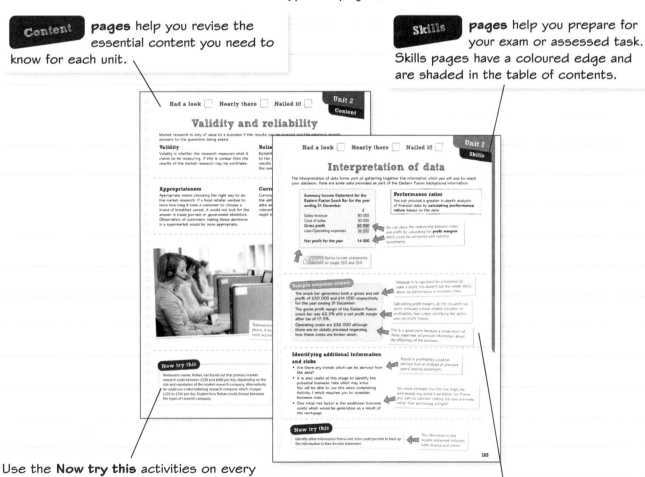

Use the **Now try this** activities on every page to help you test your knowledge and practise the relevant skills.

Look out for the **example student responses** to exam questions or set tasks on the skills pages. Post-its will explain their strengths and weaknesses.

Contents

A small bit of small print
Pearson publishes Sample Assessment Material and the Specification on its website. This is the official content and this book should be used in conjunction with it. The questions in *Now try this* have been written to help you test your knowledge and skills. Remember: the real assessment may not look like this.

Purposes of marketing

You need to understand how marketing helps businesses to develop and sell the goods and services that customers want.

Anticipate demand
Marketing aims to work out what customers might want in the future. Market research is used to ask customers questions about products and services. This helps to predict customers' needs and wants.

Recognise demand
Market research can help identify customer needs and wants that are not being met at the moment, and the sort of product or service that might fulfil these needs and wants.

> **Principles and purposes of marketing**

Stimulate demand
Businesses often use advertising and social media to persuade customers that they really want or need a product or service.

Satisfy demand
Businesses carry out market research to find out what customers think of their products and services so that they can adapt and improve them. They also use marketing to make sure customers know where they can buy a product or service.

Aspects of marketing
The UK male grooming market is expected to be worth over £1 billion by 2018. The most popular skincare products are shaving treatments, moisturisers, facial cleansers, shower gels and deodorants, and face exfoliators. Procter & Gamble UK Ltd anticipated the growth in the market and has around 31 per cent value share.

Cosmetic companies stimulate demand through product trials where samples of new products are often given away with magazines or in-store.

Now try this

Identify the starting point for a business. Where should a business begin? Explain whether it should anticipate, recognise, stimulate or satisfy demand first.

 Not all businesses are the same. New businesses might have different priorities.

Marketing aims and objectives 1

A business will have a range of marketing aims and objectives to help it grow or increase turnover and profitability. On this page and the next, you will revise the six main marketing aims and objectives.

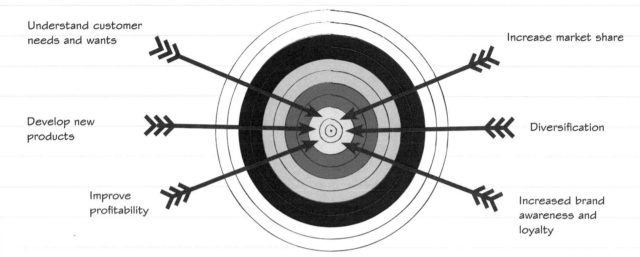

Understand customer needs and wants

Develop new products

Improve profitability

Increase market share

Diversification

Increased brand awareness and loyalty

What are aims and objectives?

An **objective** is usually a simple, short-term goal.

An **aim** is a more complicated, longer-term goal.

Understand customer needs and wants

As part of its marketing role, a business needs to identify its typical customer. Understanding customer behaviour enables a business to operate and develop to serve its customers.

Supermarkets and other large retailers offer online shopping, home delivery and customer collection. They often have 24-hour opening. This matches customer needs and wants.

Develop new products

When customers' needs and demands are identified the business may find that a new product or service is required. Being the first to offer a product or service can mean massive sales and profits.

Identifying market needs

Apple constantly develops new products and services. Being innovative gives the company a huge advantage over its competitors.

Improve profitability

More sales can mean more profit. Greater profits can also be made by setting the selling price much higher than the cost of making the product or delivering the service. Marketing can help to convince customers that a higher price means a better quality product.

Premium products

Branded petrol and diesel such as Shell or BP is usually more expensive than unbranded fuel from Asda, Tesco or Morrisons. The branded fuel is sold as a premium product.

Now try this

Describe why being innovative is so important for a business.

 Think about why it's better for a business to be first to sell the product in the market place.

Marketing aims and objectives 2

🔗 **Links** Look at the marketing aims and objectives on page 2 as well.

Increase market share

All businesses have competitors and must fight for their share of the sales. Increasing market share even by less than 1 per cent can mean a huge leap in sales and profits.

Smart marketing

Around 1 billion smartphones were sold worldwide in 2015. Samsung has a 21 per cent market share compared to Apple with 14 per cent. Samsung sold 210 million smartphones.

If Samsung's market share increased by 1 per cent, it would sell another 10 million smartphones.

Diversification

A business does not want to rely on sales of one product in one market. Demand could fall; competitors might take their market share. Offering different products and services in different markets is a good way to make sure that the business survives and continues to grow.

Clothing designers such as Diesel sell a wide range of fashions in different markets. They have also diversified to sell perfume.

Increased brand awareness and loyalty

A brand is a product or service which has a recognisable name and packaging. Marketing aims to ensure that customers instantly recognise the brand and choose to buy it rather than a competitor's brand.

What is brand loyalty?

Brand loyalty is a measure of how likely a customer is to buy a brand compared to competing brands. High loyalty means continued and regular sales.

Most of the major supermarket chains have customer loyalty cards. They reward customers for their brand loyalty by offering deals and discounts.

Now try this

An established car sales business wants to grow and increase its turnover and profitability. Identify four possible ways of achieving these aims and objectives.

 Think about each of the six marketing aims and objectives and match them to what the business wants to achieve.

Mass and niche markets

A mass market product or service appeals to most types of customer. A niche product or service aims to target a specific type of customer.

Mass market

A mass market is a large group of consumers with a wide range of different characteristics. Many products and services are aimed at mass markets. Products such as milk, bread or toothpaste are targeted at very large groups of consumers. In most cases, people want the same thing: to fulfil a basic need.

McDonald's in the UK

The UK burger market was worth £3.08 billion in 2015. By 2019 it is forecast to reach £3.3 billion. McDonald's and Burger King are the market leaders and they cater for the mass market.

McDonald's has 1200 restaurants and employs around 97 000 staff. It was the first real fast-food burger business in the UK.

Burgers are targeted at the mass market.

Niche market

Niche markets are smaller segments of the market. Consumers in niche markets want something different from the mainstream and are not attracted to mass market products. They expect to pay a higher price. Niche markets attract specialist businesses that have an expertise in providing particular products.

Premium burgers

In 2013, the US burger chain Five Guys opened in London. Now it has 30 restaurants across the UK and employs 1000 people.

It sells a niche market product: the premium burger. Other businesses have also spotted a growing niche market that does not want mass-produced burgers.

Premium-quality burgers are targeted at niche markets.

Now try this

A premium burger restaurant is about to open in your area. What competition is it likely to face?

Consider all of the potential competitors for similar customers.

Market segmentation

Businesses segment their markets based on a range of consumer characteristics. This allows them to target consumers within these segments.

 Age
Different age groups have different needs and spending patterns. Goods and services may be targeted at specific age groups.

 Gender
Men and women have different tastes and needs, and have different spending patterns.

 Income
This is a measure of how much a consumer has available to spend. Those with higher incomes have different spending patterns from those on lower incomes.

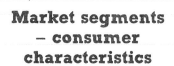 **Market segments – consumer characteristics**

 Ethnic, cultural and religious background
These influence the choice of food, fashion, preferences and other factors that affect spending behaviour.

 Buying habits
This is a measure of customer loyalty and the frequency of purchasing. Some consumers are very loyal to a brand and will buy it regardless of the price. Others will shop around for the lowest price, or make their decision based on quality or on convenience.

 Socio-economic groups
This method categorises consumers according to the occupation of the 'head of the household', usually the highest-earning person in the home. Occupation on its own is no longer considered to be a good method of segmenting consumers.

How businesses target different market segments

☑ Teenage smartphone users look for value and style. They make choices based on what they read on social media. Samsung and Abercrombie & Fitch focus on social media marketing. (age)

☑ Some retail outlets stock products aimed specifically at women, particularly in fashion. Most clothing stores have larger sections for women's wear than men's. (gender)

☑ Some supermarket chains are aimed at lower-income consumers, e.g. Aldi, while others target higher-income customers, e.g. Waitrose. (income)

☑ Halal food producers cater for specific dietary requirements. (ethnic, cultural, religious)

 Now try this

Sandi wants to open a sandwich shop in the centre of a busy town. She will make the sandwiches to order with top-quality ingredients and home-baked bread. Explain how Sandi will categorise her target segments of consumers.

Sandi needs to research the market and identify the characteristics of her target markets.

5

Branding

Branding plays a major role in marketing. You need to understand all aspects of branding.

Branding
This involves giving a product or service a recognisable identity. A brand will have its own colours, packaging and style.

Brand personality and image
The brand personality and image need to be attractive to the target market. It must be relevant to them and reflect their own preferences, needs and wants.

Unique Selling Point (USP)
There should be something special about the product or service that sets it apart from the competition. This should give it the edge when consumers are thinking about making a purchase.

Business size
Smaller businesses often lack the time and expertise to focus on marketing activity. Instead of branding and USPs, they may offer personal service or customer care. Larger businesses create and market brands with USPs to make them stand out from the competition in mass markets.

Budgets
Many businesses have limited marketing budgets and cannot afford to advertise on television or in glossy magazines. They require the highest impact for their money and market products and services using flyers, social media, email and radio.

Specialist staff
Large businesses will have specialist marketing staff. Smaller businesses may instead buy in expertise from external agencies and consultants, although specialists can be expensive.

Now try this

Choose one of the brands in the diagram above and identify the brand's USP.

 What makes the brand stand out? What are the unique elements that make it recognisable?

Internal influences on marketing

Influences within the organisation help to shape a business's choice of marketing activities.

Cost of the campaign

Effective marketing does not have to be expensive. Social media offers a cheap way to get the message across. A business needs to consider how much it normally spends and how effective the spending is in helping meet its objectives. If a business is launching a new product the key objective is increasing awareness. The business needs to calculate how many sales are needed to justify the spend.

Calculating the cost

Businesses can work out the true cost of an advert by working out how much it costs to be seen by 1000 people – this is the cost per thousand (CPT). This is calculated by dividing the total number of people who are likely to see the advert by 1000, then dividing the cost of running the advert by the answer to get the CPT. For example, a website charges £800 to feature an advertisement for a week during which time it will be seen 500 000 times. To work out the CPT:

$$\frac{500\ 000}{1000} = 500$$

$$\frac{£800}{500} = £1.60$$

In 2013, Coca-Cola had an advertising budget of around £2.5 billion, nearly 7 per cent of its total revenue. This gave it a major advantage over its competitors.

Source: http://marketrealist.com/2014/12/advertising-key-strategy-coca-colas-growth/

Available finance

Large businesses may spend a huge amount on marketing throughout the year. Most businesses have limited budgets and may only be able to afford to advertise at certain times of the year. Usually, businesses spend between 1 and 10 per cent of their revenue on marketing each year. They will want to get the best value for money.

Staff expertise

Larger businesses have a marketing department so will have the expertise in-house to run a marketing campaign. Smaller businesses may pay agencies and consultants to carry out marketing work, such as market research or writing and designing advertisements.

Size and culture of business

Marketing activities are influenced by the size of an organisation. Larger businesses will have bigger budgets, but more people will be able to influence how the marketing budget is spent.

Organisations want their marketing campaign to reflect their values and ideals. A business with a reputation for customer care would focus on this in its marketing activities.

Now try this

A business has a budget of £180 000 to spend on TV advertising. A TV station sells 30-second advertising slots throughout the day:

Time slot	Cost per 30-sec slot	Audience
Breakfast 0600–0930	£500.00	300 000
Daytime 0930–1730	£1500.00	450 000
Early peak 1730–2000	£4000.00	750 000
Late peak 2000–2300	£7500.00	900 000
Night time 2300–0600	£550.00	200 000

Careful! To carry out the calculations, begin by working out the audience sizes.

Calculate the CPT for breakfast, early peak and late peak time slots.

External influences on marketing

A number of external influences may affect a business's choice of marketing activities.

Social
- Demographics
- Lifestyle
- Age groups
- Education

Technological
- Manufacturing techniques
- Communication methods
- Use of internet and social media

Economic
- Inflation
- Interest rates
- Health of the economy
- Employment levels

External influences on marketing

Environmental
- Effects on climate and weather
- Pollution
- Recycling

Political and legal
- Type of government
- Stability of the government
- Business laws
- Regulations on competition and trading

Ethical
- Consumers' ethical demands
- Acceptable business behaviour
- Low wages and poor working conditions

Now try this

Hena is a clothing designer. She is looking for a manufacturer.
Manufacturing costs in Bangladesh are 30 per cent of the costs in the UK.
The quality is the same. Explain how the choice of Bangladesh as a location
for manufacturing might affect Hena's marketing.

 Consider ethical questions as well as manufacturing concerns.

Identifying what customers want

Market research involves gathering information about target markets, competitors and market trends, so that the business can make the right decisions.

Target markets

Market research helps a business find out about its target markets, including:

Gender   Income   Ethnic, cultural and religious background

Age ——— **Target markets** ——— Consumer behaviour

Education   Occupation

Competition

Businesses use market research to find out about what their competitors are doing or might do.

Price matching

Large supermarket chains such as Tesco and Asda regularly monitor their competitors' prices, and then offer customers money off their groceries if the price is cheaper elsewhere.

Competitor research feeds into a business's strategy.

Market trends, structure and size

1 Identifying market trends and how they are going to change over time is an important aspect of marketing strategy which enables businesses to plan for the future.

2 Market structure considers the organisation and characteristics of a market. These affect the amount of competition and the potential pricing options.

3 Market size refers to the value of the market in terms of sales and the number of competitors active in that market.

Beats Audio

Businesses need to be flexible to respond to changes in market trends. Beats Audio, a leading audio brand set up in 2006, has replaced its early products with new models to reflect changes in fashion and consumers' desire for the latest technology.

Now try this

Carrie designs greetings cards. Some designs sell well but these are boring to make. She often runs out of stock of the popular cards while having lots of cards that few people want to buy. Outline ways in which Carrie could find out what kind of cards customers want.

 Where should Carrie start and what should she consider?

Primary research

Primary research is new, fresh research collected by a business or market researcher. You need to revise the five main methods of primary research.

Links Revise the validity and reliability of research on page 13.

1 Surveys
People are asked a series of questions by post, phone or online. Often the surveys are quite long. People completing them may be rewarded with a gift or money-off voucher. Businesses can collect in-depth customer data for analysis.

2 Interviews
These are face-to-face conversations with people who are selected to match agreed characteristics (such as age or gender). They are asked a series of questions by the interviewer. Interviews enable businesses to collect in-depth opinions and ideas.

3 Observation
This involves watching people's behaviour. A supermarket has lots of security cameras and these can be used to watch store flow and how people shop. Observation is used to look at customer behaviour and habits.

Methods of primary research

4 Trials
Often a business will offer a cut price or free version of a new product to encourage people to try it. The business asks for feedback to see what people think about the product.
Trials are used to get an early indication whether customers like the product.

5 Focus groups
People selected by the business form a group and are encouraged to discuss products or services. A moderator directs the group. The group's discussions are often recorded and analysed in detail to identify attitudes and reactions and enable the business to develop products and services that meet customer needs.
Focus groups provide the business with plenty of in-depth opinions and views.

Now try this

Carrie designs greetings cards. She regularly runs out of the popular designs and is left with lots of the unpopular ones. She has decided to carry out some market research but has a limited budget. She would like to find out exactly what customers want and how to increase sales. Identify the type of primary research she could use.

Carrie wants useful information at a low cost.

Internal secondary research

Internal secondary research uses customer data and financial records already collected by the business.

Customer data and financial records

Many businesses have databases containing large amounts of information about their customers, such as their address, phone number and the number of times they have bought products or services from the business. Businesses will use this information to match products and services to customers' needs and wants to help them boost sales.

Sales records

Detailed records of sales transactions can be used as a valuable source of secondary data. For example, a business can track its sales by location, time of day or month, quantity bought at one time and how many times the same customer has bought from them.

Around 92 per cent of UK adults (46.5 million) are registered with at least one loyalty card. The most popular are Nectar, Boots Advantage and Tesco Clubcard.

Loyalty cards

Store loyalty schemes reward loyal customers with points when they buy in-store. These can be used as a discount when they purchase again. A loyalty card is used by a business to track and record an individual customer's buying habits and then to tailor the reward to the customer.

Using internal research

 Customer data
Businesses can use names and addresses to send out offers by post or by email.

 Loyalty cards
Businesses can collect detailed data on buying habits and reward customers with personalised offers and target promotions more effectively.

Use of internal secondary research

 Sales records
Using sales figures, a business can work out the busiest times of the day or month, the busiest stores and the best locations to place products. Historical sales data can also help businesses to identify market trends so they can forecast sales.

Now try this

Solid Wood Ltd is a furniture retailer. It does not have a loyalty card programme. Identify internal secondary data it might have and explain how the business could use this information.

 Think about where the business might hold data about some of its customers.

External secondary research

External secondary research is information that comes from organisations outside the business. Some organisations sell it and others offer it to businesses at no charge.

Commercially published reports

Some businesses research specialised or mass markets and then sell their findings to other businesses. The information is used to help businesses identify trends.

Government statistics

The Office for National Statistics produces a wide range of official government statistics free of charge. These provide businesses with information about social, economic and business trends.

Trade journals

A trade journal is a publication covering a specific industry (such as road haulage). It contains articles, research and news about the industry. It may also offer valuable insights into business opportunities, industry trends and competitor activity.

The Grocer is a weekly magazine for food retailers, wholesalers, suppliers, growers, food processers and manufacturers. It provides information on a wide range of topics such as food safety, prices and promotions and consumer trends.

The Grocer
www.thegrocer.co.uk   4 June 2016 | £3.95

WILLIAM REED

WE'RE REINVENTING WATER ARE YOU READY?

SUPPLY CHAIN SPECIAL

Food waste: are suppliers to blame? And how to cut it

DANGEROUS LIAISON?
The risks, benefits and significance of a potential Bayer/Monsanto tie-up .. 10
ONLINE Amazon to grab 3% share of UK grocery market in five years predicts new report 5

SOFT DRINKS Dalston Cola to scale up with Giles Brook investment 8
HEALTH & OBESITY Why artificial sweeteners are the elephant in the room in the war on sugar 19
BISCUITS McVitie's Hobnobs go gluten free 34
HOT BEVERAGES Tetley claims a UK first with functional black tea 35
FRUIT & VEG Fresh produce sales volumes up as price cuts drive consumption 38
SCOTLAND How collaboration is boosting Scottish food & drink 45
PEOPLE NEWS JW Filshill appoints Chris Miller as commercial director .. 54

I WANT THAT JOB
Area manager (operations) at MRH Retail P56

Competitors' annual reports and websites

Public companies such as Merlin Entertainments, which runs several theme parks including Alton Towers, must publish reports, updates and financial information. These appear on the company's website together with press releases and news reports. Competitors will regularly check these sources of data to collect information.

Media sources

Newspapers and magazines, television and radio programmes and news websites provide up-to-date information about business, markets and trends. The subjects are usually well researched and provide valuable information.

Now try this

Helpers Ltd provides social care, household repairs and a food shopping service for elderly and disabled customers. The business wants to offer a wider range of services to new and existing customers. Describe what it should research and the research methods it could use.

← Where should it look for data and how will it find them?

Validity and reliability

Market research is only of value to a business if the results can be trusted and the research reveals answers to the questions being asked.

Validity

Validity is whether the research measures what it claims to be measuring. If this is unclear then the results of the market research may be worthless.

Reliability

Reliability is whether the research can be applied to the whole market or all customers. Consistent results are important too: the results should be the same if the research is repeated.

Appropriateness

Appropriate means choosing the right way to do the market research. If a food retailer wanted to know how long it took a customer to choose a brand of breakfast cereal, it would not look for the answer in trade journals or government statistics. Observation of customers making these decisions in a supermarket would be more appropriate.

Currency

Currency refers to the age and relevance of the data. It is best to use the most up-to-date data as older data may no longer be accurate or relevant. The market may have changed and there might be different competitors.

Cost of research

The more customised the market research the higher the costs. Carrying out primary research takes longer and needs different skills so it is more expensive.

Secondary research is quicker and cheaper because a lot of hard work has already been done. The downside is that some commercial research companies will charge a high price for the information.

Telemarketers carry out customer surveys by phone. A business will always hope to get the most accurate results for the lowest cost.

Now try this

Restaurant owner, Rohan, has found out that primary market research costs between £250 and £600 per day, depending on the size and reputation of the market research company. Alternatively, he could use a telemarketing research company which charges £250 to £350 per day. Explain how Rohan could choose between the types of research company.

 Consider the sort of research Rohan needs to do. Also, use the points above to help you decide what questions Rohan needs answering.

Quantitative and qualitative data

Most market research uses quantitative and qualitative data to give businesses clear, reliable answers to their marketing questions. You need to revise when and where quantitative and qualitative data are used.

Qualitative data

Qualitative research aims to reveal why customers behave in certain ways and what could change their buying habits. It involves researching what consumers think, feel or do.

Qualitative data do not provide statistical data. This type of data is based on people's opinions and it might be that no two answers are the same.

Quantitative data

Quantitative research uses statistical analysis to measure how people think, behave or feel. This provides statistical results, but often the findings are hard to interpret. Quantitative data will tell you what the answer was to a question, such as 'yes' or 'no', but not why the person gave the answer.

Sources of data

A business will choose market research activities based on its need for quantitative or qualitative data.

Qualitative data

- Focus groups (group discussions)
- Individual interviews
- Participation/Observations

Quantitative data

- Surveys
- Telephone interviews
- Website monitoring
- Online polls

Combining market research

Coca-Cola uses a range of market research, including:

☑ secondary research to understand market opportunities

☑ focus groups, surveys and interviews to decide on new products, changes to existing products or packaging

☑ product trials and tests to assess the concept and get early feedback

☑ tracking performance and sales with research data from stockists

☑ social media for ongoing opinions and views of the product.

Definitions

☑ **Quantitative data** are data in numerical form which can be used to produce graphs or tables.

☑ **Qualitative data** are descriptive data which are obtained from interviews and focus groups.

Now try this

 Try and categorise the market research and what it tells the company.

A pharmaceutical company is carrying out market research:

1 The blood pressure of those given a new drug is taken one hour after each dose.

2 Each person chosen for the drug trial is interviewed by a doctor and researcher each week.

3 Each person is called on their mobile every other week and asked a series of yes or no questions.

Identify the types of market research the company is using and explain why it chose them.

Appropriate market research

Businesses need to gather sufficient information clearly focused on their marketing questions. From this, it is essential to select the right data and information ready to interpret and analyse.

Sufficient research

Many businesses fail to carry out adequate market research because they think they understand the market's needs. Insufficient market research can lead a business to believe that certain product features and benefits are far more important than is actually the case. Poor or insufficient research can result in a business making the wrong marketing decisions.

Focused research

Market research needs to have clear objectives. Specific questions need to be answered by the research to ensure it focuses on collecting the data that the business needs in order to provide answers to the questions and to meet the objectives.

Selecting and extracting data

Picking out the relevant data and then transforming them into a format that can be interpreted is essential. A great deal of information can be collected during the research but it needs to be organised and processed so that it can be understood.

Importance of market research

When the shoe retailer Brantano went into administration in early 2016, business analysts concluded that the company's market research had not alerted them to the fact that shoppers were changing their buying habits. The traditional 'bricks and mortar' retailer faced stiff competition from online retailers, and the unseasonable winter weather also affected its sales of winter shoes and boots. The company was saved but shrank from 200 to 140 stores.

Sampling and sample size

Businesses have to limit the number of people they investigate during market research. This means that they have to collect data from a sample.

The sample needs to be of a sufficient size and must be representative of the target population. Businesses need to try and work out how many responses they need to give them a reasonably accurate set of results at a cost that they can afford.

1. How accurate does the research need to be?

2. How confident is the business that it will obtain the results it needs?

Factors affecting sample size

3. The size of the budget allocated to the research

Now try this

According to the research agency AcuPoll, 95 per cent of new products that are launched each year fail. This means huge losses for businesses. Explain what might be going wrong with the market research.

 Think about bias, accuracy and sample size.

Interpreting and analysing data

Market research data need to be carefully interpreted and analysed. The data will be used to help predict events, behaviours and actions, and from this the business will develop its marketing campaign.

Analysing the data

The market research analyst sifts through all of the information and checks that the source is reliable and credible. Often they will have to use raw statistics, convert these into easy to understand facts and figures, and draw conclusions from them. Analysts require reasonable mathematical skills so that they can organise and present the information (often as graphs or spreadsheets).

Additional information

Market research aims to answer specific questions. If the answers are unclear or contradictory, then additional research may be required. Without this, the business may decide on the wrong marketing mix resulting in wasted advertising and lost sales.

Evaluating validity

In order to assess the validity of the research the analyst needs to know how it was carried out. If there are any concerns about the validity of the research, then the data might not be trustworthy.

Evaluating reliability

Once the analyst decides the market research is valid, they need to evaluate whether it is reliable. This will depend on how extensive the research was. The business will need to be sure that any generalisations made from the research will give accurate results.

 Links   For more on validity and reliability, see page 13.

How data are used

The insights from market research will enable the business to decide on the marketing mix for its campaign. The data should show:

How much customers are prepared to spend

What customers demand from the product and/or service the business is offering

How research data inform marketing decisions

The type of marketing and advertising that will be effective

What competitors are doing

Whether the products or services are rising or falling in popularity

Now try this

Describe your views on the following examples of market research:

(a) A series of face-to-face interviews with ten people out of a potential market of 1 million.

(b) Basing statistical calculations and results on data that were produced in 2009.

(c) Finding data about the French market for mobile phones and applying them to the UK.

In each case think about whether the data are valid and reliable and why.

Product life cycle

The product life cycle describes the normal stages a product or service passes through – from its development to when it is removed from the market.

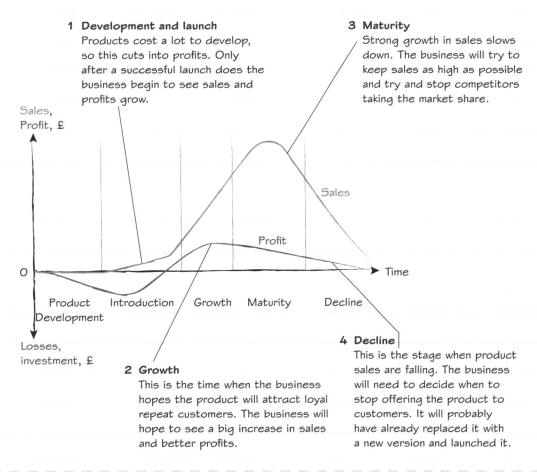

1 Development and launch
Products cost a lot to develop, so this cuts into profits. Only after a successful launch does the business begin to see sales and profits grow.

3 Maturity
Strong growth in sales slows down. The business will try to keep sales as high as possible and try and stop competitors taking the market share.

2 Growth
This is the time when the business hopes the product will attract loyal repeat customers. The business will hope to see a big increase in sales and better profits.

4 Decline
This is the stage when product sales are falling. The business will need to decide when to stop offering the product to customers. It will probably have already replaced it with a new version and launched it.

From launch to decline

1. Launch – in 2015, trade magazine *Marketing Week* surveyed 2000 UK adults about product launches: 51 per cent said that online offers and competitions were most likely to catch their attention.

2. Growth – globally, the internet is still in its growth stage. In 2014, just 35 per cent of the world had access to the internet – by the beginning of 2015 this had grown to 42 per cent.

3. Maturity – gourmet coffee machines such as Nespresso (launched in 1986) allow you to make coffee shop style hot drinks at home. The brand is firmly established and has loyal customers and steady sales.

4. Decline – Apple's iPod was launched in 2001. It has had 26 updated designs since then. Sales peaked in 2008 and have been gradually declining since then. In 2012, the iPod Touch range was launched in an attempt to revive iPod sales.

Now try this

1. Explain how a business would identify the correct stage of the product life cycle for their products and services.

2. Assess whether a business could have products or services at different stages of the product life cycle?

 Think about the product life cycle and what each stage actually means.

Suitability of marketing aims and objectives

All businesses have goals or ambitions. On this page, you will revise the types of marketing aims and objectives a business may set itself to achieve its goals.

🔗 **Links** Revise marketing aims and objectives on pages 2 and 3.

Financial objectives

These may include:
- breaking even (covering costs with revenue)
- making a profit (revenue greater than costs)
- growth (increase number of transactions).

Survival

In difficult economic circumstances a business might just have a single objective to survive. It may have to cut staff or sell assets to achieve this. New businesses will often choose survival as an objective.

Market share and customer satisfaction

Building market share takes time. It means taking customers and sales from competitors. Superior products and great customer service are very important as these should result in a good reputation, delighted customers recommending the business and an increase in sales and market share.

Ethical and sustainable objectives

A business's operations should be ethical and have a minimal impact on the environment. Bad publicity affects reputation and sales. Most businesses are keen to state that their activities are sustainable.

SMART objectives

Marketing objectives are often written with clear benefits in mind.

Specific – say what you want to achieve, e.g. to increase sales product sales compared to last year

Measurable – how you will show the objective has been partly or fully achieved, e.g. sales figures are up 10 per cent on last year

Achievable – the objective is challenging, but it can be met, e.g. employees will be able to see progress towards the objective

Relevant – the goals are clearly linked to the main objectives of the organisation, e.g. to grow the business by increasing sales and profits

Time frame – set the target dates to achieve the objective, e.g. in March next year, product sales will be 10 per cent higher than this year

Now try this

The Dartmoor Pony Heritage Trust's goal is to 'save the indigenous Dartmoor pony from extinction and to maintain its presence on Dartmoor, thus protecting our heritage for future generations'.

State the trust's three aims and objectives.

Identify the main aim and then set the objectives that will allow the company to fulfil that aim.

Situational analysis

Situational analysis involves examining an organisation's internal and external environments in order to review the current position of the business. It is an excellent starting point when designing a marketing plan. On this page, you will revise the two main types of analysis: SWOT and PESTLE.

SWOT

SWOT analysis identifies the internal and external factors that may present threats or opportunities to the business.

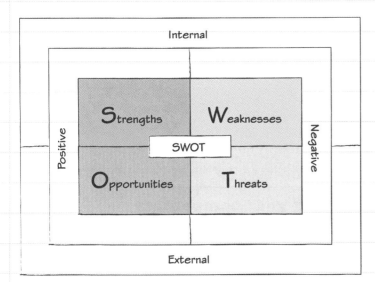

Disadvantages of SWOT

👎 It can oversimplify situations as it requires forcing factors into one of four categories which may not always fit.

👎 The analysis can be subjective. Some strength factors may not be very significant. Some factors can be either opportunities or threats; it might depend on how the business handles the situation.

PESTLE

PESTLE analysis looks at the opportunities and threats of SWOT in more detail.

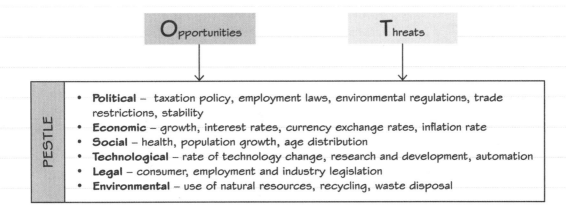

Opportunities   **Threats**

PESTLE
- **Political** – taxation policy, employment laws, environmental regulations, trade restrictions, stability
- **Economic** – growth, interest rates, currency exchange rates, inflation rate
- **Social** – health, population growth, age distribution
- **Technological** – rate of technology change, research and development, automation
- **Legal** – consumer, employment and industry legislation
- **Environmental** – use of natural resources, recycling, waste disposal

Now try this

A prosthetics manufacturer has identified these weaknesses during a situational analysis: outdated technology, poor employee skills and training, over-dependence on one specific range of prosthetics, poor quality components from suppliers and high assembly costs in UK factory.

Outline how the business could deal with each weakness.

 Think about a solution to each problem identified in the situational analysis.

Use of research data

Valid and accurate research data enable a business to identify its target markets and to carry out competitor analysis.

Target markets

It is vital for a business to identify and categorise its main customer groups so it can choose appropriate marketing activities to attract and then persuade them to make purchases. The business may identify core (regular), occasional (irregular) or rare customer types or groups.

Knowing your target market is essential when planning and developing a marketing campaign.

Identifying your target market

☑ Understand the problem that you are solving.

☑ Understand who has this problem, and who does not have this problem.

☑ Create a picture of the customer.

☑ Think about the market – types of people, geographical locations, particular/niche sectors.

☑ Do you have any areas of expertise? For example, do you have knowledge/contacts in a particular sector?

Competitor analysis

A business needs to be aware of the activities and plans of its competitors to help it prevent attempts by its rivals to take market share.

Monitoring competitors' outlets, website and press releases are all important parts of this process. Businesses will also listen to rumours or information from former employees.

Analysing your competitors

☑ Identify who your competitors are.

☑ What products or services do they offer?

☑ How do your competitors' customers rate them?

☑ Are your competitors a major threat to your business?

☑ Carry out SWOT and PESTLE analyses on your competitors to spot their strengths and weaknesses.

🔗 Links Go back and look at marketing aims and objectives on page 18 if you need to.

Branded products and services should be instantly recognisable to consumers.

T K Maxx

TK Maxx is an 'off-price' retailer. It sells designer and branded clothing and homeware up to 60 per cent less than the recommended retail price. The retailer's target customers are middle to upper-middle income shoppers who tend to be 24–35 and are fashion and value conscious.

Who are TK Maxx's closest competitors?

The look and layout of a store are designed to appeal to target customer groups.

Now try this

Matalan has over 200 stores across the UK selling discount clothing and homeware. Most stores are in out-of-town retail parks. Identify Matalan's five main competitors.

They are often located near major supermarkets, but what other competitors sell similar products to Matalan?

Marketing mix

Product is the first part of the marketing mix. You will revise all four parts over the next few pages. Product development involves designing, creating and marketing either new products or updating existing ones.

Remember the four Ps

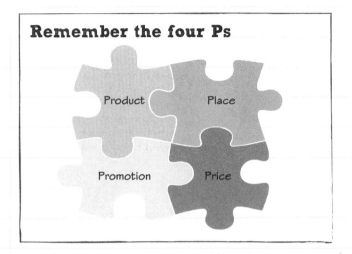

Product   Place

Promotion   Price

The product development process aims to eliminate bad ideas and to make sure that new products satisfy demand and will sell.

New product development and idea generation

▼

Screening and evaluating new product ideas

▼

Analysis of market to check whether there will be a demand for the product

▼

Product development

▼

Market testing of the product

▼

Launch of product onto the market

Form and function

Coming up with ideas for new products or services is just the first part of a complex process. If the product gets past some of the early stages a prototype needs to be developed to test whether the product meets form, fit and functionality requirements.

Branding

Branding is all about giving a name and identity to the product. It needs to be recognisable and appeal to consumers. A poor name or an unclear identity can ruin the chances of a product's success. Branding means making use of marketing, public relations and promotion to create the right image.

Links Revise more about branding on page 6.

Packaging

 Protects product during transportation and on retailer's shelf

 Protects users from hazardous ingredients or sharp edges

Purpose of packaging

 Needs to be recognisable and carry brand name and logo

 Instructions, contact details and contents printed on packaging

Now try this

For each of the four purposes of packaging outlined above, identify a product that would need this type of packaging.

 What are the functions of packaging? Why are they needed?

Pricing strategies

Setting the price – the second part of the marketing mix – is one of the most difficult concerns for a business. It needs to consider its costs, competitors and expected profit. On this page, you will revise the four main pricing strategies.

 Penetration pricing
This is aggressive pricing. The business sets its prices as low as possible to attract customers aiming to grab market share very quickly. At that point it will increase prices and hope that the customers remain loyal.

 Price skimming
This takes advantage of loyal customers. The business charges high prices for its products or services knowing that customers will still buy them. This usually means that the business has a superior product to sell compared to its competitors.

Pricing strategies

 Competitor-based pricing
This aims to match prices charged by the competition. The business will monitor prices and change them straightaway to make sure that they are not more expensive than the competition.

 Cost plus pricing
This simple pricing policy involves adding a certain percentage to the costs of a product or service to come up with the price. It takes no account of the competition or what customers might be prepared to pay.

Loss leaders

Sometimes a business will offer a small range of products or services at cost price or even less in order to attract customers to its store or website. The aim is to encourage customers to buy other products or services.

Customer reactions

Customers are very price aware. They are also price sensitive. This means that if a product price increases too much they are less likely to buy it and will look for an alternative.

Customers will sometimes ignore price if there is another reason to buy, such as fashion, convenience or a trend.

Now try this

1 Explain why a customer might be price sensitive.
2 If a business lowers the price of a product, explain what may happen to customer demand.

 Think about the benefits of the product.

22

Promoting the product 1

Promotion – the third part of the marketing mix – is any type of marketing communication that aims to inform, persuade or motivate customers to buy or support a product or service. On this and the next two pages, you will revise the different types of promotion used by businesses.

Promotional advertising

Advertising is a message paid for by a business aiming to influence customers. There are advertisements on TV, radio, social media and websites, public transport, billboards, store windows and in magazines and newspapers.

Public relations (PR)

Public relations focuses on a business's reputation. It tries to influence opinion and behaviour by providing information. PR is about trying to create goodwill and understanding among customers and other stakeholders.

Sponsorship

This involves providing financial support to organisations, individuals or events with the purpose of raising customer awareness of the business providing the sponsorship.
The business will be recognised because of its association with whatever it is sponsoring.

Globally, high-visibility sponsorship of popular and televised sports is worth £26 billion per year.

Social media

Increasingly social media is becoming one of the most important ways of promoting products and services. Growing internet access and the number of devices per household connected to the internet have driven the growth of digital advertising. Social media includes Facebook, Twitter, Instagram, LinkedIn, Pinterest, Snapchat and YouTube.

Digital advertising

According to a survey by the Internet Advertising Bureau UK, in 2014 the average UK household had more than seven devices that could connect to the internet. Advertisers spent £7.2 million on digital advertising in 2014, of which nearly a quarter was spent on smartphone advertising.

Now try this

Identify where you might successfully promote a new perfume aimed at the under-25 female market.

 Where have you seen similar promotions in the past?

Promoting the product 2

In a crowded market with thousands of advertising messages marketing experts need to be clever and try new things to get their message across.

 Links Look at pages 22–23 for more on pricing and promotion.

Guerrilla marketing

This is a low-cost advertising strategy that is unconventional. It is ideal for smaller businesses that want to make an impression and reach a large audience. It is about taking the audience by surprise by putting an advertising message in an unexpected place.

Flash-mobs or similar unconventional marketing strategies can make an impact, and provide an opportunity to exploit social media.

Personal selling

This is any face-to-face or telephone communication with a customer. It involves explaining the benefits of a product or service. The purpose is to persuade the customer to commit to buy. Salespeople are trained to answer queries and have solutions to any objections that the customer might have.

Personal selling is the oldest form of marketing and sales and in some markets it is still the most important.

Product placement

Businesses pay for their products or services to be featured in television programmes or movies. Product placement:

- raises brand awareness to the audience
- shows the brand being used
- aims to change perceptions of the brand.

Brand spotting

The James Bond movie, *Spectre*, had 17 major product placements. The brands paid nearly £100 million to see their cars in action, and have their watches or clothes worn by the stars.

Now try this

Identify **four** types of business or types of product or service that would benefit from personal selling.

 Some products and services need personal selling techniques to explain them and match the ideal product or service to the customer's needs.

Promoting the product 3

Digital marketing includes any type of internet, social media or smartphone marketing. Corporate image is the ideal impression that a business wants to create and put across to customers.

 **Links** Look at pages 22–24 for more on pricing and promotion.

Digital marketing

Digital marketing involves promoting products and services using online channels. Businesses use their databases to target customers with promotions relevant to them, the idea being they will be more likely to make a purchase.

Pay-per-click, pay-per-sale, or pay-per-lead – website owners are paid for each customer they direct to another site selling products or services.

Mobile and apps – clickable advertisements and apps that direct customers to make a purchase.

Online video and viral – posting video clips and pictures to encourage sharing.

Online articles – feature a product or service like a news story.

Digital marketing media

Social media marketing – placing display advertising on social media or setting up a page on social media.

Search engine optimisation – ensuring that a website will be found in a search featuring relevant key words.

Display advertising – banner or block advertisements on websites that can be clicked on to redirect customer to another site.

Email marketing – advertising messages and offers sent to potential customers on an email database.

Corporate image

Corporate image is how the business is perceived by the public. It is a combination of the business's brands, its identity, use of media and other factors. Businesses will spend a large percentage of their marketing budgets trying to create and maintain a good corporate image. Having a good corporate image is vital in competitive markets as it can give a business a major advantage.

Changing an image

In 2014 McDonald's began the slow process of trying to change its corporate image from 'fast food' to 'good food served fast'.

For some time, the burger chain had been criticised for its high-fat, high-calorie menus.

2014 saw the first cucumber sold by McDonald's as the corporation began to routinely offer salads instead of fries as a side order. McDonalds also exchanged the red in its logo for a deep green to emphasise its environmental credentials and greener practices.

Now try this

According to a survey, in 2014 around 55 per cent of businesses were using social media to engage with their customers and generate sales leads. Explain what is meant by 'engage with their customers' and 'generate sales leads'.

 What are the main objectives of most businesses?

Place and distribution

Place – the final part of the marketing mix – involves ensuring that products and services are available to customers at the right place and the right time. On this page, you will revise distribution channels.

Distribution channels

This is the physical movement of products from the manufacturer to the end user (customer). Most businesses will use some kind of distribution channel. This means that the product will pass from one business to another along the channel. In some cases, a business in the channel will do something to the product (such as cook it, or package it). Other times they will just pass the product on to other businesses.

Direct to end users

Business to consumer: some products can be distributed straight from the manufacturer to the end user. Direct distribution is used by large and small businesses: mail (using catalogues and brochures); online (using websites with shopping carts); and auctions (through sites such as eBay)

Business to business: the buyer (business) will receive the products straight from the manufacturer.

Retailers

Traditional 'bricks and mortar' retailers are in convenient locations, allowing the end user to see a product before they buy it. They offer a wide range of products or services from many different manufacturers. **Online retailers** allow consumers to buy a wide range of products and services at a time and place that is convenient to them. Traditional retailers often have their own websites.

Wholesalers

Wholesalers usually buy direct from manufacturers and then sell on to smaller businesses such as retailers. They hold stock for the manufacturer and distribute their products to customers. The manufacturers prefer this as the wholesaler will buy their products in bulk.

Multiple distribution

Most businesses now use a wide range of different distribution systems at the same time. They may sell direct via their own website and use wholesalers to distribute products. Any use of other businesses in the distribution channel means that the products are being indirectly distributed.

Now try this

1 Explain the main differences between direct and indirect distribution.

2 Give an example of a business that might use a multiple distribution channel.

 Think through the characteristics of the types of distribution and how and when they are used.

Extended marketing mix

As marketing has become more complex, interrelated factors – people, physical environment and process – have been added to the marketing mix.

 Links Check you have revised the marketing mix on pages 21–26.

People

This factor focuses on the quality of the employees that create, manufacture, sell and service products and services for customers. It refers particularly to employees that have any form of interaction with customers. The better quality the employees the better the experience for the customers.

High-quality employees ensure a better customer experience.

Physical environment

The physical environment is where customers buy a product or experience a service. In the traditional retailer, they want a well-laid-out store where they can comfortably browse and look at products. On a website, they will want an easy-to-navigate site with clear information and a simple buying process.

Airport facilities

Heathrow Airport has a broad range of facilities for passengers passing through the airport. Wi-fi, parking, food and drink, duty free shopping and a comfortable departure lounge are all examples of providing a suitable physical environment.

Process

Customer service plays an important part in the buying process and customer after sales service. This factor also looks at the way the business handles complaints, how it identifies customer needs or wants and how it handles the ordering and customer interaction process.

Consistent quality customer service illustrates attention to process detail.

Now try this

Identify and briefly describe the seven Ps of marketing.

 What are the key elements of the marketing mix?

Marketing messages

A good marketing campaign will send a clear message to its target audience. Creating the right balance in the marketing mix is essential to achieve this goal.

Be straightforward
and to the point

Identify the target market
– this makes it easier to create an appealing message

Marketing messages need to...

Offer a solution to the 'problem'
that the market is experiencing by showing:
- the solution has worked for other people
- the business and the product or service is different

Identify the 'problem'
that the target market experiences

Product decisions

Make sure that the product brand, name and position are right. It is important to check various product or service factors:

- Functionality
- Styling
- Quality
- Safety
- Packaging

Price decisions

This means getting the pricing structure right to match the qualities of the product and at the same time checking the prices charged by competitors:

- What are the marketing objectives of the price?
- What is the price likely to achieve?
- Can the price vary?

Promotion decisions

- Where are potential customers most likely to see the message?
- What is the ideal balance of advertising, sales promotions, personal selling and public relations?
- How big is the budget and how long will the campaign last?
- How will it be evaluated?

Place decisions

The product or service has to be in the right place at the right time; otherwise the rest of the marketing mix decisions are worthless.

- What is the most suitable distribution system?
- How are similar products or services distributed and does it work?

Now try this

A new live music club, 365live, has a limited marketing budget but it wants to get its marketing mix right. The club is located in the centre of a busy, culturally diverse city. Describe how you might create their marketing message and organise their basic marketing mix.

Identify the club's key marketing message and how it will get that across to the target audience.

Media and budgets

A business needs to know the key characteristics of its customers so it can choose the right media to reach them. The size of the budget will determine the length and spread of any media campaign.

Media choice

The choice of media for a marketing campaign will depend on the habits of potential customers. The business can match its profile of target customers against the profiles of the media owners' audience. In theory this will give them a good fit.

Selecting the ideal media balance depends on several factors.

Campaign budget

After a campaign message is created and marketing objectives decided, the next step is to work out how much it might cost to achieve that goal. Marketing budgets have to cover the costs of research, advertising, promotion, use of social media and public relations.

Each media choice has a cost, and some offer better value than others. The business needs to select the media that are the most likely to deliver the campaign message successfully within its budget.

Allocating the media budget

Depending on the industry, marketing budgets may be as low as 1 per cent of sales revenue or as high as 30 per cent.

☑ New businesses might spend up to 50 per cent of their sales income on marketing.

☑ Smaller businesses may try and match the spending of their closest competitors.

☑ Budgets can depend on the size of the business, its sales revenue and how much competition there is in the market.

Choosing the right media

BRAD – the British Rates and Data directory – offers businesses planning a marketing campaign profiles on 12 800 media titles. The choice of media may be huge, but there are ways to narrow this down.

Where do competitors advertise?

What are the common words and phrases used when customers search online for a product or service like that offered by the business?

How to select the right media

Research members of the target audience to discover what they watch, read and listen to, and which websites they visit

Use BRAD to find out advertising information, such as advertising rates and geographical coverage

Now try this

365live has decided that social media is a good way to promote the club. Explain how the club could use social media.

Social media is a good fit for the club. Outline the features of social media that would be useful to it.

Timelines and evaluation

Timelines refer to the length and phases of a campaign. A business will monitor the effectiveness of the campaign as it develops to enable it to evaluate whether it has the desired impact.

Campaign timelines

Most marketing campaigns are divided into phases. Businesses will buy advertising space and run the messages for a period of time. Often, other media will be used at the same time to support them. Timelines may focus on the launch date of a product or service or a significant date such as Christmas or the summer holiday season.

Independent music release campaign – timeline

10 weeks from release – choose track to lead radio campaign, research PR targets, upload tracks and artwork.

8 weeks from release – book Facebook and Google advertising, send track to radio stations, start using social media.

4–6 weeks from release – send out tracks to newspapers and magazines, upload video to YouTube and social media.

2 weeks from release – arrange interviews; offer free downloads, T shirts or gig tickets to early buyers. Release tour dates.

Release week – live promotion in digital store, radio interviews and offer free live sessions to media.

Monitoring campaigns

Monitoring the campaign is important as it may be necessary to make changes if something is not working. Monitoring allows the business to check the effectiveness of the different phases of the campaign and which elements of it have the greatest impact.

Daily monitoring

Facebook – number of clicks on links, messages commented on, messages liked

Twitter – number of times hashtag used in tweets, retweets, clicks on links, Twitter users involved

Social media campaign – daily monitoring

Blog – new subscribers, posts shared and new comments

YouTube – new subscribers, ratings and comments

Evaluating campaigns

Evaluation means comparing the results of the campaign against its objectives. This may be extra sales or increased market share. Marketing campaign effectiveness is not always about how much extra revenue is generated.

Non-revenue based success

This can include:

- ✓ number of hits on the website
- ✓ use of codes and coupons to see where actual sales and sales leads have come from
- ✓ how long visitors spend on the website and view products and services offered in addition to direct sales and ad-clicks.

Now try this

A small business had sales revenue of £88 000 last year. This year the sales revenue has been £122 000. The main difference is that the business ran a marketing campaign for the first six months of the year. Identify the factors the business needs to consider when evaluating whether the increase in sales is as a result of the marketing campaign.

Think about what the question tells you about the business. What has been achieved and why? What else does it need to know to understand whether the increase in sales is due to the marketing campaign?

Appropriate marketing campaigns 1

On this page, you will revise how marketing activity supports brand value and the importance of sustainable marketing.

Brand value

Brand value is the premium placed on a product or service as a result of its reputation. This is the present value (and the future value) of cash that a brand generates. You can see the link between marketing activities and brand value in the diagram:

Marketing activity promotes the brand to audiences

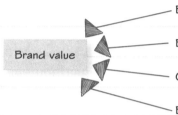

Brand value

Brand image – how the audiences view the brand compared to competitors

Brand equity – customers preference for the brand compared to competitors

Customer behaviour – changes in customer behaviour due to their preferences

Brand value – increased cash flow from changes in customer behaviour

Sustainability of activities

Sustainable marketing or green marketing looks at the ways that products and services have an impact on society or the environment. Sustainable marketing is all about focusing on the positives of a product or service, clearly stating that it seeks to minimise any negative impacts.

Ecover's Ocean Plastic bottle

Ecover makes sustainable cleaning products – from the sourcing of its ingredients through to the speed at which they biodegrade after they've been disposed of. Its Ocean Plastic bottle is made of recycled plastic, 10 per cent of which has been collected from plastic found floating in the sea.

Green ice cream

Ice cream maker Ben & Jerry's aims to make the 'best possible ice cream, in the nicest possible way'. Ben & Jerry's puts values at the heart of their sourcing decisions and has a long history of fighting for social justice, from Marriage Equality and animal welfare to championing equal access to democracy. In 2006 Ben & Jerry's was the first company to introduce a Fairtrade vanilla to the UK, and now their full flavour family is Fairtrade certified. In 2015 Ben & Jerry's launched the 'Save Our Swirled' campaign, calling on its fans across the globe to join the climate justice movement, and pledging to increase energy efficiency and shrink the company's carbon footprint.

Ben & Jerry's promotes its energy-efficient 'cleaner, greener freezer'.

Now try this

Explain how Ben & Jerry's 'cleaner, greener freezer' supports its brand value.

← Identify the key message and explain how it relates to brand value.

Appropriate marketing campaigns 2

Marketing campaigns must be able to adapt to internal and external changes while remaining in tune with the goals of the business.

Responsive marketing campaigns

Marketing campaigns need to be flexible and able to respond to internal or external changes. Campaigns might need to be delayed, brought forward or even scrapped.

A range of alternatives and back-up plans will need to be created should a major part of the campaign need to be changed at short notice.

Internal change

Marketing campaigns are organised in advance and things can change within the business. Priorities and budgets may change. It is therefore important to make regular progress checks and ensure that the campaign is still relevant and affordable.

External change

Campaigns are organised in order to achieve certain goals. They may make assumptions about the market and the activities of the competition and if these change, the campaign may need to adapt.

Organisational goals

Marketing campaigns should constantly be checked against the business's mission statement to ensure that they reflect and support the goals of the organisation.

IKEA's mission statement

The IKEA concept, or mission statement, is to provide a range of home furnishing products that are affordable to many people, not just a few. This is reflected in all of their marketing campaigns.

Now try this

Give two examples of external threats or changes that could impact on a marketing campaign.

 Unexpected external threats can have a direct impact on a marketing campaign.

Legal and ethical campaigns

Marketing campaigns will fail if they are not suitable for their target markets. They must also be ethical and comply with legal regulations.

Target markets

A combination of market research and SWOT analysis should reveal the likely characteristics, needs and wants of customers in a business's target markets. It can then produce persuasive and effective messages for each marketing segment.

 Look at marketing aims on page 18.

One company, different markets

TUI, the travel company, owns First Choice and Thomson. First Choice is targeted at younger customers and is more family orientated. Thomson is focused on catering for older and wealthier customers. Both brands offer differentiated products and personal services targeted at specific markets.

Legal regulations

According to UK law all marketing and advertising has to be:

- an accurate description of the product or service
- legal
- decent
- truthful
- honest
- socially responsible (it should not encourage illegal or unsafe behaviour).

Ethics

This generally means:

👍 be truthful

👍 have high personal standards

👍 be clear when the business is advertising and when it is providing news or entertainment

👍 treat consumers fairly

👍 never compromise the privacy of customers

👍 comply with regulations and standards.

The Fairtrade Foundation

When you see the Fairtrade mark on products like chocolate, coffee and bananas, you know that the farmers who produced the ingredients will have received a guaranteed minimum price. This ethical standard also means that workers' rights are protected. Farmers and workers receive additional money to invest in social, environmental and economic developmental projects to improve their communities.

Fairtrade helps small farmers around the world get fair terms of trade for their products and better working conditions.

Now try this

In 2016, a premium burger restaurant chain ran an advert showing a picture of a burger with the slogan: 'Vegetarians. Resistance is futile.' Although not illegal, the company apologised and ended the campaign. Discuss why you think it may have decided to do this.

 Think about the negative impact that the advertising campaign may have had and the publicity it might have received.

Your Unit 2 external assessment

You will have six hours for research and preparation and three hours to complete both activities in the set task in Unit 2 supervised assessment. The task will be based upon a case study or a business scenario.

Part A: Preparing for the set task

Two weeks before the supervised assessment (Part B), you will be given a taskbook (Part A) containing the set task brief and information. You will use this to carry out research in preparation for Part B.

Below is a revision task brief, which follows a similar model to the real set task brief you'll receive. You'll work on this revision task over the next few pages to help you understand how to approach the assessment.

> • You have been asked to prepare ideas for a marketing campaign for a small drinks manufacturer.
> • You are required to research the soft drinks market.
> • You should research and analyse one marketing campaign relating to the soft drinks market and its associated costs.

DO NOT WRITE IN THIS AREA

🔗 **Links** See page 38 for the revision task information.

You will also be provided with some further information in Part A. For the purposes of this revision task, this will be facts and statistics about the soft drinks market.

You will be expected to carry out your own preparatory work on the brief and information provided in Part A. You will be given about six hours to do your Part A advance preparatory research.
You may prepare up to six sides of A4 research notes to take into the supervised external assessment.

Part B: The set task

The set task in Part B of your assessment is divided into two activities worth a total of 70 marks: Activity 1 has 34 marks and Activity 2 has 36 marks. This will be completed under supervised conditions.

Manage your time!

You will have three hours to complete the activities. You should aim to spend just under 1 hour 30 minutes on each one. Remember to allow time to read through your work before you hand it in.

Completing the set task

In the supervised assessment period (Part B), you will be required to prepare:

• **Activity 1:** A rationale for your marketing campaign

The rationale may include such elements as:
• marketing aims and objectives
• research data on the market and competition
• a justification for your rationale.

• **Activity 2:** A budgeted plan with a timescale for your marketing campaign

A plan for a marketing campaign may involve:
• determining the budget for the campaign
• identifying the stages in launching the campaign
• allocating responsibilities to specialist staff involved in the marketing campaign.

Additional information

Your answer booklet for Part B will contain additional information about the case study. Read this information carefully before starting to complete Part B.

Now try this

Choose two different types of soft drinks and compare and contrast the features of their marketing campaigns.

Try to identify differences relating to their target markets, the key advertising messages, the use of social media, promotional offers.

Preparing for assessment

To complete your set task, you will need to use a range of skills to research, analyse and evaluate market research data in order to devise a marketing campaign.

 Research skills
Use the set task brief and information provided in Part A to research the market.

 There's more on research skills on page 37.

 Analytical and evaluation skills
As part of the preparation (Part A) for the supervised set task, you will need to analyse and evaluate the market research data you have collected so that you have a clear understanding of the market for the product or service.

 There's more on analysing market data on page 39.

Skills required for external assessment

 Time management skills
When the supervised assessment (Part B) begins first read through what you are required to prepare in Activities 1 and 2. Use your preparatory notes to identify the areas that you will cover in each of the activities. You will need to organise yourself to ensure you complete the activities in the allocated time.

 Presentation skills
Your marketing campaign is a business document and should be set out using standard business conventions including headings and numbered sections. It should refer to marketing principles and use appropriate marketing terminology.

 Communication skills
Correct spelling, punctuation and good grammar coupled with the ability to use business terminology with confidence in an appropriate setting, forms the basis of all business documents.

Now try this

Review your own strengths and weaknesses against each of the skills required in the external assessment.

 For each weakness think about what you could do to improve your skills.

Part A: Preparing your support material

Below are some examples of the areas you might wish to prepare notes on, although these will be dependent on the product or service identified in the set task brief in Part A.

Data analysis – the market
In this area you could look at market size by sales turnover and volume; main producers and their market shares; product share; market trends.

 Revise marketing aims and objectives on pages 2 and 3.

Data analysis – consumers
In this area you could look at market segmentation by age, gender, lifestyle, income and try to identify the characteristics of the main consumers of the product.

 Revise market segmentation on page 5.

Data analysis – product
You may find it useful to look at how a similar product or service already on the market has been marketed; its key features; the routes to market; how successful it has been.

 Revise market segmentation on page 5 and branding on page 6.

Data analysis – social and economic factors
Try to look for any factors in the economy or any changes in consumer tastes and preferences which may impact upon the product.

 Revise external influences on marketing on page 8.

SWOT analysis of main producers
Complete a SWOT analysis on the market leaders in the industry. These businesses will be the ones that provide the greatest threat to the success of your marketing campaign.

 Revise SWOT and PESTLE analyses on page 19.

Costings
As well as market research, use the internet and other research sources to try and get an idea of the costs of the different aspects of a marketing campaign including printing costs, trade fairs, promotional gifts and web design.

  Revise internal influences of marketing on page 7 and media and budgets on page 29.

Now try this

Try to think of another aspect of research which may be useful when preparing for your external assessment.

 Another way to approach your research for Part A is by looking at the four Ps which make up the marketing mix.

 Revise the marketing mix on pages 21 to 27.

Part A: Research skills

You will need to research the market of the product or service given in the set task brief in Part A. Effective research skills will help to ensure you're well prepared for the assessment.

 Links The worked examples in Unit 2 are based on the revision task on the soft drinks market on page 34 and the revision task information on page 38.

The research process

This flow chart will help you to approach your research in a methodical way.

 List the main areas of your market research, e.g. size of the market; market segmentation; market leaders and competitor analysis

 Identify any emerging trends in the market; what are the growth areas in the market? What factors are influencing market growth in key segments?

 Find out the ways in which different types of soft drinks are marketed

 Use the marketing mix to identify the key features in marketing different types of soft drinks

 Identify the main elements of your marketing campaign

 Justify the main features of your marketing campaign

Planning your research

Effective research requires a **plan**. The first step is to draw up a list of questions which will form the basis of your research activities, e.g. What is the size of the speciality soft drinks market? You could produce a **mind map** to jot down your ideas. Number the research activities in your mind map in order of priority. You can amend your research plan as you access more information.

Research sources

You need to be able to distinguish between the four main types of research.

Links Revise primary and secondary research on pages 10 to 12.

Identify your research

As you answer your research questions, remember to identify the source of your information or data.

Sample notes extract

Research plan

Research questions	Information required	Source
Size of market?	Sales volume Sales value Market trends	Marketing associations
Composition of market?	Main companies Market share	Annual reports

 Using a table for the research plan in Part A means that it is easier to record the results of your research and check the progress of your research activities.

 Don't worry if at this stage you have too much information – you can extract the main points from your Part A research at a later stage.

Now try this

Complete the research plan above based upon the requirements for the revision task brief on the soft drinks market.

 You could add a fourth column to the table in which you record the results of your research findings.

Part A: Using your research

With the set task brief, you'll be given data about the market on which to base your research in Part A. From your research results, you'll need to select the most important and relevant information for your marketing campaign.

Revision task information

The soft drinks market
Retail value: £15.6bn
Sales volume: 14.5bn litres
Annual growth 2010–2015: 2.1%
Number of businesses: 103
Market leader: Coca-Cola
Growth trends 2013: bottled water (+10.4%);
still juice drinks (+6.2%); energy drinks (+5.1%)
49% of carbonated drinks in the UK are low or no calorie
Source: British Soft Drinks Association (BSDA).

Using research results

Use your research results to identify:

☑ market trends

☑ different consumer groups and their characteristics

☑ how general economic factors influence the behaviour of producers and consumers

☑ general trends in society which may impact on the marketing campaign.

Sample notes extract

Two aspects stand out from the data:

1 The soft drinks industry is a growth industry.

2 Consumers are becoming more health conscious when making their purchasing decision.

Action: Follow these points up in my own research.

This learner has identified good points to follow up for a potential marketing campaign. They could also research the composition of the market and find out the strength of Coca-Cola, the market leader.

Once you have completed a preliminary analysis of the market data you were given in Part A you could then begin to look at the social, market and economic trends which may influence the product. You might find it useful to compile a table like this in order to identify the specific questions you will consider when conducting your research.

Sample notes extract

Trends	Examples	Key questions to consider
Social trends	Changing lifestyle choices Impact of technology Specific industry issues	What is the influence of these social factors on specific segments of the market? Are there any emerging trends in society which will influence the market, e.g. health concerns (level of sugar in soft drinks)?
Market trends	Demographic profile Growth segments Target demographic (age, gender, income)	What parts of the market are growing/declining? What are the potential opportunities for a new business to enter the market?
Economic trends	Unemployment rate Inflation Rates of interest Consumer confidence	What is the impact of the economic trends on the level of disposable income and discretionary spending and how does this impact upon market demand?

Now try this

Give one example of an external market trend which will impact on the soft drinks market.

Think about emerging social trends that will impact on the demand for certain types of drinks.

Part A: Analysing market research data

You will need to analyse your market research findings in Part A to provide the basis of the rationale and justification of the different elements of your marketing campaign.

 Links Revise interpreting and analysing data on page 16.

How to analyse data

Once you've classified your data, you will need to analyse them.

Analyse data
- Compare, e.g.
  - income of different consumer groups by age
  - consumer demand in different regions.
- Recognise patterns, e.g.
  - does demand increase if income increases?
  - what is the relationship between price and demand?
- Predict consequences, e.g.
  - a 10 per cent increase in advertising revenue will increase sales turnover by 2 per cent.

Evaluate data
- Weigh up evidence.
- Draw conclusions.

Sample notes extract

The soft drinks market in the UK is highly competitive with over 100 producers although the market is dominated by Coca-Cola which could impact on the opportunities available to new producers to enter the market. Also, where there is a dominant supplier in the market it can gain a competitive cost advantage in terms of supplies and distribution costs.

The increase in the sales growth of bottled water (+10.4%) and low-calorie drinks confirms that diet and health remain high on the consumer agenda. The growth in still juice sales (+6.2%) and energy drinks (+5.1%) may reflect the changing lifestyle of younger people.

The soft drinks industry grew by 2.1% over the five-year period up to 2015 despite the uncertain economic times with prices under pressure and tight consumer budgets.

 Links See revision task information on page 34.

This learner's approach to analysing their market research findings in Part A is analytical because it:

👍 **classifies** different aspects of the data (the market; the consumer; social and economic trends)

👍 **compares** the sales growth of different products

👍 **recognises patterns** such as health conscious consumers buying more bottled water and low-calorie drinks

👍 **predicts consequences** since it may be difficult for a small producer to enter the soft drinks market

👍 **evaluates** the data to draw conclusions such as the industry continued to grow despite the negative economic climate.

Now try this

Apart from the number of producers, identify another factor which makes the soft drinks industry difficult to enter.

 Think of the impact of different elements of the marketing mix.

Part A: Applying marketing principles

In the external assessment, you will need to base your marketing campaign and marketing materials on sound marketing principles. Remember to use appropriate marketing terminology.

Marketing principles

One of the main marketing principles is the **marketing mix**. All marketing campaigns are based around this and you will find it useful to base your marketing campaign around the four different elements in the mix.

Links Revise the marketing mix and the extended marketing mix on pages 21 and 27.

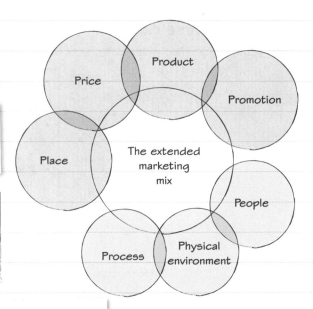

Marketing terminology

To remind yourself of marketing terms, make a glossary. Group the terms into different themes and then describe each term in your own words.

The traditional model of the 4Ps has been extended to 7Ps to take account of the service sector.

This learner has practised using marketing terminology by summarising the results of their research in their prepared notes.

Sample notes extract

The UK soft drinks market is highly competitive, offering the consumer a significant number of differentiated products. In addition, the market share taken up by large businesses makes it difficult for a new soft drink to enter the market at the introduction phase of its product life cycle.

The marketing mix model can be used as the basis for developing a marketing campaign. For example, in terms of the **product** the new producer could establish a USP focused upon its target demographic (**people**).

Establishing an internet presence via a website and using social media to promote viral advertising can be an effective marketing strategy (**promotion**).

Web analytics can also be used to determine the number of hits and conversion rates which can be monitored against targets in the marketing plan (**place**).

When writing out a summary of your research from Part A, try to identify how different features of the marketing mix can be applied to your research findings.

The learner has used appropriate marketing terminology throughout.

Now try this

Write two sentences relevant to the case study which include the marketing terms **market segmentation** and **demographic profile**.

Make a list of other marketing terms which would be relevant to this case study.

Part B: Using additional information

In the external supervised assessment (Part B), you will be given additional information about the set task which you will need to take into account when preparing your marketing campaign. Look at the revision task and information below to understand what approach to take.

Task

You will need to refer to the additional task information below and the notes of any preparatory work completed in Part A.

ACTIVITY 1

Prepare a rationale for the marketing campaign for the 'Samji' energy drink. This should include:

- Marketing aims and objectives
- Research data on the market, to include
  - an analysis of your research using appropriate tools
  - target market
  - size, structure and trends
  - competition
- Evaluation of the reliability and validity of the information researched
- Justification for your rationale.

ACTIVITY 2

Prepare a marketing budget plan and timescale which will support your marketing campaign for the 'Samji' energy drink. This should be based on your rationale in activity 1.

Task information

Brother and sister, Sami and Jenni Usman, have formed a partnership to market a new energy drink called 'Samji', an organic low-calorie yoghurt-based fruit drink sourced from a women's collective in South-East Asia. The new drink contains special herbs and spices which have been medically proven to safely increase energy levels with no harmful side effects. They wish to target women who are actively engaged in sport or who participate in keep fit activities. They believe their drink can have the same success as sports and energy drinks currently on the market.

The specific aspects you will need to cover in your marketing campaign in Part B include:
- marketing objectives
- an analysis of your market data
- how you will reach your target market
- how you will evaluate your marketing campaign.

You will need to consider how the budget will be allocated to the various marketing activities in your marketing campaign.

You will need to synthesise this new information with the research you did in Part A.

Question 1 is based on the task information provided in Part B.

Synthesising the information

Once you have read the additional information and activities, the next stage is to synthesise the information, i.e. bring it all together.

Try compiling a list of key questions (similar to those here) based upon the product and your own research data, as this learner has done.

Sample notes extract

Key questions

1   THE PRODUCT – what are its key features? Can you identify its USP? Is there a target market?

2   THE MARKET – what is the potential size of the target market? Are there any trends identified in the target market? What is the level of competition in the market? Who are the main rivals?

Question 2 is based on your preparatory notes and the set task information provided in Part A.

Now try this

Complete your plan for the two activities in the soft drinks revision task.

You will not be required to submit the plan so don't spend too much time on the presentation format.

Part B: Synthesising your ideas

You will have a lot of data and information drawn from a variety sources which need to be brought together to formulate your rationale and develop the marketing campaign in Activity 1.

The product's USP

The additional information provided a profile of the characteristics of 'Samji' energy drink:

👍 Organic

👍 Healthy

👍 Ethically sourced from women's collective

👍 Contains special herbs and spices

👍 No harmful side effects

👍 Increases energy levels

👍 Medically proven

👍 Safe

You can combine some of these factors together to identify the USP.

Links Revise USPs on page 6.

The target consumer

One way you can try to identify the target market is to **visualise** the target consumer based upon the profile of the characteristics of the 'Samji' energy drink and think of some key words to describe them:

Young women – trend setters 18-25 years old

Fit and healthy lifestyle

Samji target consumer

Active

City-living professional

Image and health conscious

Extracting data from market research

You are now in a position to review the market research data you compiled, in this case for the 'Samji' energy drink.

You should have collected information about market segmentation as part of your Part A research. You will need to focus on any information that applies to your target market.

Sample notes extract

<u>Research notes</u>

2014

UK soft drinks industry worth £15.7bn

14.8 billion litres of soft drinks consumed

Low-calorie drinks account for 57% of the market

Energy drinks account for 4.1% of the market (up from 2.7% in 2008)

Consumption of energy drinks grew by 5.3% to 600 million litres in 2014

Source: British Soft Drinks Association Annual Report, 2015
http://www.britishsoftdrinks.com/write/MediaUploads/Publications/BSDA_Annual_Report_2015.pdf

Sample response extract

<u>The rationale</u>

The soft drinks industry is a growth industry with a trend towards health-conscious, life-style drinks. The industry has an estimated worth of £15.7 billion per year with over half (57%) of the total soft drinks market accounted for by low-calorie drinks. Although the size of the energy drinks market is relatively low (4.1%), there is the potential for market growth (5.3% growth in 2014). An opportunity exists for the introduction of a new energy drink with a marketing campaign focused upon 18–25-year-old females coupled with a marketing message of an action-sport brand and where the desire for a healthy living lifestyle may take a priority over product price.

Once you have completed your research in Part A, you should start to put together a **rationale** for your marketing campaign by summarising what it will try to achieve.

Now try this

Analyse the market research you have collected to identify any other data which would support the rationale of the proposed marketing campaign.

 Identify market size, growth and demographics.

Part B: Developing your campaign

Once you have written the rationale, you will be ready to develop your marketing campaign. The diagram below shows the stages involved.

  1 Produce the marketing message

2 Decide the marketing mix

 3 Select media

Links Revise marketing messages and the marketing mix on page 28.

The marketing campaign

Links Revise media and budgets on page 29.

 6 Evaluate the campaign

 5 Prepare a timeline of key dates when marketing activities are to take place

 4 Allocate the campaign budget

  Links Revise evaluation on page 30.

Links Revise timelines on page 30.

The marketing message will form the basis of all marketing activities and consists of six steps.

Sample response extract

<u>The marketing message</u>

The marketing message for the 'Samji' energy drink will focus on '<u>increasing your energy levels</u>' in order '<u>to keep fit and stay healthy</u>', by enjoying a '<u>socially responsible yoghurt-based energy drink</u>', a '<u>low-calorie drink which increases energy levels</u>' and is '<u>medically proven to be safe</u>'.

We want consumers to '<u>Try it next time you go to the gym</u>'.

Capture the attention of the market

Identify the needs of your target market

Provide a brief description of the product

Describe the benefits of the product

Give message credibility

State the action you want the consumer to take

Sample response extract

<u>Marketing mix</u>

The 'Samji' energy drink's USP is that it is medically proven to be able to safely increase energy levels (**product**); consumers are likely to pay higher prices for the drink and, although there may be the opportunity for price skimming, the first phase of the campaign will involve penetration pricing (**price**); social media will play a key part in the campaign linked to positive reviews and endorsements in lifestyle magazines (**promotion**); the product will be sold primarily through high street stores, health stores and sports clubs (**place**).

Use the elements of the marketing mix to identify how product, price, promotion and place will be incorporated into your marketing campaign in Part B Activity 1.

Now try this

 Targets should be set according to SMART principles.

State one financial target and one non-revenue target for your marketing campaign.

 Links Revise SMART objectives on page 18.

Part B: Costing the campaign

In Activity 2, the budget available to your marketing campaign will be given to you in the external assessment. For the soft drinks revision task the budget has been set at £60 000. In the assessment, you will need to show how you will allocate the marketing campaign budget.

Budget calculations

Use your research notes to calculate the costs of the different elements within your marketing campaign.

One way of making the budget decisions more manageable is to allocate a percentage of the budget to specific marketing objectives. For example, in the soft drinks revision task you may want to allocate 20 per cent of the £60 000 (£12 000) to promotional activities and gifts. You will then be able to calculate how many leaflets and gifts you could purchase with this budget allocation.

Be creative

Try to think of ways to get your marketing message across which are **cost effective** (or incur no costs at all). Examples include:

- ✓ social media including blogs
- ✓ press releases and press articles
- ✓ sponsorship
- ✓ use family and friends
- ✓ celebrity endorsements.

Sample response extract

Objective: to increase brand awareness		
Budget allocation: £15 000 (25%)		
Activity	**Costs**	**Target**
To attend 'Women in Sport' trade show	Hire of stand: £7000 Promotional gifts: £2000 Free product samples: £1500	60% brand recognition by attendees departing the venue 85% 'excellent' customer satisfaction rating after tasting samples of 'Samji'

 Identify each activity separately so you can calculate how much of the budget allocation is left over to achieve the objective – here £4500 remains out of the allocation of £15 000.

 Itemise the specific cost related to each activity so that you can monitor and adjust your budget.

 Setting and monitoring targets is a good way of assessing the impact of your budget expenditure. You could also measure total number of sales, repeat sales and market share.

Now try this

What activities would you put in place if 15 per cent of the budget in the soft drinks revision task was allocated to using the internet to promote the product?

 You need to know the monetary value of the 15 per cent before you decide the activities you will put in place.

Part B: Presenting the campaign

In the external assessment, you will be expected to write up your marketing campaign in the taskbook provided. You will not have access to a computer. A possible format is suggested below.

Number each separate section in your work and give it a heading.

Establish the rationale of the marketing campaign

- Identify no more than four aims and objectives.
- Relate your objectives to elements such as sales, brand recognition and brand awareness.

Give the marketing campaign a title.

This section forms the foundation of the marketing campaign.

Research

- Analysis of the data
- Evaluation of the data
- Include both data on products and consumers.
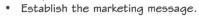

The quality of your preparatory work will be reflected in this section.

Try to identify the USP of the product in this section.

The product

- Identify the key characteristics of the product.
- Establish the marketing message.
- Determine target demographic and main characteristics.

Map the key characteristics of the product against the target demographic.

In this section of the report be specific regarding the media you will use.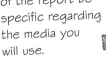

The marketing mix

- Product, Price, Promotion, Place
- Identify relevant actions in relation to each of the marketing aims and objectives.
- Identify the timeline for each action.
- Identify how the impact of the action will be measured.

Identify the routes to market, e.g. high street stores, supermarkets, sports clubs, website.

Check that the budget in the marketing campaign adds up to the budget allocation.

Budget allocation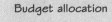

- Allocate budget against each action.

Allocate the budget to specific objectives.

In this section consider possible contingency plans if things don't go according to plan.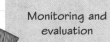

Monitoring and evaluation

- Show how the campaign will be monitored against the targets and the budget allocation.
- Revise budget on the basis of outcomes.

You may wish to retain a contingency fund to allow for any unexpected opportunities.

Now try this

State three aims and objectives of the marketing campaign for the new 'Samji' energy drink.

Start each aim and objective with 'To ...'.

45

Functions of money

As part of managing your personal finances, you need to understand what money is. On this page, you will revise the four functions of money.

1 **Unit of account**
Money can be used to place a value on goods and services. You exchange money for an equivalent value in goods and services – this is the price. In the UK, the unit of account is shown in pounds and pence.

2 **Means of exchange**
Money is used to sell, buy or trade goods and services. Money makes it simple to do this; otherwise you would have to swap products or services in order to trade (more commonly known as bartering).

Functions of money

3 **Store of value**
Money has a value. It can be stored, for example in a bank, and then used in the future to buy goods and services.

4 **Legal tender**
Money is the legal means you use to pay for goods and services. Legal tender is the national currency of a country. It is the official method of payment.

Paying with money

When you hand over a £5 note to buy a burger and fries, you are using money as a means of exchange. Money is recognised and universally accepted in all restaurants or shops. Anyone with money can walk into a restaurant or shop and exchange that money for goods or services. If you tried to exchange potatoes or flowers for a burger and fries you would run into problems – neither are common means of exchange.

Money (cash) is the universally recognised means of exchange.

Now try this

Identify the main functions of money.

 Identify what money does and what it is for in your own words.

Role of money

As part of managing your finances, you need to understand how the role of money can change. On this page, you will revise the six factors that may influence your view of money.

 Personal attitudes
- Your attitudes towards risk and reward. Will you take chances to make money, or do you prefer to play safe and save?
- How you balance the way you borrow, spend and save.

 Life stages
As you go through each of the five main life stages – childhood, adolescence, young adult, middle age, old age – your financial priorities and needs will change.

 Culture
Your background or culture, including religious beliefs or ethical principles, may shape your view of money.

Factors influencing your view of money

 Life events
Major life events such as moving home or being made redundant can affect your view of the importance of money.

 External influences
These include events outside your control, such as the state of the economy or the availability of jobs in your area.

 Interest rates
Interest rates can have a big impact on whether you decide to save or borrow. Low interest rates are good for borrowers but not for savers, while high interest rates make money expensive to borrow but savers receive more interest on their deposits.

Now try this

Identify and explain the likely financial commitments of a young adult.

For most people this is their first taste of independence, but it also means serious financial commitments for the first time as well.
What big purchases might you make as a young adult?

Planning expenditure

It's important to plan expenditure in order to avoid getting into financial difficulty. On this page, you will revise the principles you need to think about when managing your finances.

Control costs

Avoid getting into debt

Avoid legal action and/or repossession of goods or your home

Counter the effects of inflation

Remain solvent

Provide insurance against loss or illness

Why plan expenditure?

Maintain a good credit rating

Set financial targets and goals

Avoid bankruptcy

Generate income and savings

Manage money to fund purchases

Benefits of planning

Careful planning will help to ensure you have money to meet future financial needs.

👍 A good credit rating means you will be able to borrow money to fund a large purchase such as a car or your home.

👍 Money not spent on essentials can be saved and earn interest to generate an income.

👍 Savings can be used to fund purchases or be available to pay for unexpected expenses.

The risks of not planning

Failure to control expenditure may mean you are at risk of:

👎 getting into debt because you cannot pay bills

👎 having insufficient funds to pay loan repayments

👎 having legal action taken against you for non-payment of loans or losing goods that you are unable to pay for (repossession)

👎 a poor credit rating, which affects your ability to borrow money

👎 not being able to save for the future.

Now try this

Last year Ruksana took out a loan to buy a car. She has made 12 of the 36 repayments but has just been made redundant and cannot make the remaining instalments. Discuss what might happen to Ruksana.

 What will the lender do and what should Ruksana do?

Ways to pay 1

There are many different ways to pay for products and services. On this and the next page, you will revise each method, including its advantages and disadvantages.

 Cash – notes and coins
- Accepted in most places
- Can be stolen or counterfeited
- Cannot be used for online purchases

 Debit card – issued by banks
- Payment is taken directly from the cardholder's bank account
- Secure method, no need for cash
- 'Contactless' cards can be used for small amounts
- Small risk of cardholder overspending

 Credit card – issued by banks and financial companies
- Goods and services are paid for directly by the card issuer
- Cardholder receives short interest-free period, usually a month, on amount borrowed
- Card issuer charges interest on the balance outstanding after the interest-free period
- Risk of cardholder overspending and getting into debt

 Cheque – issued to bank customers
- A written order to pay a sum of money from a bank customer's account to another person or organisation (payee)
- Fairly secure method as only the payee can cash the cheque
- Once the payee cashes the cheque, it takes at least three days for the amount to be available in their account
- Although still widely used, some retailers no longer accept cheques

Payment methods

 Electronic transfer – direct payment
- Payment is made directly between bank accounts
- Easy to set up and use
- Transfer is instant
- Bank details of third party must be correct; otherwise transfer will not take place

 Direct debit – an instruction to pay
- An instruction to a bank authorising a third party (payee) to collect varying amounts of money from the person's bank account (payer)
- Simple way to pay regular bills – the amount is deducted automatically from the payer's bank account
- Payee may vary amounts making it difficult for payer to plan expenditure
- Payer must have sufficient funds in their bank account to cover the payment

 Standing order – an instruction to pay
- An instruction to a bank from an account holder to make regular set payments to a person or organisation
- Payments do not change, allowing the payer to plan their expenditure
- Payments are made automatically and continue until cancelled by the payer
- Payer must have sufficient funds in their bank account to cover the payment

Now try this

Explain the differences between credit cards, debit cards, gift cards and loyalty cards.

 These payment card types have different characteristics; they differ in terms of usage, scale, acceptance, security and costs.

Ways to pay 2

🔗 **Links** See page 49 for more ways to pay.

 Prepaid cards – cash loaded onto a card which can be used to make purchases
- Widely accepted by retailers
- Cannot spend more than the amount of cash on card – may help with control of expenditure
- If lost or stolen, the cash on the card is lost
- Some cards have set-up and transaction fees

 Contactless cards – payment is made when card touches terminal
- Fast, easy and secure
- Usually for amounts less than £30

 Charge cards – issued by financial companies
- A short-term, interest-free loan. Cardholder can buy goods and services without paying for them immediately but balance must be paid in full at end of every month
- Annual fee is payable; charge card companies require customers to have a certain level of annual income

 Store cards – issued by retailers
- Similar to a credit card but only accepted by store that issues it
- Cardholders may benefit from discounts and loyalty schemes
- Interest payable on balance unless paid off in full each month
- Risk of cardholder overspending and getting into debt

Payment methods

 Mobile banking – online banking using an app
- Bank account holder manages their account through their smartphone or tablet
- Allows account holder to check balances, make payments and transfers
- Secure, can be used wherever the account holder has access to internet
- Service limited compared with internet banking

 BACS and Faster Payments – electronic payment from one bank account to another
- BACS – takes three days to transfer payment from one account to the other
- Faster Payments – transfer takes place within two hours
- Usually no fee

 CHAPS – electronic payment from one bank account to another
- Guaranteed same-day transfer as long as bank instructed by a certain time
- A fee is charged

 **Now try this**

Give a situation when a business or an individual might use:
(a) BACS
(b) Faster Payments
(c) CHAPS.

 These are all forms of electronic payment, but they tend to be used in specific situations.

Current accounts

Banks and building societies offer a choice of four main types of current account for everyday use. You need to revise their different features, advantages and disadvantages.

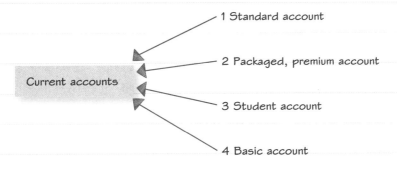

Current accounts
- 1 Standard account
- 2 Packaged, premium account
- 3 Student account
- 4 Basic account

1 Standard account

Customers must have a fair credit rating. Features include:

- no banking fees
- cheque book and bank card, often with contactless payment
- facility to set up direct debits/standing orders to pay bills
- salary can be paid directly into the account
- overdraft facilities – the interest may be high.

2 Packaged, premium account

This is similar to a standard account but offers additional features for a monthly fee. These include:

- packaged benefits such as travel insurance or discounts on goods and services – customers have to pay for these even though they may not want them
- interest on credit balances
- cash back on household bills paid by direct debit
- special rates of interest on overdrafts.

3 Student account

This is aimed at learners in higher education to help them manage their finances. It has limited features, which include:

- interest-free overdraft up to a certain limit – if you go over the limit, the interest can be very high
- debit card
- some accounts offer a free gift card or travel discounts.

4 Basic account

This is a no-frills account aimed at customers with a poor credit rating. It is similar to a standard account but with no overdraft facilities. Features include:

- no banking fees
- debit card
- facility to set up direct debits to pay bills.

Now try this

1   Describe and explain which type of current account would best suit: (a) someone with a good credit rating wanting to set up regular payments for household bills, (b) a student who has just left university and is about to start a full-time job, (c) someone with a poor credit history wanting to set up regular payments for household bills, (d) an 18-year-old about to leave home to start university.

2   Why shouldn't someone keep the same bank account their entire life?

Think of the needs of each of the customers and decide which type of account best suits these needs.

Borrowing

People need to borrow money for lots of reasons. It's important to match the type of loan with individual needs. On this page, you will revise the six main types of borrowing.

1 Overdraft

This is a short-term loan which can be used to pay bills if you are short of cash. You arrange with the bank to borrow money up to an agreed amount when the balance on your current account reaches zero.

👍 Usually free to set up. You only pay interest on the money you borrow.

👎 Interest is high and you will be charged a fee to use your overdraft. If you go over the limit or have an unarranged overdraft, there will be penalty charges.

2 Personal loan

This can be used to buy expensive items, such as household goods or a car. You borrow a fixed amount and pay it back in set monthly instalments, usually over a period of one to five years, at a fixed rate of interest.

👍 Monthly instalments allow you to plan your expenditure.

👎 There may be arrangement fees, which can add to the cost. If you fail to make payments on a secured loan, you may lose the asset it is secured against.

3 Hire purchase

This is usually used to buy a car. You put down a deposit, then pay monthly instalments over a period of one to five years. During the payment period, you hire the car; once the instalments are paid, you own the car.

👍 Allows you to buy an expensive item at an amount you can afford.

👎 While you are paying you cannot sell the car because you don't own it. If you fall behind with payments, then the lender may repossess the car.

4 Mortgage

This is a loan taken out to buy a property. It is usually for 25 years and you pay off the mortgage in monthly instalments.

👍 Allows you to buy your home and spread the cost over a long period. Fixed or tracked mortgage rates can help make payments affordable.

👎 An increase in interest rates may affect your ability to pay back the mortgage. The property is used as security for the loan. If repayments are not made, the property can be repossessed.

🔗 Links See ways to pay on page 49.

5 Credit card

You can use this to buy goods and services in shops, online, by post and on the phone. You may spend up to the amount of the credit limit on your card. At the end of each month, you will receive a statement showing how much you owe.

👍 If you pay the full amount each month, you will pay no interest.

👎 If you pay the minimum amount shown on the statement, you will be charged interest on the outstanding amount. Interest rates are higher than a personal loan.

6 Payday loan

This is a short-term loan, usually for small amounts, often when people need cash to pay bills between paydays. A fee is charged.

👍 Can help with cash-flow problems.

👎 Very expensive way to borrow.

Now try this

Gary borrows £900 from a payday lender. He pays £23.88 for every £100 he borrows. He borrows for ten months, missing three payments. He is charged £15 each time. What is the total cost of the loan?

Remember he needs to pay back the capital as well as the other costs – plus the extra three months.

Savings

If you earn more than you spend, you could save or invest the spare cash. On this page, you will revise types of saving and investment, and the risks and rewards of choosing between them.

Individual savings accounts (ISAs)

An ISA allows you to save without paying tax on the interest or profits you earn. There is a limit on the amount you can put into an ISA each year. You may need to give notice if you wish to make a withdrawal.

There are two main types of ISA.

- **Cash ISA:** a savings account where interest is paid tax-free.
- **Stocks and shares ISA:** funds are invested in shares or bonds, and profits/returns earned are tax-free.

In addition, there are now two more types of ISA.

- Innovative finance ISA: interest is earned from lending money to other people or companies through peer-to-peer lending.
- Help to buy ISA: launched in 2015 for first-time buyers to help them save to buy property.

Risks and rewards

Saving money in UK banks is generally a safe option. Investing in shares can be higher risk, as share value may fall and dividends depend on the performance of the business. Rewards for low risk investments are much lower than higher risk investments.

Deposit and savings accounts

- An easy access savings account allows you instant access to your savings. Other savings accounts may ask for notice to withdraw money. This type of account pays a variable amount of interest which is taxable.
- A fixed deposit account pays a set amount of interest over a set period of time. You are not allowed to make withdrawals during this time.

Protected savings

The Financial Services Compensation Scheme guarantees retail deposits up to £75 000 per investor per bank or building society.

Links See also consumer protection on page 58.

Premium bonds

Premium bonds do not pay interest. Instead, savers are given the chance to win a tax-free cash prize every month. Your savings are secure but you will receive no return on your money unless you win a prize.

Bonds and gilts

These are fixed interest securities issued by companies (corporate bonds) and the government (gilts). They pay investors regular interest over a set period of time, as long as the issuer is able to pay the interest. The value of bonds and gilts can fall.

Shares

Shares, or equities, give investors part ownership of a company. In return for their investment, shareholders receive payments, or dividends, per share based on the performance and profits of the business. The share value can go up or down. The rewards may be good, but shareholders can also lose their investment if the company underperforms.

Pensions

Pensions are long-term savings schemes designed to help you save for retirement. Employees pay into the state pension through National Insurance contributions.

Workplace pensions put a percentage of an employee's pay into a pension scheme, with a contribution usually added by the employer.

Some people may also pay into a private pension.

Now try this

Nigel bought 1800 shares at £2.23 each. His first annual dividend was 9p a share. Today, the share price is £2.75. If Nigel sold the shares now how much would he have made from his investment?

 Work out the initial cost and subtract this from the income from the shares and the current value.

Insurance

Insurance is a way of protecting an individual, organisation or an asset against something untoward happening. In return for a premium payment, the insurer undertakes to compensate the owner should something happen. On this page, you will revise the six main types of insurance.

 Car – three levels of cover from Third Party to Fully Comprehensive
- Must have insurance to comply with the law
- Very expensive for new or young drivers
- Insurance pay-outs rarely cover the full value of the car
- Provides protection against liability claims from other drivers

 Home and contents – can be bought separately, but is usually bundled
- Home covers cost of repair or rebuilding if damaged by storm, flood, fire, subsidence, etc.
- Contents covers loss or damage to personal possessions
- No cover for general wear and tear
- No cover if the property is left unoccupied for more than 60 days

 Life assurance and insurance – pays a lump sum or income if the individual dies
- Most only pay out in the event of death; others also cover critical illnesses
- Existing medical conditions are not covered
- Pay-out can make a real difference to families who have lost a member

Insurance

 Travel – can cover a wide variety of potential losses or problems
- Covers emergency medical expenses, personal liability, lost or stolen bags and possessions
- Covers the costs of cancellation, delays or the need to cut the trip short
- Dangerous and adventurous activities will need additional insurance
- Most pre-existing health conditions are not covered

 Pet – covers most veterinary costs
- Does not cover routine vaccinations and other treatments
- Offsets the high cost of veterinary bills and is good value
- Pre-existing conditions are not covered

  Health – only necessary if the individual wants non-NHS healthcare
- Covers some or all private healthcare costs
- Tends not to cover any pre-existing medical conditions, chronic illnesses, cosmetic surgery, check-ups or pregnancy
- Can be expensive and will rise each year as the individual gets older

Now try this

Identify the type of insurance that would cover the following situations:

(a) A family has to cancel a trip to Florida due to an illness.

(b) A driver returns to their vehicle and discovers someone has scratched the paintwork.

(c) A storm knocks off tiles from the roof of a house.

(d) A burglar has stolen a laptop from a house.

Which type of insurance is most likely to cover someone in each case?

Financial institutions 1

Financial institutions range from the Bank of England to a payday loan company. On this page, and the next, you will revise how each institution relates to the personal financial sector.

 Bank of England
- UK's central bank – regulates and supervises banks, building societies, insurance companies, investment companies and credit unions
- Responsible for maintaining the UK's monetary and financial stability
- Sets interest rates – if it increases rates, the cost of borrowing will rise
- Issues legal tender
- Independent from government

 Banks
- Owned by their shareholders
- Offer customers a range of financial services, e.g. current and savings accounts, loans
- Are reliable, secure and private
- May charge for certain accounts and services

Types of financial organisations

 Building societies
- Owned by their members (account holders)
- Provide financial services, e.g. savings accounts, mortgages
- Can offer better interest rates and savings than banks
- Fewer branches leading to poorer access

 Credit unions
- Financial cooperatives owned and run by their members
- Not for profit organisations
- Offer members savings accounts, current accounts and loans
- More limited funds and opportunities than commercial banks and building societies
- Good cooperative and group feeling

Now try this

Identify three advantages for a financial institution that offers online access.

 Think about flexibility and customer service.

Financial institutions 2

🔗 **Links** See page 55 for more on financial institutions.

 National Savings and Investments (NS&I)
* Sells savings and investment products, e.g. premium bonds, ISAs
* Money invested in products used to finance government activities
* Savings and investments are secure as government backed
* Poor interest rate, no interest payments on premium bonds
* Extremely secure and guaranteed by the government

 Insurance companies
* Businesses that offer customers protection against loss in exchange for a premium, e.g. car insurance, travel insurance
* Offer security and peace of mind
* Difficult to understand what is covered and what the conditions of insurance are

Types of financial organisations

 Pension companies
* Businesses that sell policies to customers allowing them to save into personal pension schemes in preparation for retirement
* Funds locked into the savings scheme with penalties if taken out early
* Projected income is based on figures that may change over time

 Pawnbrokers
* Individuals or businesses that loan money against the value of a person's assets, e.g. jewellery
* Interest is charged on loans for the period during which the money is borrowed
* Pawned items not bought back within a certain time may be sold by the pawnbroker to recover the debt
* Instant cash available if asset has value
* Short-term cost is high, risk of losing the asset

 Payday loan companies
* Businesses that offer short-term loans to people requiring cash between paydays
* Immediate cash available even for those with poor credit history
* Very expensive and easy to get into deeper debt

Now try this

Alice requires a small amount of instant cash to pay for a household item. Explain two ways she could get cash, and the risks.

 Which might be the least expensive option for Alice?

Customer communication

The high street banks offer customers several ways to interact with them.

Bank branch

Customers visit the bank to carry out transactions either over the counter or using automated self-service machines. They may also seek advice on financial services and products. Branch staff may try to sell additional products to customers who visit. Access is limited to branch opening hours, and customers may have to travel to get there, but the full range of services is offered.

Branches provide customers with face-to-face contact with the bank, but the opening hours are limited.

The high street bank branch allows the bank to promote its brand and encourage customer loyalty.

Telephone banking

Customers can carry out simple transactions over the phone 24/7, e.g. checking balances, paying bills. Services are automated, although some accounts allow customers to speak directly to an adviser who can provide advice or carry out transactions and other services on their behalf. Automated systems are very efficient, but customers are often confused by the options.

Online banking

This allows customers to manage their accounts on a computer or laptop via the internet. Customers can check their balance, pay bills, transfer money between accounts and seek online advice. Services are more limited than at a branch, as customers cannot pay in or draw out cash, but access to the account is 24/7.

Postal banking

Many banks still send paper copies of statements to their customers. Customers may also pay bills by cheque sent through the postal system. Cheques may be delayed in the post, but the service is useful for customers who may not have access to online or mobile banking and are unable to reach a branch easily. Most banks are going 'paperless'; this means customers will need internet access.

Mobile banking

Customers manage their accounts through a mobile device such as a smartphone or tablet using an app provided by their bank. The service is available 24/7. Services are similar to online banking. Mobile banking is very efficient, but there are concerns about security.

Now try this

Explain three reasons why a customer might want to visit a bank branch.

 Which services are better delivered face to face?

Consumer protection

There are several independent organisations within the personal finance industry set up to protect the rights of consumers. On this page, you will revise their functions, role and responsibilities.

Financial Conduct Authority (FCA)

The FCA regulates the conduct of financial services providers.

- Its role is to authorise businesses to trade, supervise their work and change poor practice through enforcement.
- It is also responsible for making sure that consumers are provided with a wide range of products and services.
- The FCA is an independent body funded by the organisations it regulates and accountable to parliament.

Financial Ombudsman Service

This is where consumers can turn if they have an unresolved complaint about the service they have received from a financial services provider.

- The ombudsman gives advice or makes decisions based on the facts, and the service is impartial.
- The service was set up by law as an independent public body. It is not a regulator and cannot fine businesses.

Financial Services Compensation Scheme (FSCS)

- This fund can pay compensation to consumers for financial loss if a financial services business is unable to pay claims against it.
- The FSCS covers claims against businesses authorised by the FCA. It is independent of government and the financial services industry.

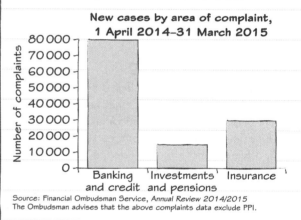

Complaints to the Ombudsman

Consumers mostly complain about charges, administration, and sales and service.

Source: Financial Ombudsman Service, Annual Review 2014/2015
The Ombudsman advises that the above complaints data exclude PPI.

Consumer credit legislation

The Consumer Credit Act (1974) regulates credit card purchases and gives consumers protection when signing loan and hire purchase agreements. It covers interest rates, credit limits, cooling off periods and access to credit files.

Office of Fair Trading (OFT)

Until April 2014, the OFT was responsible for protecting consumer interests. This part of its work is now the responsibility of the FCA.

Now try this

Fiona decided to treat herself to a large curved television. She signed a credit agreement amounting to £4600. The TV was due to be delivered in ten days. When she got home she had a chance to think about what she had done and decided to cancel the agreement. Outline her rights.

 Think about her rights under the Consumer Credit Act.

Consumer advice

Personal finance can be complicated. There are several organisations and individuals that provide financial information and guidance. You need to revise the different types of financial advice each offers.

Citizens Advice

Citizens Advice is a charitable organisation which provides 'free, confidential and impartial advice' on a variety of financial and non-financial issues, including debt, tax matters, borrowing and consumer rights. Advice may be provided online, by phone or in person. Advisers are volunteers and may not be financial professionals.

Independent financial advisers (IFAs)

These are professional individuals who give independent advice and guidance on a range of financial products, e.g. mortgages, pensions and investments. Financial advisers are regulated by the Financial Conduct Authority. Consumers pay a fee for the advice.

Price comparison websites

These help consumers find the best deal on a range of financial products, e.g. mortgages, savings, insurance. The price comparison is free, and can be accessed at any time. Consumers may need to use more than one website to find all the options available.

The Money Advice Service

This independent organisation, set up by the government, offers free and impartial advice to help people manage their money. It provides guidance on a wide range of financial matters, e.g. debt and borrowing, budgeting, saving and insurance. Advice may be provided online and by phone. The website includes a range of calculators and tools to assist users.

Debt counsellors

Organisations such as the charity National Debtline provide free debt advice and information on a wide variety of debt related topics, e.g. council tax, loans, hire purchase.

Its expert debt advisers also advise on court procedures, dealing with creditors and various debt options. The organisation is regulated by the Financial Conduct Authority.

Individual Voluntary Arrangements (IVAs) and bankruptcy

- An IVA is an agreement that an individual undertakes with their creditors to pay off all or part of their debts. The individual pays an insolvency practitioner, who then splits the payment between creditors. There are fees for this service.
- An individual who cannot pay their debts may apply to the Insolvency Service to become bankrupt. The individual's assets can be used to pay off debts and there will be bankruptcy restrictions.

Now try this

Outline the advantages and disadvantages of three of the consumer advice agencies.

 Each of them offers specialised help for particular problems.

Accounting

Accounting involves making a record of the business's financial transactions, then preparing a set of accounts from this information which may be used to evaluate the business's performance. You will need to revise the five main purposes of accounting.

 Recording transactions
Accountants record all money coming into and going out of the business. This enables them to keep track of payments received and ensure bills and taxes are paid on time.

 Management of business
The manager of a business is responsible for:
- planning – to foresee likely financial commitments
- monitoring – to check performance and spending
- controlling – to ensure sufficient funds are available to cover outgoings.

Purposes of accounting

 Compliance
All businesses have a responsibility to comply with financial reporting requirements in accordance with laws and regulations.
Internal accounting controls help to combat fraud.

 Measuring performance
Accountants measure how well the business is performing financially through its:
- gross and net profit
- sales revenue
- efficiency in collecting money owed to the business
- expenditure
- costs.

 Control
Accounting also tracks:
- trade receivables – debts that are generated by the sale of products or services between businesses (money owed to the business)
- trade payables – debts that have been created as a result of purchasing products or services from other businesses (money owed by the business).

Now try this

Explain how an accountant might check on the financial health of a business.

 Think about what an accountant is concerned with and what they might look at.

Income

Income is money received by the business. On this page, you will revise the differences between capital income and revenue income.

Capital income

This is money used to set up a business. It is a long-term investment.
Examples of capital income include:

Loan – money lent to a business by an investor such as a bank. The business will pay back the loan with interest, usually in monthly instalments over a few years.

Mortgage – loan usually used to buy property, such as a business premises. The mortgage will be secured against the property purchased. The business will pay back the mortgage with interest usually over 25 years.

Debentures – a type of bond issued by large companies to raise money. Investors receive interest on their loan which is repaid in full by the company on an agreed date.

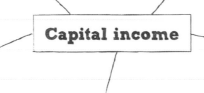

Capital income

Shares – issued by the company to shareholders who own the business. As investors in the business, shareholders may receive a dividend.

Owner's capital – the owner invests their personal savings in the business. The owner may be a sole trader or a partnership.

Revenue income

This is income received by the business on sales of its goods or services.
Examples of revenue income include:

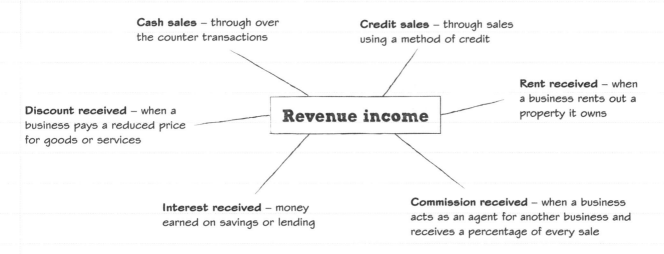

Cash sales – through over the counter transactions

Credit sales – through sales using a method of credit

Rent received – when a business rents out a property it owns

Discount received – when a business pays a reduced price for goods or services

Revenue income

Interest received – money earned on savings or lending

Commission received – when a business acts as an agent for another business and receives a percentage of every sale

Now try this

Identify which of the following are examples of capital income or revenue income:

(a) money invested by a sole trader

(b) loan received

(c) sales

(d) rent received

(e) commission received

(f) money received from the sale of shares.

 There are three of each.

Capital expenditure

Expenditure refers to items bought by the business. There are two types of expenditure: capital and revenue. On this page, you will revise capital expenditure.

Capital expenditure

These are assets – capital items – that the business plans to use over a long period of time. There are two types of assets: non-current (tangible) and intangible.

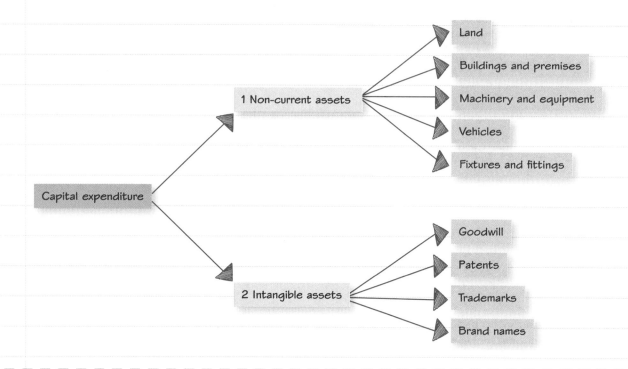

Intangible assets

These are not physical items and may be difficult to value and sell:

- Goodwill is the additional value of a business. It is a measure of the number of customers and its reputation.
- Patents, trademarks and brand names are a recognisable part of the business and have a value.

Depreciation

Some assets such as machinery and office furniture lose their value over time. Depreciation is used to show the fall in value in the business's accounts.

- Straight-line depreciation reduces the value of an asset by the same amount each year over its life.
- Reducing-balance depreciation shows the loss of value as being higher during the early years.

Now try this

Identify examples of capital expenditure:

(a) wages

(b) purchasing a vehicle

(c) building a factory extension

(d) electricity bill

(e) stationery purchase

(f) redecorating an office.

 Three of the six are capital expenditure items.

Revenue expenditure

On this page, you will revise revenue expenditure – the day-to-day costs incurred in running a business.

 Links Revise revenue income on page 61.

Rates – business tax on non-domestic property used to fund local council services

Heating and lighting – payment for services such as gas and electricity

Rent – only paid by businesses that do not own their own premises

Water – payment for supply of water to premises

Inventory – raw materials, finished products, supplies required to run a service business

Insurance – businesses are legally required to take out buildings, contents, public liability and employer's liability insurance

Discount allowed – customers receive money off goods either as an incentive to purchase or buying in bulk

Administration – paperwork required to run a business

Interest paid – on mortgages and loans

Telephone – administrative cost

Bank charges – bank account fees payable on every transaction

Postage – administrative cost

Stationery and printing – administrative cost

Wages – hourly rate paid to an employee

Salaries – annual sum of money, divided into equal monthly payments, paid to an employee

Revenue expenditure

Straight-line depreciation

Reducing-balance depreciation

Marketing – costs related to promoting and selling goods and services

Links For more on this go to page 76.

Links For more on this go to page 76.

Links Go back to Unit 2 and revise marketing.

Now try this

Identify examples of revenue expenditure:

(a) stationery

(b) buying a patent

(c) new office furniture

(d) bank charges

(e) rent

(f) updated computer system.

 Three of these are examples of revenue expenditure.

Internal finance

Some businesses are able to generate their own finance which they use to fund expenditure. On this page, you will revise internal sources of finance and their advantages and disadvantages for the business.

 Retained profit
Some of the profits are kept in the business and not distributed to the owners or shareholders. The money is retained for reinvestment in the business.

👍 Does not have to be repaid and no interest payable.

👎 Not available to new businesses and many companies may not make sufficient profits.

 Net current assets
This is money that is immediately available to the business, e.g. cash, which can be used to cover day-to-day expenditure. It also includes assets that can quickly be turned into cash, such as invoices that are due for payment.

👍 A quick way of raising money. Selling off inventory reduces the costs related to holding it.

👎 May have to accept a lower price for its inventory.

Internal sources of finance

 Sale of assets
Vehicles, buildings, machinery or equipment can be sold to give the business cash. It may take time to sell assets and sometimes the amount received may be lower than their actual value.

👍 A good way of raising funds from assets that are not needed any longer.

👎 Not all businesses have surplus assets that they can sell. May be a slow method of raising funds as some assets may take time to sell.

Useful formulae

profit = sales revenue – total costs

net current assets = current assets – current liabilities

New and small businesses

Many internal sources of finance are not available to new or small businesses. They have not been running for long enough to have much retained profit. They may lack cash nor have many assets to sell off.

Now try this

Over the last three years a manufacturing business has retained 20 per cent of its profits. Explain why it may have chosen to do this.

 Why might the business need this money in the future?

External finance 1

Many businesses need external sources of finance to fund their activities. On this page and the next, you will revise the wide range of finance available from individuals and organisations.

Owner's capital
Existing investors put more money into the business. This is a long-term option, with few additional costs. Limited by the funds available to the owners.

Loans
This is money borrowed at an agreed rate of interest. It tends to be a medium- to long-term source of finance. Repayments are spread over a period of time allowing the business to budget. Interest payments can be high and lenders might want security on the loan. There are two types of loans: fixed-interest loans, and variable-interest loans where the rate of interest changes over the term of the loan.

Hire purchase
This allows the business to obtain assets by paying a deposit then making regular payments. Unlike leasing, the asset is owned by the businesses once all of the payments have been made. This is a medium-term source of finance. It is relatively expensive compared to buying in cash.

Crowd-funding
This involves raising funds online by asking people to invest a small amount of money each. Rewards are offered, or the investment is in effect an advance order for the product or service at a discounted price. This tends to be a short-term source of finance.

External sources of finance

Debt factoring
This involves selling the business's invoices to a third party. The debtor now owes money to the factor agency and they will pursue payment. This is a short-term funding option.

Venture capital
This is funds from a professional investor in return for a share of the ownership of the business. The investor will want to be involved in the decision making. Venture capital tends to be a long-term investment.

Mortgages
This is a loan that is secured on a property. The business will own the property after the last payment has been made. It is a long-term source of finance. The business has immediate use of the property with the payments spread over time. It is expensive compared to cash and if repayments are missed the property can be repossessed.

Now try this

Pavel wants to organise a loan with his bank. He has been offered two options. One is to have a fixed-interest loan and the other a variable-interest loan. Explain what these two options mean and what might happen in each case if there was an increase in the base rate of interest?

The two types of loan have different features and conditions. Consider the characteristics of each type of loan in terms of financial planning.

65

External finance 2

 Links Revise also external finance on page 65.

Trade credit

The business has use of goods immediately and pays the supplier 30–90 days later. It is a short-term source of finance. The business is able to sell on the goods before they pay for them. It is good for cash flow and no interest is paid. The business will not receive cash discounts for prompt pay and it will need to pay on time.

Leasing

Leasing allows the business to obtain assets (like renting) without paying a large lump sum. It is arranged through a finance company. Set repayments are made. It is a medium-term source of finance. The business can have modern equipment and the payments are spread out. Leasing can be expensive and the asset never belongs to the business.

Grants

Grants are government payments to businesses which are given with conditions (e.g. creating jobs or locating somewhere). They do not have to be paid back, but only certain businesses may be able to access the grants.

External sources of finance

Donations

These are rather like grants but they come from charities and other organisations rather than government.

Invoice discounting

Instead of buying a business's outstanding invoices (debt factoring), the organisation lends against the value of outstanding invoices for a fee. This is a short-term option with the advantage that the business is still managing the relationship with the customer. The biggest disadvantage is the loss of some profit.

Peer-to-peer lending

Small investors use an organisation to help them find businesses to invest in and that organisation takes a fee for matching the investor to the business. This is a long-term funding option.

Now try this

Pavel needs to pay his suppliers, but has to wait for his own customers to pay their invoices. Recently, some customers have been delaying their payments. Explain how Pavel could pay his creditors' invoices more promptly.

There are three methods he could consider. Think about which methods already relate to his customers.

Cash inflows

Cash flow forecasts aim to predict the money flowing in and out of a business to ensure it stays solvent. On this page, you will revise inflows or receipts coming into a business.

Cash sales
Goods and services paid for at the time of sale using cash or debit card

£ £ £ £ £ £ £ £ £ £ £

Credit sales
Goods and services paid for following purchase, e.g. by credit card

£ £ £ £ £ £ £ £ £ £ £ £

Inflows/Receipts
£

Loans
Money borrowed by the business from an external source

£ £ £ £ £ £ £ £ £ £ £ £

Capital introduced
Funds invested in the business by the owner or shareholders

£ £ £ £ £ £ £ £ £ £ £ £

Sale of assets
Money received from selling an asset, e.g. machinery

£ £ £ £ £ £ £ £ £ £ £ £

Bank interest received
The business may store money in a savings account on which the bank will pay interest

£ £ £ £ £ £ £ £ £ £ £ £

Cash inflows

Now try this

A business had cash sales of £25 000 in May. In the same month it spent £15 000 on raw materials. It began the month with an opening balance of £5000. Rent, rates and other running expenses were £2000. Identify the cash inflows.

 Work out which of the figures are actually inflows and not outflows.

Cash outflows

On this page, you will revise outflows or payments going out of the business.

Links Revise also external finance on page 66.

Outflows/Payments

£

Cash outflows

£ £ £ £ £ £ £ £ £ £ £ £ £ £ £ £ £   Cash purchases
£ £ £ £ £ £ £ £ £ £ £ £ £ £ £ £ £   Credit purchases
£ £ £ £ £ £ £ £ £ £ £ £ £ £ £ £ £   Rent
£ £ £ £ £ £ £ £ £ £ £ £ £ £ £ £ £   Rates
£ £ £ £ £ £ £ £ £ £ £ £ £ £ £ £ £   Salaries
£ £ £ £ £ £ £ £ £ £ £ £ £ £ £ £ £   Wages
£ £ £ £ £ £ £ £ £ £ £ £ £ £ £ £ £   Utilities
£ £ £ £ £ £ £ £ £ £ £ £ £ £ £ £ £   Purchase of assets
£ £ £ £ £ £ £ £ £ £ £ £ £ £ £ £ £   Value Added Tax (VAT)
£ £ £ £ £ £ £ £ £ £ £ £ £ £ £ £ £   Bank interest paid

Cash and credit purchases

Anything a business buys is an outflow whether it is for use by the business or for resale, e.g. raw materials, stationery.

Rent, rates, salaries, wages and utilities

These are all regular outflows. The business must have cash to cover these.

Purchase of assets

These are small and large expenditures on items, from computer printers and telephones to vehicles and expensive machinery and buildings.

VAT

Value Added Tax is charged on most goods and services. A business must be registered for VAT if its sales go over the VAT threshold (£82 000 in 2015). The business adds VAT on to the cost of its goods and services.

Now try this

Adejola runs a second-hand furniture business. He buys a table and five chairs in August for £110 cash. The following day he agrees to sell them to a regular customer at £40 for each chair and £95 for the table. However, the customer can only pay him half in cash straightaway and the remainder in September. A week later Adejola buys another six chairs for £140 and sells them to the same customer for £35 each. The customer pays the balance of the first purchase and promises to pay Adejola for the six chairs in October. Calculate how much Adejola receives from the customer by the end of September.

Carefully work out how much money Adejola receives from the customer, stage by stage.

Cash flow forecasts

Cash flow forecasts are used by businesses to identify potential problems with cash flow. This will enable them to plan, monitor and control spending more effectively.

Format of forecast

Opening bank balance
Itemised receipts or cash inflows
Total of receipts added to opening balance
Itemised list of payments
Total of payments or cash outflows – this is then deducted from the total of the receipts
Closing balance – this is calculated by adding the net cash flow and opening balance together. This becomes the opening balance for the following month

Entering data

It pays to be systematic when constructing a cash flow forecast, as it is important for the figures to be correct.

Consider:

✓ Are the figures realistic?

✓ What do the figures actually show?

How could potential cash flow problems be resolved?

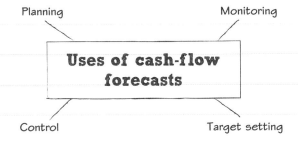

The flow of cash into and out of a business has to be carefully managed. Having too little cash means that suppliers, and even employees, may not be paid on time.

Profit and cash

Businesses selling lots of products and services may have major cash flow problems. If the business is selling products and services and recording them as being sold they may be short of cash if they have sold them on credit as they will not have yet received the money. They will need to replace the inventory but as they have not been paid for items they have already sold, they may not have funds to do this.

Benefits and limitations

Cash flow forecasts should help the business predict when they might have cash flow problems. If the business has predicted and planned for its financial needs, then banks may extend overdrafts or offer loans.

Cash flows fail to consider that a business can delay payments to increase their net cash inflows and that it can buy using a leasing arrangement to avoid using cash.

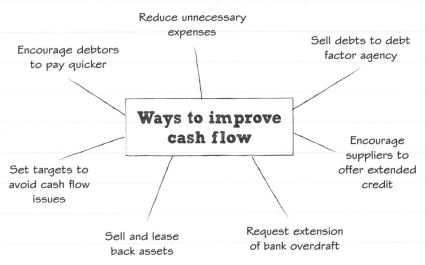

Now try this

Jermaine designs and manufactures dog coats. He has a contract with a chain of pet stores worth £1200 per month, and he also has a website, with a monthly income of £1500. Calculate Jermaine's monthly inflow and his annual cash inflow.

Work out the monthly figures first and then the figure for the year.

Costs and sales

Break-even analysis identifies the point at which a business's costs are matched by the money it receives from sales. Below this point the business is losing money and above this point it is making a profit. On this page, you will revise costs and sales.

Costs

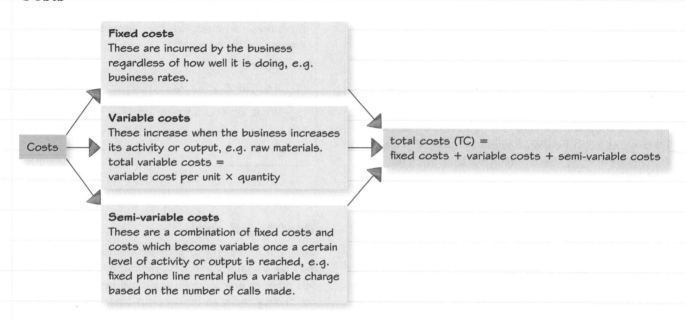

Costs

Fixed costs
These are incurred by the business regardless of how well it is doing, e.g. business rates.

Variable costs
These increase when the business increases its activity or output, e.g. raw materials.
total variable costs =
variable cost per unit × quantity

Semi-variable costs
These are a combination of fixed costs and costs which become variable once a certain level of activity or output is reached, e.g. fixed phone line rental plus a variable charge based on the number of calls made.

total costs (TC) =
fixed costs + variable costs + semi-variable costs

Sales

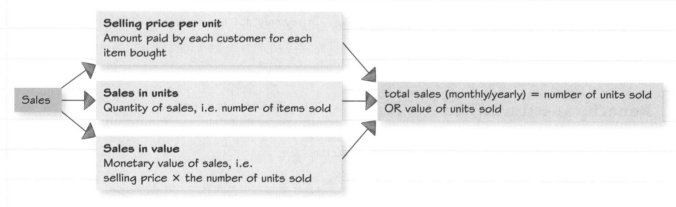

Sales

Selling price per unit
Amount paid by each customer for each item bought

Sales in units
Quantity of sales, i.e. number of items sold

Sales in value
Monetary value of sales, i.e.
selling price × the number of units sold

total sales (monthly/yearly) = number of units sold
OR value of units sold

Total revenue

Total revenue (TR) = Quantity of goods sold × Selling price per unit

Break-even point

Total revenue (TR) = Total costs (TC)

Now try this

Calculate the total revenue of a business that has sold 12 000 units at £12.45 per unit.

Multiply the units sold by the price per unit.

Break-even analysis

You need to revise how to calculate a business's break-even point using both the break-even formula and a break-even chart. On this page, you will also revise profit and loss and how to calculate margin of safety.

Calculating break-even using formulae

A factory making plastic chairs has a maximum capacity of 10 000 units per year. It has fixed costs of £12 000. Selling price per unit is £8 and variable cost per unit is £4.

> contribution per unit = selling price − variable costs per unit

£8 − £4 = £4 contribution per unit

> total contribution = contribution per unit × number of units sold

total contribution at maximum capacity = £4 × 10 000 = £40 000

> break-even point = $\dfrac{\text{fixed costs}}{\text{contribution per unit}}$

break-even point = $\dfrac{£12\,000}{£4}$ = 3000 units

> margin of safety = sales − break-even level of output

at maximum capacity = 10 000 − 3000 = 7000 units

> months to break even = $\dfrac{\text{break-even units}}{\text{units produced per month}}$

production is 834 units per month (i.e. $\dfrac{10\,000\ \text{units}}{12\ \text{months}}$)

months to break even = $\dfrac{3000}{834}$ = 3.6 months (or just under 4 months)

Break-even chart

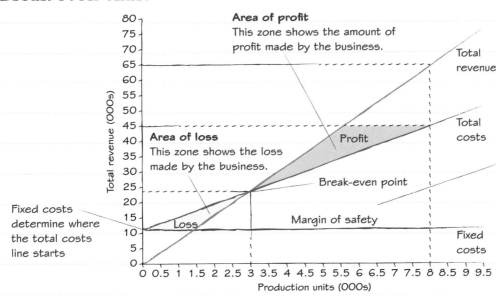

Now try this

Look at the graph and answer the following questions.

(a) State the profit or loss when 8000 sales have been made.

(b) State the margin of safety at 8000 sales.

 Carefully study the graph and check your calculations.

Using break-even

Break-even is a valuable management tool used by businesses to plan, monitor, control and set targets. As part of break-even, contribution per unit has both limitations and benefits.

Planning and monitoring

- **Planning** – break-even helps the business to work out how many items it needs to sell over a certain period to cover its costs and to use this information to set a price that will enable it to make a profit.
- **Monitoring** – break-even alerts the business to potential problems, e.g. increased fixed or variable costs or a fall in sales, allowing it to take steps to fix them in good time.

Control and target setting

- **Control** – break-even can be used to identify where costs are increasing, allowing the business to take action to control this.
- **Target setting** – break-even helps a business to set targets for sales, unit costs, contribution and profit.

Contribution – benefits and limitations

Contribution pays for the business's fixed overheads, so it is an important measure.

👍 A business is able to see whether the products it produces actually cover their own variable costs.

👍 This is used to set the price of the product in relation to direct production costs.

👎 Contribution per unit may be very low, so the business will need to sell a large number to cover the fixed costs.

👎 Contribution per unit on certain products may be extremely high.

👎 In each case the contribution per unit is distorted and may not be valuable.

Preparing, completing and analysing

It is necessary to go through a series of stages to work out the break-even point:

- The variable costs relate to the additional costs incurred per unit.
- Total costs are the total of these two figures.
- Total revenue is calculated by multiplying the number of units sold by the price the business received for them.

Remember that if a business makes no units they will still have to pay fixed costs but their revenue will be zero.

Revising break-even

Break-even may have to be recalculated where there is a change in:

- selling price – if the selling price is increased total revenue will be greater and rise more quickly. If it falls then total revenue will drop
- fixed costs – total costs will increase if fixed costs increase
- variable costs – these will affect the total costs line, shifting it up if unit costs increase and down if they fall.

Now try this

Using the information you have been given about establishing the break-even point, explain what a business would need to change in order to make more profit.

 What should they do to the selling price, the fixed costs, market share and supplier costs?

Statement of comprehensive income

At the end of its financial year, a business will produce a statement of comprehensive income – also known as a trading profit and loss account – which records sales revenue and expenses and shows how much profit or loss the business has made. On this page, you will revise the various elements of an income statement and how to calculate gross profit and profit or loss.

Purpose and use

The statement sets out the business's revenue and expenses. It shows whether a business's turnover has grown or shrunk and where costs have been incurred. Of particular importance is the amount of net profit and how the business has used it.

Calculations

The business's income from sales minus its direct costs is equal to its gross profit. From this gross profit figure other costs are deducted, such as rent and wages. This produces the operating or trading profit.

To work out the net profit before tax the sales of any assets or profits are added. The business then pays tax on its net profit.

The remaining figure is its profit and the business needs to decide what to do with it.

Calculation of profit or loss

There are different types of profit:

- Gross profit – the net sales minus the cost of goods sold
- Operating profit – the gross profit minus any selling or administrative expenses
- Net profit – the operating profit minus any other expenses before tax
- Net profit after tax – the final profit figure once the business has met its tax liabilities
- Loss is calculated similarly with the assumption that expenses exceed income or funds generated from sales.

Adjustments for depreciation

On an income statement it may be necessary to show a fall in the value of assets. Few assets last for an indefinite period of time and their value drops as they age. These include machinery, equipment, furniture and vehicles.

Remember:

- If the asset is depreciated too quickly then profit will appear to fall.
- If the depreciation is too slow then it will inflate the business's profits.

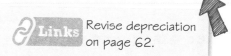 **Links** Revise depreciation on page 62.

Adjustments for prepayments and accruals

The statement has to include expenses, whether or not they have been paid.

Prepayments occur when the business pays for something in advance, e.g. the rental of a telephone line. An accrual occurs when an expense has been incurred but has not yet been paid, e.g. a phone bill.

Interpretation, analysis and evaluation

Interpreting statements is not always straightforward. External factors like inflation can have an impact. Many businesses will also try and bring sales forward that really belong to the next trading period, but are shown here to increase turnover and profit.

This statement on its own will not tell you exactly how a business is performing. It needs to be compared with about five years to show a real trend.

Now try this

A business pays its rent annually on 1 May. This is £22 000. It is preparing an income statement at the end of November and the business needs to work out its prepayment of rent. Calculate how much prepayment has been made by the business on its rent on 30 November.

 Remember to calculate one month first to allow you to calculate how much the prepayment is.

Statement of financial position 1

A statement of financial position (SOFP), also known as a balance sheet, shows the assets, liabilities and capital of a business – its value – at a specific point in time. On this page, you will revise the various elements of a financial statement.

Key relationships

The SOFP shows how a business has raised capital and how it has used it.

- Assets are equal to liabilities.
- Total assets of the business are equal to the fixed and current assets.
- The liabilities are equal to the share capital, borrowings, other creditors and reserves.

Importance

The SOFP shows:

- the actual value or worth of a business
- progress when compared over a number of years
- whether the business is borrowing money and will be vulnerable if the interest rate increases
- whether the business is using short-term (e.g. overdrafts) or long-term (e.g. mortgages or loans) loans.

Other information

- It shows the state of the business at a particular moment in time; before or after could be very different.
- It only shows financial dealings. It does not show how well the business is being managed.

Reading and interpreting

- It is possible to use it to make an assessment of both the short- and long-term financial position and strategy of the business.
- In the short term it shows short-term debt and the current assets used to pay these debts.
- The longer term position can be seen by examining the fixed assets, capital and reserves.

Fixed assets and capital

Fixed assets are those items used by the business to generate income. Acquiring fixed assets means that the business is intending to improve its performance and output.

If a business borrows money to buy assets then it is vulnerable to interest rate changes; it is safer if it has used share capital or reserves.

Reserves

Reserves are funds that the business has set aside with the intention of spending it on an asset or to make a payment to its shareholders.

Now try this

Organise these current assets from most liquid to least liquid:

- bank balance
- stock
- debtors
- cash in safe

 Think about how easy it is to turn the asset into money. Include the terminology within your answer.

Statement of financial position 2

Each item, whether an asset, liability or capital, is detailed on the statement of financial position (SOFP). They are accurate at the same point in time.

Non-current assets

Non-current assets are those that are not intended to be converted into cash in the short term:

- They can be tangible or intangible.
- They can depreciate in value (for tangible assets).
- They can be depreciated for intangible assets (amortised).

The non-current asset can be valued at its net book value, which is the cost of the asset before it has been depreciated.

Current assets and liabilities

Current assets are those that are intended to be converted into cash in the short term.

Current liabilities are short-term debts.

Current assets	Current liabilities
• Inventories • Trade receivables • Prepayments • Money as cash or in the bank	• Bank overdraft • Trade payables • Accruals

Net current assets and liabilities

Subtract current liabilities from the current assets. If the figure is positive then it shows that the business has a surplus of working capital to cover its liabilities.

If the figure is negative (in other words, the liabilities are greater than the assets) then the business does not have any working capital and is unlikely to be able to cover its current liabilities.

Non-current liabilities

Non-current liabilities are those that are due after more than a year. A business may have arranged a long-term bank loan, or perhaps it has a mortgage. It will be paying instalments on those borrowings, but the full amount or balance is not due within the next 12 months.

Net assets

Net assets are also known as net worth. It is the total assets of a business (its current assets plus its fixed assets) minus its current liabilities.

current assets + fixed assets – current liabilities = net assets

Capital

Capital is either cash or other assets that have been introduced to the business, or removed from the business:

- **Opening capital** – the value of investment by the owners
- **Transfer of profit or loss** – the statement of comprehensive income shows the profit or loss of the business
- **Drawings** – funds that could be either salary or wages taken by the owners
- **Closing capital** – equal to the opening capital plus or minus any of the above figures

Now try this

Erdem's business is at the end of its first year of trading. He has £110 000 of assets and £80 000 of liabilities. What important information can be discovered from the difference between these two figures?

 Calculate his net assets.

Statement of financial position 3

It may be necessary to make adjustments on the statement of financial position (SOFP) in order to ensure that any income or costs related to the accounting period are correctly stated.

Straight-line depreciation

$$\text{asset purchase price} - \frac{\text{estimated salvage value}}{\text{estimated useful life of asset}}$$

$$= \text{annual depreciation}$$

Calculation

A business buys a computer network for £5000. It estimates that the computer system will be worth around £200 scrap value. The business has always replaced its computer network every three years to keep up to date. Therefore:

$$£5000 - £200 = \frac{£4800}{3} = £1600 \text{ depreciation per year}$$

Reducing-balance depreciation

The reducing-balance method is slightly more complicated as it requires a series of calculations every year.

Calculation

If an asset's value is £10 000 and the reducing-balance percentage is 10 per cent then the depreciation at the end of the first year is £1000. This brings the net book value of the asset down to £9000. At the end of the second year applying a 10% depreciation reduces the value of the asset by £900. This means the net book value is now £8100.

Prepayments

These are used when an invoice has been paid in advance of the current accounting period.

Calculation

Lucia pays her business's water rates for the year of £144 in April. She is preparing her statement of financial position in July. By how much should she adjust the water rate payment? April to July is four months so she has prepaid eight months, totalling £96.

Accruals

These are stock, assets or other items that have been received from a supplier but the invoices have either not been received or are not yet due.

Calculation

Lucia pays her rent quarterly, which is £3000 each quarter. She paid the last rent in May, covering March, April and May payments. The next payment is due at the end of August. If she were completing her statement of financial position at the end of July she will have already had two months of rent owing but not yet paid. This would be an adjustment on the SOFP.

Interpretation and analysis – key aspects to consider

- **Profitability of the business** – measured by its profit margins, mark up and efficiency in using capital
- **Liquidity** – the business's ability to be able to cover its current liabilities by its current assets
- **Efficiency** – the business's ability to collect and pay debts and its use of stock

Evaluation – key points to consider

- **Cash conversion** – how quickly does the business turn stock into cash?
- **Fixed assets** – the value of fixed assets needed to generate sales
- **Return on assets** – how much is earned from the assets
- **Intangible assets** – what value is there in the business of its intellectual property and its goodwill?

Now try this

Ashton has just bought an asset that has cost him £12 750. He estimates that the scrap value at the end of five years will be just £250. How would you go about working out the straight-line depreciation per year on this asset?

 Work systematically by figuring out the total depreciation over the five years first.

Gross profit and mark-up

Businesses use four profitability ratios to measure how well they are performing. On this page, you will revise gross profit margin and mark-up and how to calculate them.

Gross profit margin

This enables a business to work out the gross profit on goods sold after deducting their cost. Gross profit is measured as a percentage of revenue.

A business can improve its gross profit margin either by increasing sales, or by reducing its costs.

Mark-up

The mark-up is the percentage added to the cost to create the selling price. Gross profit is measured as a percentage of cost of sales.

The larger the mark-up, the greater the gross profit.

Gross profit margin formula

$$\frac{\text{gross profit}}{\text{revenue}} \times 100$$

Mark-up formula

$$\frac{\text{gross profit}}{\text{cost of sales}} \times 100$$

Calculating gross profit margin

A business has a gross profit of £6000 on sales of £10 000. The gross profit margin is:

$$\frac{£6000}{£10\,000} \times 100 = 60\%$$

For every £1 that the business makes in sales 60p is gross profit.

Calculating mark-up

A business has sales revenue of £100 000. It shows a gross profit of £20 000 on those sales. The mark up is:

$$\frac{£20\,000}{(£100\,000 - £20\,000)} \times 100 = 25\%$$

Now try this

1 Jak spent £100 000 on stock over the course of the year. His sales revenue was £500 000. Unfortunately, one of his product lines was faulty and he was forced to refund £50 000 to customers. Calculate Jak's gross profit margin for the year.

2 A business has sales of £96 000. It shows a profit of £12 000. Calculate the mark-up.

1 Don't forget to take off the £50 000 in lost sales for the gross profit as well as the revenue!

2 Try and remember how to use the formula.

Profit margin and ROCE

On this page, you will revise two further profitability ratios – net profit margin and return on capital employed – and how to calculate them.

🔗 **Links** See gross profit and mark-up on page 77.

Net profit margin

This ratio measures the profit made by the business after all expenses have been deducted – net profit. For this reason, it is considered to be a more accurate measure of efficiency and performance than gross profit margin ratio. It is measured as a percentage of revenue. If net profit falls, the business may take steps to reduce its expenses.

Return on capital employed (ROCE)

Investors and owners put capital into a business in the hope that this will enable it to make a profit. From this profit, investors expect a return (profit) on their investment. This ratio measures the return on capital as a percentage of the capital employed, and shows how efficiently the business uses the money invested. A high profit from a low investment means the business is performing well.

Net profit margin formula

$$\frac{\text{net profit}}{\text{revenue}} \times 100$$

ROCE formula

$$\frac{\text{net profit before interest and tax}}{\text{capital employed}} \times 100$$

Calculating net profit margin

A business has sales of £90 000, with expenses (rent, rates and wages) of £60 000. The net profit is £90 000 – £60 000 = £30 000. The net profit margin is:

$$\frac{£30\ 000}{£90\ 000} \times 100 = 33.33\%$$

For every £1 of sales, 33p is net profit.

Calculating ROCE

Two business owners invest £120 000 into a new business. In the first year, the business shows a profit of £440 000. ROCE is:

$$\frac{£440\ 000}{£120\ 000} \times 100 = 366\%$$

For every £1 of capital invested, the owners received £3.66.

Now try this

1. Rav borrows £96 000 to set up his new business. He puts £13 000 aside as a contingency fund and invests the rest in equipment and machinery. At the end of the first year his business has created a profit of £92 000. Calculate the ROCE.

2. Rav's profit of £92 000 was on sales of £226 000. Calculate his net profit margin.

 Match the figures you need to the right formula to make the correct calculation.

Liquidity

Liquidity ratios allow you to measure the ability of a business to be able to pay its short-term debts. You need to revise current and the liquid capital ratios, and how to calculate them.

Current ratio

This is also known as the working capital ratio. It measures a business's assets compared to its liabilities and shows whether a business is being managed properly.

Ideally a business should have £1.50 of assets for every £1 of debt. So the ideal ratio is 1.5:1. If it has less than 1:1 it will struggle to pay its debts. It will not have sufficient current assets to cover current liabilities.

Liquid capital ratio

This is sometimes known as the liquidity ratio or the acid test ratio. It removes inventory from the calculation as this may be difficult to quickly turn into cash to pay a debt.

The ideal ratio is 1:1. If a business has less than this it will have problems paying off its current liabilities.

Current ratio formula

$$\frac{\text{current assets}}{\text{current liabilities}}$$

Liquid capital ratio formula

$$\frac{(\text{current assets} - \text{inventory})}{\text{current liabilities}}$$

Calculating current ratio

A business has current assets amounting to £46 000. Its current liabilities are £39 000. The current ratio is:

$$\frac{£46\,000}{£39\,000} = 1.18:1$$

The business has just enough current assets to cover its debts.

Calculating liquid capital ratio

The same business has £3800 tied up in inventory. The calculation for the liquid capital ratio is:

$$\frac{(£46\,000 - £3800)}{£39\,000} = 1.08:1$$

The business has just enough to cover its short-term debt, just over 1:1.

Now try this

A business has current assets of £77 000 and short-term debts of £56 000. It has £22 000 of unsold inventory.

Calculate:

(a) its current ratio

(b) its liquid capital ratio.

 Make sure you have the right figures for each of the calculations.

Efficiency

Efficiency ratios enable a business to measure how efficiently it manages its finances and uses its inventory. On this page, you will revise the ratios, and how to calculate them.

Trade receivable days

This ratio measures the average number of days debtors take to pay their invoices.

The formula is:

$$\left(\frac{\text{trade receivables}}{\text{credit sales}}\right) \times 365$$

Payment terms vary from industry to industry. A high number of days usually indicates the business is not controlling its debt collection. This may cause cash flow problems.

Calculating trade receivable days

A business has trade receivables of £2300. It has credit sales of £43 750.

$$\left(\frac{£2300}{£43\,750}\right) \times 365 = 19 \text{ days}$$

On average, the business is receiving payments from debtors 19 days after the invoice has been sent. Assuming that the industry standard is 30 days, the business is handling its debtors very well.

Trade payable days

This ratio measures the average number of days for the business to pays its supplier (creditors).

The formula is:

$$\left(\frac{\text{trade payables}}{\text{credit purchases}}\right) \times 365$$

Businesses with cash flow problems are likely to take longest to pay.

Calculating trade payable days

A business owes its creditors £5600 and spends £37 990 with suppliers throughout the year.

$$\left(\frac{£5600}{£37\,990}\right) \times 365 = 54 \text{ days}$$

On average, the business is taking 54 days to pay. If it has credit terms of 30 days, then the business may have cash flow problems.

Inventory turnover

This ratio measures the average number of days a business holds its stock (inventory), and helps it to determine when to reorder. Where a business uses perishable supplies, inventory days will be low. A high number of days may mean that the business has money tied up in stock.

The formula is:

$$\left(\frac{\text{average inventory}}{\text{cost of sales}}\right) \times 365$$

Calculating inventory turnover

A business has inventory of £16 550 in its warehouse. Over the year it spends £92 700 on stock.

$$\left(\frac{£16\,550}{£92\,700}\right) \times 365 = 65 \text{ days}$$

On average, stock has a life of 65 days. Over the course of the year the business would need to order 5.6 (6) times to stay in stock. It also shows that stock is being turned around on a regular basis.

Now try this

Fran runs a market stall. She doesn't have a warehouse or store room; all her stock is kept in her small van. This means that she has to buy stock from the cash and carry quite often. Her yearly sales cost is £76 450. On average she holds £3200 worth of stock. Calculate her inventory turnover.

 You need to work out how many days it takes for her to sell her stock.

Limitations of ratios

Ratios can give useful insights into a business's performance, but they have limitations as a management tool, which you will revise on this page.

 Ratios are averages – figures used for ratio calculations are taken from across the business which may hide the fact that one part is performing well and another poorly.

 Ratios highlight problems but don't explain them or provide solutions to fix them.

 Ratios are based on data which may have changed – the figures come from the statement of financial position which values the business at a specific point in time and may no longer accurately reflect its situation.

 **Limitations of ratios**

 Accounting practices used by the business may distort its performance – figures in the accounts might be misleading.

 It may be difficult to compare ratios with those of competitors – accounting practices between businesses may vary and the data used may no longer show a rival's true situation.

 Poor performance does not always mean the business is failing – the market may be very competitive and lower profits are expected until the market grows or competition lessens. Newer businesses may be investing heavily to establish themselves in the market.

Ratio formulae

Gross profit margin: $\dfrac{\text{gross profit}}{\text{revenue}} \times 100$

Mark-up: $\dfrac{\text{gross profit}}{\text{cost of sales}} \times 100$

Net profit margin: $\dfrac{\text{profit}}{\text{revenue}} \times 100$

ROCE: $\dfrac{\text{profit}}{\text{capital employed}} \times 100$

Current ratio: $\dfrac{\text{current assets}}{\text{current liabilities}}$

Liquid capital: $\dfrac{(\text{current assets} - \text{inventory})}{\text{current liabilities}}$

Trade payable days: $\left(\dfrac{\text{trade payables}}{\text{credit purchases}}\right) \times 365$

Trade receivable days: $\left(\dfrac{\text{trade receivables}}{\text{credit sales}}\right) \times 365$

Inventory turnover: $\left(\dfrac{\text{average inventory}}{\text{cost of sales}}\right) \times 365$

Now try this

Ushma is thinking about investing in her friend's business. Outline the value and limitations of business performance ratios to help her make a decision.

 Think about whether the performance ratios tell the whole story about a business.

Your Unit 3 external assessment

You will have two hours to complete the Unit 3 external assessment. You will be required to answer short factual questions and more in-depth questions where you will apply your knowledge in different business situations. You will need to answer all questions.

Marks allocated and timing

The paper is divided into two sections worth a total of 100 marks.

Section A Personal finance	6 questions	36 marks	45 minutes
Section B Business finance	8 questions	64 marks	1 hour 15 minutes

Remember your calculator

You must bring a calculator into the external assessment because some of the questions will require you to perform calculations based upon business data.

Command words

These are the words used in questions that tell you what is required in your response. Command words:

- indicate how much **detail** is required in the question
- identify the **approach** you should take to answering the question
- determine the number of **marks** allocated to the question
- indicate how much **time** you should spend on each question.

ALLOCATION OF MARKS

Command words can be ordered into a hierarchy – see opposite – which shows how the marks are allocated between different types of questions.

Questions allocated the highest number of marks

Mark allocation depends upon the complexity of the calculation

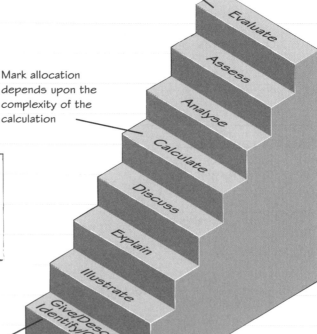

Evaluate
Assess
Analyse
Calculate
Discuss
Explain
Illustrate
Give/Describe/Identify/Outline

Questions allocated the fewest marks

Now try this

Explain why you think a question which requires you to 'describe two factors' has a higher mark allocation than a question which requires you to 'identify two factors'.

Think about what is required in terms of the knowledge and understanding you have to show in answering the question.

Preparing for assessment

Below are some tips to help you plan and prepare for your Unit 3 assessment, and guidance on good exam technique.

Plan

1 Don't leave everything to the last minute.

2 Group together some of the topics so that you can start to identify relationships and how things fit together.

3 Prepare an outline schedule of how you will allocate your time between the various topics.

4 Using a spreadsheet is a good way to prepare your revision schedule.

5 Revise your plan on the basis of changing circumstances.

6 Reward yourself for sticking to the plan.

Prepare

1 Make sure you are familiar with the specification for this unit.

2 Practise answering sample test questions in a given amount of time.

3 Review your answers to see how they could be improved.

4 Make a note of your weaknesses and work on them.

5 Create a study group with some of your friends.

6 Don't be afraid to ask for help.

Skills progression

The command words in Box A require high levels of subject knowledge whereas the command words in Box B require you to APPLY this knowledge to compare, interpret and weigh up different courses of action.

Box A
Give/outline/identify
Illustrate
Explain
Calculate

Application of knowledge →

Box B
Discuss
Analyse
Assess
Evaluate

How to approach your revision

Think of revision as a four-stage process:

1 FACTS ▶ 2 KNOWLEDGE ▶ 3 UNDERSTANDING ▶ 4 APPLICATION

Success in the external assessment will rely on your ability to recall facts and apply this knowledge in different business situations. For example, you will recall facts to answer 'Give one feature of an individual savings account (ISA)'. You will need to apply this knowledge – interest earned on an ISA is tax free – in different situations, e.g. by weighing up the pros and cons of ISAs against other forms of savings and investments in terms of risk.

Exam technique

1 Focus on the command words for each question. Spend a little time thinking about what the question is asking and the best way to approach it before starting to write.

2 If you can't think of an answer to a question, move on to the next question. Save enough time to return to those questions you haven't answered.

3 Keep an eye on the time so that you answer all the questions.

4 Allocate your time according to the number of marks available for each question.

Now try this

Use a spreadsheet to devise an outline revision plan.

Manipulate the spreadsheet so it can automatically revise the times spent on specific activities.

'Give' or 'Identify' questions

'Give' or 'identify' questions require you to recall key facts about a topic. They are worth two marks. Here are two examples:

1 Give two advantages of contactless cards.

2 Identify two risks covered by an insurance policy.

Make sure you read and understand what the question asks you to give or identify. You will lose marks if you misread the question. When asked to state two 'advantages', be sure to give advantages not disadvantages.

Questions which rely on your ability to recall facts carry the fewest marks because they don't require you to expand on your answers.

Links See page 48 for information on planning expenditure.

Worked example

A high street bank is planning to produce a leaflet aimed at school-leavers about to start their first job.

Give two reasons why you should plan your personal finances.

2 marks

Throughout the exam paper, you will be provided with scenarios such as this. Scenarios provide background to the following question or group of questions. Some questions will have their own scenario.

Sample response extract

1 To avoid getting into debt

2 To generate income and savings

The learner has succinctly met the requirements of the question by briefly giving two reasons. This answer would be awarded two marks.

Where a question has several possible correct responses, make sure you only give the number asked for – there are no marks for additional answers.

Worked example

The owner of a dry cleaning business plans to install a new steam cleaner. A colleague has suggested she should lease the equipment.

Identify two advantages of leasing as a form of business finance.

2 marks

Links Links to page 66.

Spend only a minute or so on recall questions. If you don't immediately remember the answers, then move on to the next question and remember to come back later.

Sample response extract

1 Does not require a large outlay of cash

2 Equipment can be updated at the end of the lease period

Don't be tempted to add anything to the points you have identified – in answering these types of questions there's no need to expand your answers. For example, if you had expanded on your first advantage by writing 'Does not require a large outlay of cash which means that it does not have a negative impact upon working capital', you would be stating two separate points – one relating to cash and one relating to working capital.

Now try this

Identify **two** ways a business could finance the purchase of capital equipment.

Underline the key words in the sentence.

'Describe' or 'Outline' questions

'Describe', 'Outline' and 'Illustrate' questions require you to give a brief summary or description of an aspect of personal or business finances. They are worth two marks. Here are two examples:

1 Describe the role of an independent financial adviser (IFA).

2 Outline why a business should produce a cash flow forecast.

You should aim to write a maximum of two sentences for these types of question. Since they are worth two marks you need to make specific points which relate to each other.

Whereas 'Give/Identify' questions rely purely on factual knowledge, 'Describe/Outline' questions require you to apply your knowledge.

Worked example

Links Revise current accounts on page 51.

A high street bank is planning to produce a leaflet aimed at school-leavers about to start their first job.

Describe the features of a current account. **2 marks**

Sample response extract

Your salary can be paid directly into a current account. Cash can be obtained from a cash dispenser using a cash card and the account can be managed online with regular payments being made automatically via standing orders and direct debits.

This is a good answer because it captures the four features of the current account in two succinct sentences:

1 Paying money into the account
2 Managing the account
3 Accessing cash
4 Paying bills

It would have been acceptable to use other examples of each of these features, e.g. in terms of managing the account, the purpose of bank statements could have been included and, with regards to paying bills, bank debit cards could have been mentioned. Since this is a two-mark question, you don't have to include all the examples.

Worked example

Links See statement of financial position on page 74.

Kevin Sharpe started his own printing business a year ago and has asked his accountant to explain to him the purpose of the financial statements that need to be produced.

Outline the purpose of the statement of financial position. **2 marks**

As well as reading the question carefully to make sure you understand what is required, you need also to read the context or scenario on which it is based. Doing so may help you shape your answer more closely to the question.

Sample response extract

The purpose of a statement of financial position is to identify how much the business owns (its assets) and how much it owes (its liabilities) from which can be determined the value of its working capital, the business's ability to cover its debts and the value of the equity in the business.

This is a good answer because it uses business terminology – assets, liabilities, equity and working capital.

It shows an understanding of the importance of working capital (to pay short-term business debts) and a knowledge of the accounting equation: assets = liabilities + equity.

The question isn't asking you to comment on the structure of the SOFP so you don't have to include details of current and non-current assets and liabilities.

Now try this

Describe the features of a debenture.

Link together some of the features using a maximum of two sentences.

'Explain' questions

'Explain' questions require that you link together a chain of related facts in a logical order. They are worth four marks. Here are two examples:

1 Explain why personal data should be protected when using online banking.

2 Explain two benefits of opening a building society deposit account.

> Make sure that the points you raise are logically ordered.

> You might find it useful to jot down the points you want to raise and then see how you can link them together.

Worked example

>  **Links** Links to page 54.

Maria has recently left school, started a job and bought her first car. She now wants to purchase a motor insurance policy.

Explain two factors which affect the car insurance premiums paid by young drivers.   **4 marks**

> This is a good answer because it clearly sets a context for how insurance premiums are calculated. Once this has been identified it then becomes relatively straightforward to identify the relationship between risk and insurance premiums in the context of young drivers.

Sample response extract

Insurance premiums are directly related to the level of risk involved in the insurance policy. In motor insurance the main risks are to property (the car), the person (the policyholder/ driver) and third parties (those affected by the actions of the policyholder). Newly qualified drivers, such as young people, have less driving experience and are classified as being 'high risk' resulting in higher premiums. Secondly, an analysis of motor insurance claims indicates that the number and value of insurance claims are proportionately higher for younger drivers and, as a result of the higher risk, their insurance premiums are higher.

> Notice how the answer has been logically put together – the higher the risk, then the higher the premium.

> Don't include anything in your answer that is not asked for in the question, for example, how a young driver can pay a lower premium by taking out different types of motor insurance policies.

> Try using the chain of reasoning model when answering 'explain' questions.
>
> 1 Identify key terms 2 Describe the relationship between the terms
> 3 Explain how one factor can influence another 4 Draw together your conclusion.

Answering 'Explain' questions

✓ Use business terminology.

✓ Consider if there is a direct and indirect relationship.

✓ Make sure your conclusion is logically consistent.

> Remember
> 'Explain' questions require you to:
> ✓ show clear details to support your opinion or view
> ✓ understand relationships.

Now try this

Explain the difference between a bank loan and an overdraft.

> Refer to the 'chain of reasoning model' when answering the question.

'Discuss' questions

'Discuss' questions require you to consider different aspects of a topic, how they link together and their importance in order to give a balanced point of view. They are worth six marks. Here are two examples:

1 Discuss two different types of insurance that could be considered by a young couple who have recently taken out a mortgage to purchase their first home.

2 Discuss the importance of retained profit as a source of finance available to a business.

You are not required to reach a conclusion in 'discuss' questions but make sure you include the important points in your discussion.

 'Discuss' questions will usually focus on a particular theme or topic so make sure that you don't stray off the point.

Worked example

 Links See external finance on page 66.

> Sonia Ali wants to start her own jewellery business but is finding it difficult to raise the finance to support the venture.
>
> Discuss how peer-to-peer lending may be able to help Sonia.   6 marks

This extract starts by 'setting the scene' for the discussion – the reason why small firms find it difficult to obtain business finance.

Sample response extract

> ... Small firms can find it difficult to obtain finance because there is a high risk of business failure. As a result, securing the finance may result in high borrowing costs. Peer-to-peer lenders are financial intermediaries who attract funds by offering high rates of interest to savers who are willing to lend to small businesses.

The extract then goes on to provide a succinct summary of the role of peer-to-peer lenders.

The complete answer was good because it went on to discuss how a small business can access the funds from the peer-to-peer lenders but ended with a warning of the risks of peer-to-peer lending which may deter some savers from using this form of saving.

Worked example

 Links See page 69 for cash flow forecasts.

> Greg Sterling's bank manager has suggested that he should include a cash flow forecast in his business plan.
>
> Discuss two ways Greg could use a cash flow forecast.   6 marks

The first way of using a cash flow forecast is clearly signposted and identifies how business activities can be planned on the basis of the information in the forecast.

Sample response extract

> ... Greg could use this forecast to **plan the business** by identifying any months where the cash outflows are greater than the cash inflows so that he can make adjustments to his business plan. Although it is a forecast, Greg must ensure that his figures are as accurate as possible; otherwise the cash flow forecast will not accurately represent what is likely to occur.

Since this is a 'discussion' question it is useful to include the reference to why the forecast should be as accurate as possible.

The second part of the response went on to consider how the business could use the cash flow forecast to **monitor** the business.

The question only asked for two ways of using a cash flow forecast. Other ways include **controlling** and **monitoring.**

Now try this

Discuss why a person should consider purchasing a travel insurance policy when arranging a family holiday.

Consider the potential risks of travelling abroad.

'Calculate' questions

'Calculate' questions require you to perform several calculations within a business scenario. The number of marks will depend on the calculation's complexity. Here are three examples:

1 Calculate the return on capital employed (ROCE). `3 marks`

2 Calculate the adjustment for depreciation using the reducing-balance method and amend the statement of financial position. `4 marks`

3 Calculate the revised net profit margin after taking into account the changes in inventory levels. `8 marks`

You would need to perform a straightforward calculation based on extracting the figures for capital and net profit from a set of data.

This would require you to extract data from a table, perform a calculation and present financial data in an appropriate format.

This would involve you performing a more complex set of interrelated calculations.

Worked example

Mary Brindley is the owner of Jazzy Covers Ltd which specialises in designing covers for mobile phones. Mary set a target for the net profit margin of 18% in Year 1 and 20% in Year 2.

The company's financial data at the end of Year 1 was as follows:

Jazzy Covers Ltd	
Sales	£250 000
Cost of sales	£165 000
Wages	£18 000
Rent	£10 000
Office expenses	£7000
Utilities	£5000
Insurance	£1500

a Calculate the company's net profit margin in Year 1 and interpret its performance. `3 marks`

b If sales and the cost of sales in Year 2 remain unchanged, calculate the changes to total expenses that would have to take place in order achieve the target net profit margin. `8 marks`

Show your workings.

You will need to understand business terminology so that you know the correct data to extract from the business scenario.

Sample response extract

Sales	£250 000
Cost of sales	£165 000
Gross profit	£85 000

Total expenses =

£18 000 + £10 000 + £7000 +£5000 + £1500
= £41 500

Net profit Year 1 = £85 000 – £41 500
= £43 500

Net profit margin for Year 1 = $\frac{43\ 500}{250\ 000} \times 100$
= 17.4%

Interpretation: The net profit margin achieved in Year 1 was 0.6% below the target profit margin of 18%. On sales of £250 000 the net profit would have to be £45 000 in order to achieve the target net profit margin, i.e. $\frac{45\ 000}{250\ 000} \times 100 = 18\%$

Required net profit margin = 20%

Net profit required to achieve a net profit margin of 20% =20% of £250 000
= £50 000

Gross profit remains at £85 000 therefore to generate a net profit of £50 000 expenses would need to be £35 000 (£85 000 – £35 000 = £50 000)

Reduction in expenses required in Year 2 = £41 500 – £35 000 = £6500

This is a good answer because the calculations are correct and it shows an understanding of the relationship between gross profit, expenses, net profit and the net profit margin.

You will improve your answer if you show the steps you used to calculate your answer.

Now try this

Calculate the liquid capital ratio using the following figures: Assets £20 000; Inventory £10 000; Liabilities £5000.

You may be asked to interpret the results of your calculations in the external assessment.

'Analyse' questions

'Analyse' questions require you to interpret and study relations in business scenarios and to use data to identify key trends and interrelationships. They are worth eight marks. Here are two examples:

1 Analyse the effect of changes in a business's current ratio.

2 Analyse the contribution of break-even analysis to business planning.

Focus your answers to 'analysis' questions on trends and relationships rather than explaining what the terms mean.

This type of question will not always involve financial data. It can also consider topics such as analysing the reasons for poor business performance.

Worked example

Set out below are the ratios relating to Lovell's Supermarket:

Lovell's Supermarket	
Operating profit margin	3.6%
Average inventories turnover period	18 days
Average settlement period for trade receivables	2 days
Current ratio	0.8 times

Analyse the financial ratios of Lovell's Supermarket.   **8 marks**

This is a good answer because it relates the analysis of the financial ratios to the sector in which the business is operating (low profit margins).

Sample response extract

... The grocery business is highly competitive and to generate high sales volume it is usually necessary to accept low operating margins (3.6%). The inventories turnover period is also quite low (18 days) which points to the supermarket's inventory control systems being efficient, ensuring that stock sold is replaced in good time so that there are no shortages on the shelves.

The answer clearly relates the importance of efficient inventory control for a supermarket.

The answer comments on each ratio in turn and analyses the implications for the business.

A similar approach was taken in the rest of the answer and included an analysis of the impact of a low inventories turnover and a low average settlement period for receivables on the current ratio.

Now try this

Analyse the effect of poor trade receivables control systems on a business.

Consider the impact on a business's financial statements.

'Assess' questions

'Assess' questions require you to weigh up the positive and negative aspects of a topic or situation and give your conclusion. They are worth ten marks. Here are two examples:

1 Assess the use of hire purchase when purchasing a consumer durable.
2 Assess the use of venture capital as a form of business finance.

Try to use 'qualifying words' when you answer an 'Assess' question, e.g. 'However', 'But', 'Although'. This will enable you to balance a positive aspect by introducing a negative aspect which is central to answering 'Assess' questions.

Worked example

> Martin has recently passed his driving test and is looking at the options available to him to purchase his first car.

Assess the options available to an individual who wishes to finance the purchase of a new motor car.   `10 marks`

🔗 **Links** See page 52 for borrowing.

The learner has weighed up the good points and negative points if an individual uses their savings to purchase the motor car.

Sample response extract

... If the individual has sufficient savings they could pay for the car without having to take out a loan. However, although they would not have to pay any interest on the loan, their reduced savings balance would gain less interest and they may also face financial difficulties if any unexpected expenses arose in the future.

Note the learner's use of qualifying words to provide a balanced assessment.

Worked example

🔗 **Links** See pages 77–78 for calculating profit.

> Hayley started her own fabric design company last year and now wants to measure how well the company has performed in its first year of operation.

Assess the use of profitability ratios in measuring the performance of Hayley's business.   `10 marks`

The learner has identified how profitability ratios are measured and their link with the financial statements.

Sample response extract

... Profitability ratios express the profit made by a business in relation to other key figures in the financial statements. The net profit margin, for example, is a measure of how much profit is generated by each sale taking into account the cost of the sale and the expenses incurred. However, it does not provide a measure of the business's efficiency or liquidity.

The learner assesses the use of the net profit margin but then qualifies this benefit by saying what the net profit margin cannot be used to measure.

The learner went on to raise the use of other profitability ratios including ROCE and mark-up; but countered this by identifying the importance of setting targets, identifying trends and the importance of industry benchmarks.

Now try this

Assess the use of break-even analysis in business planning.

Use some 'qualifying words' in your answer.

'Evaluate' questions

'Evaluate' questions require you to come to a reasoned judgement from your own assessment of a set of alternatives. They are worth 12 marks. Here are two examples:

1 Evaluate which insurance policies would be most suitable in these circumstances.
2 Evaluate the performance of the business with reference to its profitability and efficiency.

Worked example

> Zahra's grandparents have given her a gift of £5000 for her 21st birthday. Zahra wants to invest the money but is unsure about whether to open a savings account or buy shares.

Evaluate the relative merits and drawbacks of savings accounts and shares.

12 marks

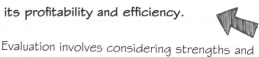

Evaluation involves considering strengths and weaknesses or identifying advantages and disadvantages and looking at alternatives. You will need to form a judgement based upon the points you have raised in your answer.

 Links See page 53 for savings.

Sample response extract

An individual can either choose to save the money in a savings account or invest the money in the shares of a public limited company.

 The opening paragraph summarises the alternatives available to a person with money to invest.

With a savings account you obtain a rate of interest but with shares you receive a share of the profits.

Rates of interest may vary according to the period of time you lock away your money. For example a three-year fixed-term savings account will pay a higher rate of interest than an instant access account. Shares receive dividends based upon the profits made by the company.

 Paragraphs 2 and 3 look at the advantages of savings accounts and shares, how they generate financial returns and the factors which influence the size of these financial returns.

Savings are relatively safe forms of investment although inflation can reduce the value of returns over time. Although shares are riskier investments they have the potential to receive greater rewards than the same level of savings if the company makes very large profits. In addition there is the opportunity for capital gains with shares since their value may increase on the stock exchange.

Savings accounts and shares both involve risks. For example a fixed-rate savings account will not benefit if general interest rates rise. The real return on savings accounts will also be affected by the level of inflation. With shares, falling profits will mean lower dividends and a fall in the value of the shares on the stock exchange.

 Paragraph 4 considers the potential disadvantages by looking at the risks involved of both savings accounts and shares.

Investment decisions are based upon an individual's attitude to risk. An individual who likes taking a risk and is willing to accept a loss is more likely to purchase shares whereas an individual with a more cautious approach to investing would opt for a savings account.

 The final paragraph concludes with an overall summary that evaluation of the merits of savings accounts and shares has to be undertaken with reference to a person's attitude towards financial risk.

Now try this

Evaluate the use of ratios when assessing business performance.

 Ratios can be used to measure profitability, efficiency and liquidity.

Management and leadership

Over the course of time business experts have put forward definitions of management and leadership. A manager's role is to plan, organise and coordinate work. A leader's role is to inspire and motivate others. You need to revise the definitions of management and leadership.

 Management by objectives
- Managers set objectives for employees to achieve business goals.
- Relies on delegation, as employees take responsibility for achievement of objectives.
- Employees have some independence to achieve objectives.

 Situational leadership
- Employees are followers who may or may not have the ability and willingness to do a job.
- Managers adopt different ways to get employees to do their jobs.

 Contingency leadership
- Managers identify the type of problem and either resolve it themselves or seek employee collaboration.
- Sometimes managers may need to be autocratic and instruct employees to carry out tasks; at other times they may give employees greater freedom.

 **Definitions of management and leadership**

 Functional management
Each manager manages a limited range of activities and uses their knowledge and understanding to direct employees.

 Transformational leadership
Leaders who believe their job is to inspire and motivate others to work hard.

 Action-centred leadership
For every job, managers must balance three main management responsibilities:
- Achieving the task
- Managing the team
- Managing individuals

 Transactional leadership
Leaders who believe employees have to be rewarded in order to work.

Now try this

Identify the key differences between a leader and a manager.

Consider what a manager does. What things need putting in place to ensure that the goal is achieved? What might those things be?

Think about what is required of a leader in terms of motivation and ensuring the employees meet the targets that they are given. How might they do this?

Management functions

Managers combine financial, physical, information and human resources in order to achieve their goals. This involves a complex mix of different functions.

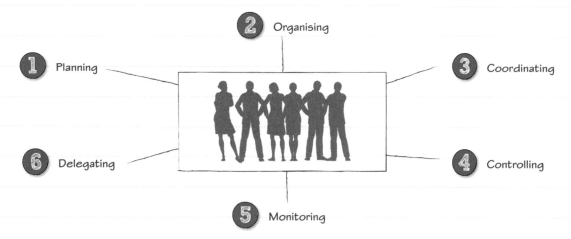

1 Planning

Planning involves:

- determining the business's goals
- working out a strategy to achieve the goals
- designing a plan to implement the strategy.

2 Organising

This is one of the main jobs of a manager and involves arranging relationships between human resources and other resources in order to accomplish goals.

3 Coordinating

Closely related to organising is the function of coordination. This means having the right people in the right place, with the right skills, at the right time. It means making sure that when a job needs to be done the resources are there to ensure it happens.

4 Controlling

This is about ensuring that all of the activities going on in the organisation are aimed at meeting the organisation's goals. It is also about making sure that each individual resource, whether human or financial, is performing to the best level.

5 Monitoring

Monitoring involves systematically checking on progress or performance. It means ensuring that once resources have been set to accomplish a goal they are actually accomplishing that goal or moving towards it.

6 Delegating

This involves giving someone the power and authority to carry out a task or activity on the manager's behalf.

A manager cannot directly lead all activities and has to rely on others, such as junior managers, supervisors and team leaders, to accomplish goals under their direction.

Now try this

The functions of a manager are important and often interrelated. When a manager is trying to accomplish a new goal, explain which of these functions is the most important.

Think about the function that would help you most and enable you to achieve your goal as a manager.

Leadership functions

Leaders aim to inspire, accomplish goals, find efficient ways to do things and empower others. You need to revise the functions that enable them to do this.

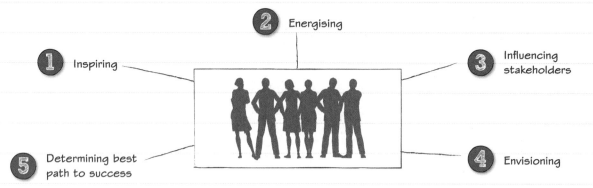

1 Inspiring
2 Energising
3 Influencing stakeholders
4 Envisioning
5 Determining best path to success

1 Inspiring

A leader will try to motivate individuals to do or feel something and to believe that all goals are achievable. Inspirational leaders set the pace of change. They have a belief in the future and try to connect individuals to show that what they are doing has a meaning.

2 Energising

This aims to give individuals the drive and will to accomplish goals. A good leader will make people feel much more able and more powerful to be able to achieve targets.

Energising leadership is all about mobilising and focusing activity and effort.

3 Influencing stakeholders

A good leader will direct the activities of stakeholders – individuals and groups who have an interest in the business – and mobilise their support. They will try to ensure that the shareholders or owners of the organisation are rewarded for their investment by showing good profits.

4 Envisioning

This is one of the most important functions of a leader because it means that they are able to create an image of the future and then develop a strategy to achieve it. They have to communicate this to others and convince them to buy in to the vision. A good leader would be able to create a clear strategy to achieve the vision.

5 Determining best path

A business's future, or problems it may be facing, presents the leader with options. Choosing the most effective path or route is a major function of the leader. They then need to convince others to see that this is the right way forward, and in so doing get the support that they need to ensure success or solve the problem.

Leadership

Leadership is not a personality trait, although elements of someone's personality can make them a better leader, such as being charismatic.

Leadership does not have to come from being in a position of power. It is more about the ability to get things done.

Now try this

Explain why leadership is so important to an organisation.

 What important functions does a leader fulfil?

Business culture

Every organisation has its own distinct personality, or business culture. Business culture is the style and way things are done within a company based on its values, beliefs and attitudes. It influences all business decisions and functions and how the company is managed. On this page, you will revise how business culture influences all aspects of an organisation.

① Vision, mission and values

② Management practices

③ Policies and procedures

④ Management styles

⑤ Structure of the workforce

⑥ How people work

Business culture

1 Vision, mission and values

A business will have an ideal view of what it wants to achieve and how it wants to achieve it – its vision. This can be found clearly expressed in a mission statement. The business will also have a set of values or ethos – how it intends to do business and what it stands for.

2 Management practices

The business culture influences how the organisation is managed. Decisions will be made in line with the culture that has been created, e.g. a business that values ethical behaviour would always make management decisions to avoid situations where its activities could be considered unethical.

3 Policies and procedures

The day-to-day decisions and activities of an organisation will reflect the business culture. Ways of handling problems or situations will also take this culture into account.

4 Management styles

Certain management and leadership types suit some business cultures better than others, e.g. an authoritarian manager would not work well in an organisation that values democracy and participation of the workforce.

5 Structure of the workforce

Some organisations have very rigid structures with several layers of management. Power and authority filters down the organisation to order and instruct those lower down.

Smaller and more modern organisations have flatter structures. Much of the work is carried out in teams and the distance between an employee and the owners may not be great as they probably work together every day.

6 How people work

Business culture determines how people work. Some organisations offer flexibility. Staff will be able to work flexible hours, job share, work from home or work as a member of a team rather than on their own. Others will have a more rigid existence. Staff will have their own desks. They will be required to work certain hours and their views and opinions may not be valued.

Now try this

Identify the advantages of having a business culture.

Think about how having a business culture helps employees and customers. Some industries will adopt different cultures that are more suited to their type of customer and employee.

Management and leadership styles 1

There are seven different types of leadership style.

 Autocratic
An autocratic leader has total authority and control over decision making. They will control employees and monitor them. Autocratic leaders are often found in construction, manufacturing and the military.

 Democratic/Participative
A democratic leader encourages freedom and discussion. They are often dynamic leaders and can operate in rapidly changing business environments. Democratic leaders are often found in the creative industries, e.g. advertising, design.

 Paternalistic
A paternal leader acts as the father figure and takes care of their employees' needs. They expect employees to trust them and to follow their instructions. The bond between employees and the leader is very strong, e.g. the owner of a small family-run business.

 **Laissez-faire**
A laissez-faire leader allows things to take their own course without interference. They give employees an opportunity to take responsibility and instead focus on motivating and providing a sense of direction. Laissez-faire leaders are often found in industries where the employees are experienced, highly skilled or well educated, e.g. experienced sales teams, car or machine repairs.

 Transactional
A transactional leader states the goals and objectives from which activities are then organised. Employees carry out activities in exchange for rewards, e.g. for pay and performance. Example: Lord Alan Sugar.

 Transformational
A transformational leader focuses on the hearts and minds of employees. They aim to give them satisfaction, motivation and achievement. The leader shows trust rather than trying to control, by empowering employees to do the job themselves. Example: Steve Jobs (Apple).

 Charismatic
The charismatic leader tends to have commitment, passion and the ability to hold on to their beliefs. They are persuasive and appealing and are able to use their skills to get people on their side. They are usually confident, optimistic and good speakers. Example: Sir Richard Branson (Virgin).

Leadership continuum for management behaviour

Autocratic ←———————————————————————→ Democratic

- sole decision maker
- sells decisions to others
- presents decisions and invites questions
- presents problems and requests suggestions
- defines problem and asks for group decision
- allows full freedom of action

Now try this

Organisations with many local branch offices give these outlets the power and authority to govern themselves and to make decisions without having to refer to senior management. Explain why an organisation would risk allowing its branch managers to make decisions.

 Do you think the local managers usually come up with the right solution?

Management and leadership styles 2

Managers and leaders have many different roles to fulfil. The spider diagram below identifies the varied skills across many different areas that managers and leaders are expected to have. On this and the next pages, you will revise the skills managers and leaders require to be successful in their roles.

1 Set objectives
2 Motivator
3 Decision maker
4 Team builder
5 Lead by example
6 Consult with others
7 Problem solver
8 Value and support others
9 Manage conflict
10 Build positive interpersonal relationships
11 Use emotional intelligence
12 Communicator
13 Provide feedback

1 Set objectives

Objectives are goals or activities that need to be completed within a given time frame or by a particular deadline. This could be a 30-second call answering rule in a call centre or a same-day despatch in a mail order department. Managers must set clear, measurable and achievable objectives.

2 Motivate

Managers need to encourage or motivate their employees to perform their job roles well. This may involve praise, constructive feedback, opportunities to learn new skills, ensuring work is interesting and giving them autonomy to complete tasks. A motivated employee who is enthusiastic about their role will be more effective than one who feels undervalued.

Now try this

Explain why motivational techniques such as job enrichment, enlargement or rotation are of great value to an organisation as well as to the employee.

 Think about why adopting these techniques would lead to a happier employee and more successful organisation.

97

Management and leadership styles 3

🔗 **Links** Refer to the spider diagram on page 97 as you revise management and leadership skills.

3 Make decisions

Decision making is a key skill, as managers will have to:

- identify the issue
- gather information
- weigh up options
- choose the right course of action to suit the circumstances.

Decision making may have to be made in difficult situations and sometimes the decisions will not be popular.

4 Support teamwork

Effective team working increases a business's productivity and performance. A team builder needs to ensure that team members establish good working relationships and are willing to take on responsibilities, while minimising potential conflict. Managers have to accept that they will have to delegate some responsibility to the teams, but to give them clear instruction and support when it is necessary.

5 Lead by example

The manager acts as a role model for employees. By setting the right example, the manager shows they have the abilities to do the job, demonstrates that they are in charge and are able to deal with even the most difficult situations.

6 Consult with others

The manager is recognised as experienced or an authority on a particular area. They are able to give clear and objective views and are used as a primary information source. They do not seek to impose their views but give their opinion when asked. On other occasions, they will need to consult with others, e.g. financial specialists.

7 Solve problems

This is a major managerial skill. The way in which a manager handles a problem will depend on how well they are able to anticipate problems and how responsive they are.

There is no real problem-solving model that works in all situations, but the most important thing is for the manager to collect as much information about the problem as possible and then assess, analyse and evaluate that information before attempting to come up with a solution.

8 Value and support others

An effective manager should always be focused on the opportunity to develop other individuals in the organisation. This means placing a value on others' opinions and experience, as well as supporting them to develop. This may involve sharing information with their team, having regular conversations about employees' career goals and interests and asking employees to feed back at regular intervals on progress.

Now try this

Research suggests that coaching is the most important function of a manager to ensure employees' career development. What is coaching and do you think managers actually have the time for this role?

Coaching is about supporting employees but it also involves other employees' time. Think about the benefits and drawbacks of this function.

Leadership skills

🔗 **Links** Refer to the spider diagram on page 97 as you revise management and leadership skills.

9 Manage conflict

Conflict may occur within teams and between teams. A good manager may be able to anticipate potential conflict and deal with it before it becomes an issue. Where a conflict arises, a manager will need to listen very carefully and understand both sides before encouraging a resolution or compromise.

10 Build positive relationships

Positive interpersonal relationships are the foundation of effective communication and understanding. Relating to others is an important skill to learn. It means being able to be both a leader and someone that is dependable and confident.

11 Use emotional intelligence

Emotional intelligence is about being able to understand and manage not only your own emotions but those around you. Those with a high level of emotional intelligence are aware of their own feelings, what they mean and how they can affect others.

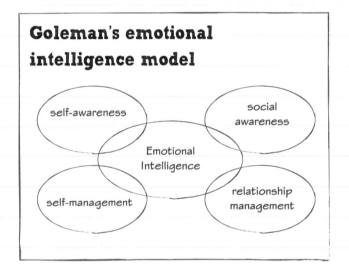

Goleman's emotional intelligence model

self-awareness — social awareness — Emotional Intelligence — self-management — relationship management

12 Communicate

Communication is an important skill as it means that the manager is not only able to get across orders, instructions and requirements but they are also able to express their ideas, values, vision and opinion.

Individuals learn from communication with their managers and interaction through verbal communication in particular helps boost morale and loyalty.

13 Provide feedback

Feedback involves giving an employee a response to a particular activity, conversation or task. It is an ongoing training tool. From feedback employees learn what they are supposed to do and how they are supposed to do it. Feedback can be negative or positive.

Negative feedback	Positive feedback
Involves pointing out what someone has done wrong and how to change it.	Builds on the individual's strengths. They are praised for good performance.

Now try this

Sheryle uses what she calls the sandwich method for her feedback. She slips in a negative comment between two pieces of positive feedback. How do you think employees would respond to this kind of approach?

 Do you think the employees will recognise this approach? What will they do?

Human resources

Managing human resources efficiently is central to the success of any organisation. Businesses need to ensure they recruit the right people to meet the needs of the business plan.

Factor of production

Human resources, or labour – one of the four factors of production – is a flexible resource which can be used to complete many functions and tasks within an organisation when used alongside other economic resources.

Labour market analysis

To help them make the right employment decisions for the business, managers analyse labour market trends at an international, national or local level, and within their industry sector. They will also look at economic trends and the supply of skilled workers to help them understand the implications for their workforce.

Forecasting labour demand

The UK Commission for Employment and Skills (UKCES) produces projections on the size and shape of the labour market as far ahead as 2024. These consider employment forecasts by industry, occupation, qualifications, gender and employment status. Managers will use these data to predict future employee skill needs.

Sources of data

The primary sources of information on labour market analysis are the extensive government statistics.

The main statistics are compiled by:

- ✓ The Office for National Statistics
- ✓ The Learning and Work Institute
- ✓ The Trade Union Congress
- ✓ The Institute for Employment Studies
- ✓ The Chartered Institute of Personnel Development
- ✓ The UKCES Department for Business Innovation & Skills.

Business planning and human resources

The human resources (HR) function is responsible for recruiting the right number of individuals with appropriate skills and abilities to ensure the business has the human resources necessary to fulfil the organisation's objectives within the business plan. It is also responsible for developing the workforce through education and training, and for retaining and promoting talented employees. Market analysis may also lead HR to plan for redeployment of staff and redundancy.

Globalisation and HR planning

HR planning may involve:

- recognising the requirement for additional language skills in the workforce
- moving skilled employees or managers from one country to another
- understanding the different requirements and standards relating to employment in different countries
- monitoring the labour market in different countries.

Now try this

Data from The Office for National Statistics for the beginning of 2016 show that 31.39 million people were in work in the UK. This was 588 000 more than the year before. Nearly 23 million were working full time. If this trend were to continue, explain what would be the implications for HR.

 What will happen if HR finds it hard to attract employees?

Human resource planning 1

Human resource planning is the process of ensuring that the right numbers of people with the right skills are employed in the right place at the right time. On this page, you will revise how HR identifies the business's workforce requirements.

Nature of work and characteristics

Job description
- Outlines requirements of job role
- Can be used to match characteristics of individual to carry out role

Nature of work and characteristics required to perform work role

Experience
An individual may have practical experience of having done the work in the past, but may not necessarily have qualifications. They will probably have the kind of skills that an employer is looking for. They may need some retraining and will probably be more expensive than an inexperienced candidate.

Person specification
- Outlines key characteristics, skills, experience and aptitude of individual required

Skill levels

Fundamental awareness – individual has common knowledge or understanding of basic techniques or concepts ▶ Novice – trainee ▶ Intermediate – will have some competence but may need occasional help from expert ▶ Advanced – can perform work without assistance ▶ Expert – recognised authority; provides guidance to others

Educational level

Some job roles will have minimal educational requirements. Other jobs will require basic educational standards in English, Mathematics and other core subjects.

Jobs related to a particular skill will require qualifications, particularly those that are technical.

Aptitude

Aptitude is a natural ability to be able to do something. It is about showing a flair for doing something and being interested in progressing in it.

Aptitude tests are used by many organisations to see if they are hiring the right person. It is one thing to look at someone's achievements but their aptitude shows whether the individual could learn or develop in the future.

Now try this

If an organisation is looking at assessing people before it offers them a job, outline what the organisation should think about first.

Think about what is required from the employee and the job role. How can the organisation ensure that the person is right for the job before employing them?

Human resource planning 2

In an increasingly changing employment market businesses look for a more flexible workforce and employees look for more flexible employers. On this page, you will revise how HR plans the structure of the workforce.

Flexibility

Flexibility aims to provide a business with an adaptable approach to its use of employees. At busy times, employees within a multi-skilled and adaptable workforce can be moved to deal with critical job tasks that are under pressure. Team working can also speed up progress.

Core and peripheral workers

- Core workers are essential to the running of the business. They hold strategic job positions and will be employed on full-time permanent contracts.
- Peripheral workers support core workers. They may be part time or have flexible working hours. The number of peripheral workers may change according to the needs of the business. They may not undertake the essential tasks of the business.

Full and part time

- Full-time workers usually work 35 hours or more per week.
- Part-time workers work less than this but there is no specific number of hours. They offer the employer flexibility to cover busy periods, and provide extra skills and experience.

Both full- and part-time workers are permanent employees.

Sub-contracting

A sub-contractor is an individual employed by the business to do a specialist activity that cannot be done by its own workforce. Sub-contractors are not directly employed by the organisation. They are often:

- self-employed or part of another business
- not necessarily entitled to the same rights as other workers (e.g. the minimum wage)
- responsible for their own tax and National Insurance.

Zero-hours contracts

Zero-hours or casual workers are on call when the organisation needs them, but the organisation does not guarantee to give them a specific number of hours' work per week. Workers get paid only for the hours they work although they are entitled to the national minimum wage. Individuals can refuse to work when asked.

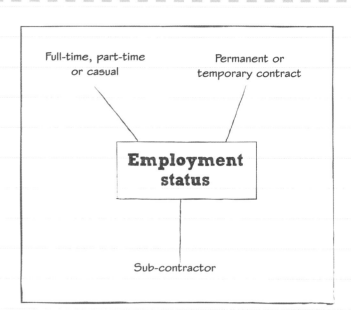

Now try this

A business is thinking of using zero-hours contracts. Identify the advantages of zero-hours contracts for (a) the business and (b) its employees.

 Although zero-hours contracts might seem unfair, some employees prefer them. Why might they prefer them?

Human resource planning 3

Some employees are taken on to cover for staff shortages, while other employers use temporary or agency staff as a means of outsourcing human resources. On this page, you will revise more aspects of HR planning.

Temporary staff

Temporary employees are hired for limited periods of time, perhaps over a seasonal period, or to cover for staff shortages or when traditionally the business has been exceptionally busy.

Temporary workers can be valuable, not only to take up the slack but also to see if they would be suitable for full-time posts should they come up in the future.

Agency staff

Agency staff are used to fill temporary gaps in the workforce. They are employed indirectly through an employment agency, which provides businesses with suitable candidates for the job role. Although the business does not need to give agency staff the same benefits as permanent employees, it may be more expensive to hire agency staff.

HR issues at an operational level

Businesses have to make human resource decisions at an operational level. If a business takes on additional employees to carry out specific work then HR has to ensure that there is sufficient supervision and increased training for these individuals.

At an operational level HR handles recruitment, interviewing and will maintain records, as well as dealing with payroll issues.

Productivity

Businesses will try to work out the labour costs per unit of production and try to reduce this or make it as efficient as possible. Productivity can be measured in terms of:

- output per hour
- output per job
- output per worker.

HR will monitor productivity to see if additional training or supervision is needed.

Labour turnover

Labour turnover is the measure of the rate at which employees are leaving a business. The lower the turnover the better. HR would investigate when turnover is high and act on the findings.

Calculating labour turnover

 $\dfrac{\text{Number of employees who left organisation}}{\text{total (average) number of employees}} \times 100$

(this gives a percentage figure)

 $\dfrac{\text{number of employees who left organisation}}{\text{total number of employees}}$

Now try this

The HR department for a building contractor is asked to find eight bricklayers. The contractor wants them to work a 20-day month. Over this time the eight bricklayers will be expected to lay 120 000 bricks. Explain how HR would work out the productivity per worker per month and what would it mean.

Calculate the average number of bricks laid per worker per month and assess whether it is a good indication of productivity.

103

Human resource planning 4

Many of the problems that human resources faces are recurring ones. On this page, you will revise some final aspects of HR planning.

Skill shortages

Forecasts in labour demand should alert employers to potential shortages of skilled workers. By monitoring the skills of current employees and those who are leaving, HR can build a picture of skills within the business which will allow it to plan recruitment and training.

Construction skills

In 2016, the UK faced its biggest skills shortage of plumbers, builders and engineers for 30 years.

Workplace stress

Around 100 million working days are lost annually in the UK as a result of stress. HR is responsible for looking after the well-being of the workforce, and should advise on how to reduce workplace stress.

Absenteeism

Businesses can calculate the level of absenteeism by dividing the number of staff absent by the total number of staff and multiplying it by 100. Where a business has high absenteeism, it may produce a strategy to reduce this.

Is the job stressful, boring or physically demanding?

Do some areas of the business have higher rates of absenteeism than others?

Reasons for absenteeism

Does an individual's personal circumstances affect their rate of absence?

What motivators are available?

Motivation

Motivation of employees needs to be long lasting, as it is related to high performance and productivity. HR planning involves creating a situation where employees have a positive attitude to work and feel a commitment to the organisation through provision of personal development, incentives and a pleasant working environment. Above all employees need to believe that their individual roles are not only valued but crucial to the organisation.

Links For more on motivation, see page 107.

Engagement with culture

HR planning needs to show that the business culture is an asset because it sets out the organisation's values and beliefs, along with its purpose.

Employee satisfaction

HR planning should aim to ensure that the employee has a positive attitude towards their work, their position and the organisation.

Now try this

1 If on average employees work for 47 weeks a year and work a five-day week, then the total number of days worked per year per employee is 235. A business has 38 workers and the number of full-day absences over the course of the year was 612. Calculate the absentee rate for the year as a percentage.

2 What are common reasons for absenteeism?

Calculate the level of absenteeism by dividing the number of days absent by the total number of days worked and multiplying it by 100.

Maslow and Herzberg

A successful business is likely to have a motivated workforce. On this page, you will revise Maslow's and Herzberg's theories which look at how to motivate employees and how to keep them motivated and productive.

Maslow's Hierarchy of Needs

Maslow's theory is shown as a pyramid. Starting at the base, employees must satisfy their basic needs first before they can move onto the next level. By helping employees to meet important needs at work, employers are able to create and support a highly motivated and happy workforce that will be very productive.

Self Actualisation

Esteem Needs
Self-esteem
Recognition
Status

Social Needs
Sense of belonging
Love

Safety Needs
Security
Protection

Physiological Needs
Food
Shelter
Warmth

Herzberg's Two Factors

According to Herzberg, employees need a mix of motivators and hygiene factors to be fully satisfied at work.

1 Motivators – factors that actually motivate workers.

2 Hygiene factors – features of the workplace that help to make workers feel good. They do not motivate employees, but may cause them to feel more or less satisfied or dissatisfied.

Motivators

- ☑ Achievement – employee has to feel that something has been accomplished
- ☑ Recognition – employee has to feel that their role is important and appreciated
- ☑ The work itself – employee has to feel they have enough freedom to make their own decisions
- ☑ Responsibility – employee must be responsible for the work and given ownership
- ☑ Advancement – employee has to feel that they have a chance of promotion

Hygiene factors

- ☑ Wage or salary paid
- ☑ Bonuses/commissions paid
- ☑ Working conditions
- ☑ Quality of supervision
- ☑ The working environment
- ☑ Job security

Now try this

Herzberg suggested that businesses should focus on dealing with demotivated employees and rearrange work. Explain how this could be done.

 Outline the practical steps that the employer could take.

105

Taylor and Mayo

Scientific style experiments have been applied to management, motivation and performance to see if there is a single formula to make it work. On this page, you will revise the management theories of Taylor and Mayo.

Taylor's Scientific Management

Taylor assumed that employees only work for money. He came up with simple work methods to reduce the time a task took to complete. Organising the tasks was down to managers and supervisors. Encouragement to work harder and the promise of additional benefits, he theorised, would make employees sufficiently motivated to work harder. Taylor discovered that employees would only work harder when they were being supervised, but would return to their normal pace of work once the supervision was removed.

Time and motion

From Taylor's work the practice of time and motion evolved. This involves a detailed study of a task, breaking down each action or movement and timing it so as to work out exactly how long each part of the task takes and come up with a more efficient method.

The first production line for cars, designed by Henry Ford, was based on Taylor's principles.

Mayo's Hawthorne Experiments

Mayo adopted the scientific theory of Taylor, but he made changes to lighting, heating and the availability of refreshments. Each time he made a change the rate of productivity increased. He was puzzled, so he reversed his actions by removing tea-breaks and reducing the level of lighting, but productivity continued to increase. What was happening?

Mayo continued his investigations and was finally able to suggest:

- output and motivation improved when employees were being observed
- some employees pressurised others to work hard.

Mayo had discovered the power of team working.

Informal groups

Mayo realised that being a member of a group actually determined the output or productivity. This was because the individual was expected by the group to do a fair day's work. These informal groups never appear on organisation charts.

Now try this

Taylor viewed all work as input, process and output. So he assumed that humans were rather like robots and all that he was concerned with was the work and productivity. But humans are not robots. Describe other factors that need to be taken into account.

Can everyone do things at the same pace and accuracy? Think about whether money is the only motivator.

Motivating employees

Motivated employees work harder and feel closely connected to the business. You need to revise how motivation affects business performance and the type of motivators businesses use.

Motivation and performance

Employees are not just driven by money. Motivation can be activated by factors related to the work itself or the rewards that an employee gets for doing it. These motivators do not fit neatly into financial or non-financial motivators. Motivation and, as a result, performance needs to be a combination of approaches.

Lack of motivation

Businesses need to recognise what demotivates employees and may damage business performance:

- ✓ Failure to recognise and reward performance
- ✓ Failure to deal with performance problems
- ✓ Unfair treatment
- ✓ Unnecessary policies and procedures
- ✓ Constantly changing goals and objectives
- ✓ Poor quality feedback from management

Financial motivators

Bonuses – paid when goals or objectives are met

Commission – a small percentage of sales value paid to the employee that made the sale

Performance-related pay – additional payments made to employees who have reached specific goals

Time-off in lieu (where overtime pay is unavailable)

Financial motivators

Benefits – e.g. subsidised travel, company cars, reduced interest loans

Pensions – although businesses are legally obliged to have a pension scheme, enhanced pensions are often part of a financial package

Overtime – additional hours paid at a higher rate

Extrinsic rewards – a reward that is related to job performance and needs to be given every time an employee achieves a task, e.g. a bonus or commission

Intrinsic rewards – personal satisfaction from doing a job well, e.g. recognition or praise

Non-financial motivators

Responsibility

Job satisfaction – may be achieved through job rotation, job enlargement, job enrichment, teamwork

Sense of achievement

Non-financial motivators

Recognition or praise

Non-financial incentives, e.g. private healthcare, subsidised canteen

Good working relationships

Sense of self-worth

Now try this

If a bank were to offer lower cost loans and mortgages to its employees, explain why they might not be as attractive as they may initially appear.

 And if the employee left the bank...

Skills requirements

A business needs to ensure that its employees have the appropriate skills and qualifications to carry out their job roles. The spider diagram below outlines the range of techniques used to meet skills requirements.

 1 Recruitment
In most organisations, the human resources (HR) function will handle the recruitment process. Departments and teams will outline the type of person they need and the skills required. HR will try and find suitable candidates to match them to the job. It will also organise and supervise the selection process.

 2 Upskilling
This enlarges the range of skills of employees to make them more technically able.

4 Training
In-house and external accredited and non-accredited training programmes ensure that employees remain up to date with developments and/or have appropriate qualifications.

3 Reskilling
This retrains employees in new skills.

 5 Outsourcing
Some organisations outsource certain functions to outside suppliers as this may be the most efficient and cost-effective way of meeting skill requirements, e.g. customer services and support.

 6 Changing job roles
HR will try to ensure that the right person with the appropriate skills is in the right role in the organisation. This is a more efficient use of skills and talent and also ensures that employees are fulfilled.

 7 Restructuring
Restructuring is an internal change in the way that the organisation functions. HR steps in to organise the whole process of changing departments, teams and work groups. Restructuring can mean a better use of skills, but it might mean that skills are lost if employees leave.

Now try this

Explain how the HR department in an organisation could ensure that the business has the skills it needs.

 What is the mix of managerial techniques used to achieve this important task?

Training

Businesses need to ensure that employees are up to date with new technology, techniques and skills, policies and procedures. On this page, you will revise the different types of training.

Training needs analysis

Training needs analysis (TNA) seeks to identify existing skills and skills gaps in the workforce and is used to determine training requirements. TNA may be used to identify levels of competency and how skills relate to achieving the business's objectives.

Specific issues regarding the nature of training, including its location, availability of trainers, materials and support required is also considered.

Internal/external training

- Internal training takes place at the business's premises. It may be delivered by a member of staff or the business may pay an expert trainer to come to its premises.
- External training takes place off site. Staff may attend a commercial or private training centre or college.

On-the-job training

Employees are trained in a realistic working environment under supervision in order to acquire the skills needed for the job.

👍 Familiar working environment
👍 Training to approved employer standards
👍 Lower cost
👍 May be guided by familiar supervisors
👎 Supervisor may not be a qualified trainer or up to date
👎 Insufficient time if business is busy
👎 Bad habits may be passed on
👎 Space needs to be allocated for training as it will usually involve both practical and theoretical elements

Off-the-job training

Delivered through employee attendance at training colleges and other external training agencies. Training may also take place on the business's premises but away from the work area.

👍 Fully qualified, expert trainers
👍 No distractions from daily tasks
👎 Working (training) environment will be unfamiliar
👎 Higher cost

Coaching and mentoring

Coaching and mentoring are closely linked.

- Coaching aims to build an individual's confidence. The coach encourages the individual to look for solutions to their own problems. It is normally an informal process which may be linked to an appraisal system.
- Mentoring aims to give guidance, support and knowledge to an inexperienced employee through an experienced member of staff.

Effectiveness of training

Ultimately training will be judged by improvements in performance and effectiveness. For example, customer service training should result in fewer customer complaints and more efficient handling of customer queries. Manufacturing training for production line workers should result in fewer defects and faster output.

Now try this

Describe the main differences between on-the-job and off-the-job training.

 Think about the skills that a person can acquire with on-the-job training and also what might be better taught off-the-job.

Performance appraisal

Performance appraisals provide a way to monitor and evaluate an employee's performance against a set of targets in a given job role, and are usually carried out annually or half-yearly. The spider diagram outlines the four main purposes of appraisals.

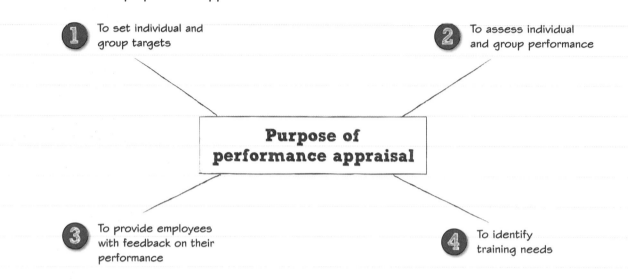

1. To set individual and group targets

2. To assess individual and group performance

Purpose of performance appraisal

3. To provide employees with feedback on their performance

4. To identify training needs

1 Individual and group targets

At their appraisal, each employee (the appraisee) agrees with their manager (the appraiser) a set of individual and group targets which they are expected to achieve over the course of the next work period and before the next scheduled performance appraisal.

2 Individual and group performance

Individual and group targets are assessed at the beginning of each performance appraisal. The appraiser will compare actual performance with the targets that were set in the previous appraisal. A grading system is used to indicate which targets have been met, missed or exceeded. This will include the appraisee's contribution to meeting group targets.

3 Providing employee feedback

Good managers should regularly feed back to employees on their performance, conduct and progress. A performance appraisal is a formal opportunity to do this. Feedback should be constructive and supportive, and offer guidance on particular areas of performance that could be improved.

It also provides the appraisee with an opportunity to request support and advice.

4 Training needs

The appraiser should evaluate areas of strength and weakness highlighted in the appraisal to help identify whether the appraisee requires upskilling, reskilling or further training.

 Revise upskilling, reskilling and training on page 108.

Now try this

Outline the factors an organisation should consider when carrying out an appraisal.

← Consider what the manager will need to discuss with the employee in order to assess their performance and also decide what might need to be done to improve it.

Types of appraisal

Performance appraisals are an essential part of managing and evaluating employees. You will need to revise these methods of appraisal.

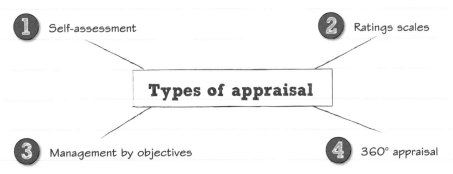

1 Self-assessment

2 Ratings scales

Types of appraisal

3 Management by objectives

4 360° appraisal

1 Self-assessment

This is where the employee evaluates their own performance against individual and group targets. Sometimes businesses provide self-assessment questionnaires as preparation for the performance appraisal.

2 Ratings scales

These evaluate an employee's performance, based on a set of criteria. The appraiser ranks the appraisee on their merit and capabilities of carrying out the activities involved in their job role. Ratings scales are usually associated with a subjective evaluation by the appraiser.

3 Management by objectives (MBO)

Management by objectives involves setting goals and monitoring the performance of individuals.

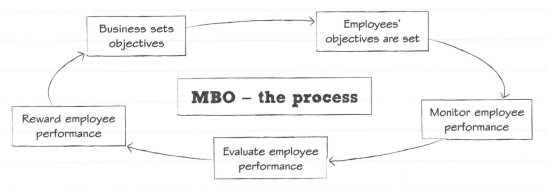

Business sets objectives

Employees' objectives are set

MBO – the process

Reward employee performance

Monitor employee performance

Evaluate employee performance

4 360° appraisal

A standard 360° appraisal involves face-to-face feedback sessions, where the appraisee can ask their own questions as well as listen to feedback. Many businesses prefer a more sophisticated system in which employees are evaluated by a number of individuals, including senior staff and colleagues, who could be peers and junior staff below the appraisee in the organisation. The data collected are used to identify development and training needs.

The employee and 360° appraisal

Begin with an open mind:
1 Self-evaluate honestly.
2 Suggest a plan of action.
3 Mentally prepare to receive feedback.
4 Accept all feedback as being constructive.
5 Analyse the feedback.

Now try this

If you were deciding which performance appraisal system to use and had ruled out using management by objectives, explain which other method you would choose.

Think about which system offers the most information and will be the most beneficial to the business.

Impact of appraisals

In theory, appraisals should benefit both employees and employers. On this page, you will revise what can be achieved when an appraisal system is used.

The individual

For many employees a performance appraisal represents one of the only opportunities to have a focused conversation with their supervisor or manager. It is usually a positive experience that looks forward to improvements, opportunities and motivation.

The business

For supervisors and managers, it is a formal situation that enables them to make a face-to-face objective assessment of the value of an employee. It should identify where to best deploy the employee and whether any future training or development is needed.

Motivation and satisfaction

Appraisals can have a major impact on motivation and satisfaction. Employees feel that the organisation is genuinely interested in their individual performance and development. This can be a positive thing as it will improve the individual's sense of worth, commitment and belonging.

During an appraisal employees can be recognised for their efforts.

Training and development

Appraisals offer a great opportunity to agree on individual training and development needs.

They often link performance outcomes and future career aspirations. For the organisation appraisal data can show the overall demand for training and development.

Employee evaluation

Appraisals are used to examine and evaluate the performance of individuals. This can be stressful for both the manager and the individual. Evaluation if carried out fairly should be objective and lead to encouraging and developing individuals.

Now try this

In 2014 the professional services multinational, Deloitte, surveyed 2500 organisations across 90 countries. Only 8 per cent of the companies thought appraisals were really effective, and nearly 60 per cent thought they were a waste of time. Explain how you would defend the use of appraisals.

 Think of the major advantages for both managers and employees.

Managing change

Businesses have to be adept at managing change. If they don't adapt to challenging situations, they may fail to be successful or even to survive. On this page, you will revise internal and external factors that may influence a business to make strategic changes.

Internal factors likely to cause change

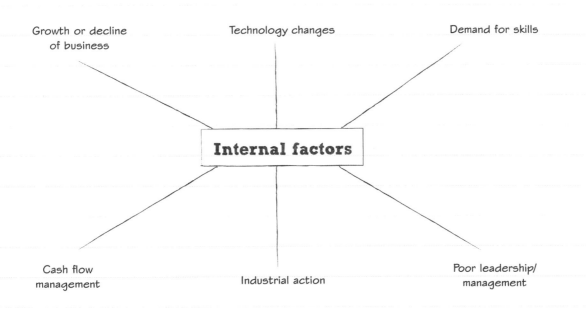

Growth or decline of business

Technology changes

Demand for skills

Internal factors

Cash flow management

Industrial action

Poor leadership/ management

External factors likely to cause change

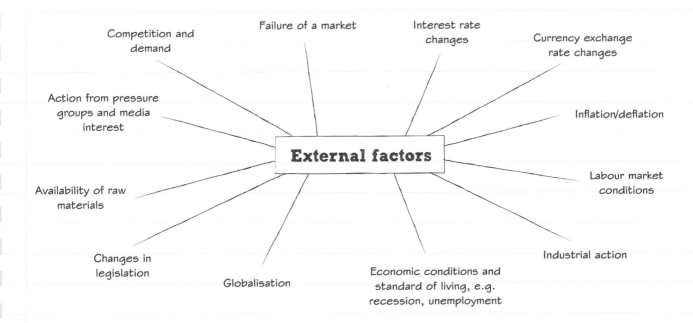

Competition and demand

Failure of a market

Interest rate changes

Currency exchange rate changes

Action from pressure groups and media interest

Inflation/deflation

External factors

Availability of raw materials

Labour market conditions

Changes in legislation

Globalisation

Economic conditions and standard of living, e.g. recession, unemployment

Industrial action

Now try this

Explain why some retail businesses in small towns resist the opening of discount supermarkets, such as Aldi or Lidl.

 Think about the number of customers and the effect that extra competition will have.

Stakeholders and change

Stakeholders are individuals or groups that are affected by or who have an interest in a business. On this page, you will revise how stakeholders may influence change.

1. Owners and managers
2. Employees
3. Financial institutions — **Stakeholders** — 4. Government
5. Regulators
6. Customers

1 Owners and managers

- A sole trader or owner of a small business will influence its objectives and direction. Larger businesses, with shareholders, may be influenced by the board of directors or the shareholder with the largest holding.
- Senior managers plan business strategy while middle and junior managers are responsible for the day-to-day running of the business and employee supervision.

2 Employees

Employees have an obvious connection with the business and have considerable influence. The business pays them wages or salaries in exchange for their work. The business also offers them job security. In exchange, however, the performance and profitability is dependent on the employees. They produce output and they meet deadlines and delivery dates.

3 Financial institutions

Many businesses have loans, mortgages and overdrafts. Finance providers may demand change if the business struggles to repay loans or mortgages. Many financial institutions also invest in larger businesses. As shareholders they exert an influence and may push for change. The Bank of England sets the Bank Rate, so it too has an influence on businesses.

4 Government

The government is the source of all laws and regulations that govern the way in which businesses operate. It can affect the business in a variety of ways:

- Taxes paid to central and local government, including VAT
- Consumer protection legislation
- Employee legislation
- Regulations regarding the environment
- Through its economic policies.

5 Regulators

Some industries have regulatory organisations that aim to ensure customers receive the highest standards of service, e.g. Ofcom. Regulators set out a range of technical and legal requirements, which businesses must comply with, and also demand levels of service and compensation in cases where customers are treated unfairly.

6 Customers

Customers or users of a service may demand change at certain times if they feel that a business no longer offers the products or services that they expect. Where a business fails to respond to customer demand, it may lose its customers to other suppliers. This means that customers are important stakeholders.

Now try this

Describe how a business can identify its stakeholders and outline how much influence they have.

 Where would the business begin to identify the stakeholders, and then how would it assess their power?

Quality standards

There are three main recognised quality standards. Businesses awarded these standards have demonstrated best practice in certain areas, and this may enhance their reputation with consumers and suppliers.

 BSI (British Standards Institution) standard BS7850-1:1992

This is a total quality management (TQM) standard. It provides guidance to management on how to make the organisation's structure, management and quality systems more effective. At the same time the changes can meet the objectives of the organisation through maximising their use of resources.

 ISO (International Organisation for Standardisation) ISO 9000:2015

This is designed to clarify and standardise quality terms. It is also there to try to suggest a structure that can be adopted by organisations to introduce:
- quality management
- quality control and quality assurance
- quality planning
- quality improvement.

 Kite marks – Investors in People (IiP)

Investors in People is awarded to organisations that lead, support and improve people's capabilities to achieve high performance. The objective is to encourage continuous improvement so that organisations have a clear vision how to use their resources in the most effective way and best use the talent of their employees.

Now try this

The private healthcare company BUPA achieved IIP in 2000. BUPA claimed that job satisfaction steadily increased after gaining the kite mark. Identify the benefits for the organisation.

 Think about the benefits for the organisation and individuals related to greater job satisfaction.

Quality culture

Developing a quality culture means making sure that quality systems are an integral part of a business's values, beliefs and habits. On this page, you will revise aspects of quality systems.

Setting quality standards

Product and service quality are extremely important as they can set the business apart from its competitors. Quality control and quality assurance should filter down into the values, beliefs and ideas of all employees to drive a quality culture and ensure defective products or services are rejected.

Quality standards

Quality control – only parts and components that conform to given specifications are used in the production process and only products that conform to the specifications leave the system and become available to customers.

Quality assurance – a series of planned and systematic activities aiming to ensure that quality requirements are always met.

Managerial commitment and staff buy-in

Managers set quality standards and need to demonstrate the importance of quality to all staff.

Employees also need to embrace quality and feel that they can play a direct role in keeping quality standards high.

Quality circles

Quality circles are small groups of employees who meet regularly to identify quality problems, investigate solutions and make recommendations.

Partnerships with suppliers and customers

- Businesses need to be assured about the quality of products or services received from suppliers. This may include simple issues such as confirming delivery times and specifications. Increasingly, businesses are monitoring supplier performance and may expect suppliers to be accredited with quality standards.
- Customers will have expectations as to the quality standards of products and services supplied. Businesses need to be aware of their customers' needs, wants and requirements.

Transparent and open communications

Communication is all about the sharing of information and ideas. When an organisation wishes to develop a quality culture it needs to ensure that the information is received as it is intended.

Employees, suppliers, customers and other interested groups will often judge the quality of an organisation by the communications that they have with it.

Now try this

One way a business can introduce a quality culture is to compare how they do things with the most successful and profitable competitor in the same market. Outline the advantages and disadvantages of taking this approach.

Consider both the good and bad aspects of copying the way another business operates. Is it always good to just copy or should you be doing more as a business?

Quality management

Quality control, lean manufacturing and Six Sigma are all techniques of quality management.

Quality control

Quality can be controlled at one of four quality control stages.

 1 By prevention – trying to avoid problems from happening in the first place.

 2 By detection – making sure that faulty products never reach the customer.

Quality control

 3 By correction – stepping in to offer a repair solution with no argument with the customer.

 4 By improvement – trying to stay ahead of customer expectations by eliminating potential problems by continuous improvement.

Lean manufacturing

Lean or stockless production aims to improve profits and returns on investment through:

- reduced inventory levels and turnover rate
- improved product quality
- reduced production and delivery lead times.

Lean manufacturing includes JIT and Kaizen.

JIT and Kaizen

- Just in time (JIT) is designed to allow high-volume production, while ensuring that minimal inventories of raw materials, work-in-process and finished goods are held by the business.
- Kaizen seeks to involve individuals from across the organisation at every level of the organisation. The goal is to work together in order to achieve improvements without having to make large capital investments.

Six Sigma

Six Sigma is a quality process used by businesses to identify and remove the causes of defects to ensure the final product is as close to perfect as it can be. By eliminating defects, manufacturing costs should fall as there is less waste and time lost. Fewer faulty goods also means higher customer satisfaction.

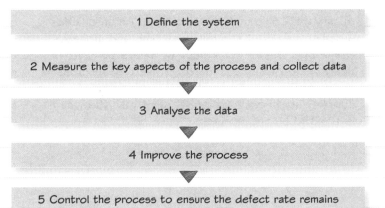

1 Define the system

2 Measure the key aspects of the process and collect data

3 Analyse the data

4 Improve the process

5 Control the process to ensure the defect rate remains as low as possible

Now try this

Explain why a factory using lean production techniques needs to have very good relationships with its suppliers.

 Consider response times.

Benefits of quality management

Managing quality well, both within the organisation and externally by involving suppliers and customers, will bring benefits to the business.

Zero defect production and output quality

The key elements are to avoid errors and make manufacturing processes as fool proof as possible. By minimising the number of defects, the business will be able to improve the overall quality of its products and experience fewer manufacturing problems. This will ensure that products reach customers in a fit state. The business will benefit from greater efficiency, customer satisfaction and maximised profits.

Continuous improvement

The business continually monitors processes and identifies areas which require improvement. The root causes of substandard performance are evaluated and action taken. Performance is measured to ensure the problems have been resolved. Having achieved this improvement, more goals are set and the cycle of continuous improvement continues. The business benefits from more efficient working, better productivity and less waste.

Reduced inspections

Once quality systems have been put in place, the business will still regularly monitor progress, often through random selection of a number of products from each batch to test them. Businesses committed to continuous improvement may not be subject to as many inspections by external regulatory bodies.

Improved efficiency and profitability

The ultimate goal of quality management techniques is to improve the efficiency of the business. In eliminating defects and thereby reducing waste, returns, complaints and other problems, the business will maximise its profits.

Supplier engagement and satisfaction

Businesses depend on their suppliers to provide quality materials and parts on time. An unreliable supplier may cost the business time and money. Some businesses will expect suppliers to have accredited quality standards. While the business needs to be satisfied with its supplier, the supplier also needs to be satisfied with the way it is treated by the business.

Customer involvement and satisfaction

Improved products and services often have their roots in suggestions and demands made by customers. Successful businesses listen to their customers. They run systems such as customer relationship management through which they collect customer views and test them to see if they are widespread. From this, the business will try to create new products and services in order to keep customers happy.

Now try this

When a business chooses a supplier, explain why price may not be the only determining factor.

 Is a low price of value to the business if the quality is poor?

Had a look ☐   Nearly there ☐   Nailed it! ☐

Your Unit 6 external assessment

For this unit you will be assessed through completion of a set task. The task will be based upon a case study or business scenario.

Your set task

The supervised set task consists of two activities. These will ask you to look at specific managerial issues within a case study and make recommendations to resolve them. You will be expected to apply your knowledge of managerial principles and refer to the set task information and prepared notes to help you produce:

Activity 1: Formal report – a report written in appropriate business language, layout and style

Outcomes

Activity 2: Presentation – a visual presentation including slides and speaker notes

The documents must be produced using word-processing, spreadsheet or presentation software. The taskbook (Part B) will tell you which documents you will need to submit.

Part A: Preparing for the set task

Two weeks before the supervised assessment (Part B), you will be given a taskbook containing the set task brief and information you need to prepare (Part A).

> Over the next few pages, you'll work on this revision task similar in style to one you might be given to help you understand how to approach the assessment.

DO NOT WRITE IN TH

You are working as a trainee journalist for *The Business Journal*, a magazine read by business managers. You have been asked to prepare a set of background papers for the editor of the magazine who is writing an article on business mergers.

You will need to identify the managerial issues in the case study and prepare yourself to complete tasks based on the content of Unit 6.

You will be expected to carry out your own preparatory work on the brief and information. You may prepare up to two sides of A4 notes to take into the supervised external assessment, to complete the set task in Part B, and you will be given about six hours to do your research.

Part B: Completing your set task

You will have three hours to complete your set task in your supervised assessment. The set task is divided into two activities worth a total of 88 marks. Both activities are allocated 44 marks.

Manage your time!

You should aim to spend just under 1 hour 30 minutes on each activity. Remember to allow time to read through your work before you hand it in.

Now try this

Give four 'good practice points' when completing a time-constrained case study.

 Think of some of the functions of management.

Part A: Approaching the case study

The activities in the supervised set task will be based on a case study given in the set task information in the Part A taskbook. On this page you will look at how to approach reading through the set task information provided in Part A.

Approaching your task

The focus of the set task in Part B is to apply your knowledge of the principles of management to a specific business scenario. When reading through the set task information provided in Part A, try to follow this six-step process:

Read through the case study material

 Read it through carefully and identify the main points.

The case study in Part A could contain:
- a background to the features of a particular industry
- a set of management issues faced by a business in the industry
- a set of charts and tables.

Assess the impact on the business of any issues

 Weigh up the positive and negative aspects.

Focus upon the central themes which are emerging in the case study.

Analyse management information

 Identify, compare and weigh up data and relationships between variables.

Highlight the implications for management which emerge from your analysis.

Identify relevant leadership and management concepts

 Apply your knowledge of management and leadership to real life business issues.

Identify the management theories that could be applied to the case study.

Evaluate alternative management responses

 Come to a reasoned judgement from an assessment of the alternatives.

Each alternative will have potential benefits, drawbacks, limitations and risks.

Recommend your proposals

 You will need to be prepared to justify these proposals.

Highlight how your proposals will address each of the management issues you have identified.

Now try this

Write a set of bullet points identifying three management theories which could be relevant to a case study involving employee motivation.

 Don't be tempted to write a long explanation of each theory.

Part A: Preparing your notes

You need to prepare two sides of A4 notes from the task information (provided in Part A) to take into the supervised assessment (Part B). On this page, you will look at how to make comprehensive and well-structured notes to help you effectively complete the activities in the assessment.

Task information

Here is an extract from the information which accompanies the revision task on page 119. The first part of the task information will set the context for the other data and information provided.

Bradbury and Bestle case study

Bradbury plc has opened discussions with one of its main competitors Bestle plc with a view to agreeing to a formal merger under one management team. Both businesses manufacture confectionery and Bradbury plc consider that the merger of both businesses would enable significant costs savings to be made which could be passed on to the consumer in the form of lower prices. Efficiency savings could also be ploughed back into the business to invest in research and development into new products geared towards the growing Chinese economy.

The workforce in both companies are concerned about the possible implications of the merger and union representatives have asked management for urgent talks to discuss the situation. It is rumoured that Bradbury plc's American owners, the multinational Prestlock Industries, will move production out of the UK if the merger does not go ahead.

Making structured notes

When you receive the task information you will **not** be given the two activities you will be required to complete until the start of Part B supervised time. You will need to prepare your notes by identifying the managerial issues in the case study and then considering the business principles to be applied. The key questions to the right will help you to do this. Make notes on each question using bullet points as in the example below.

1 What are the key management themes in the case study?

↓

2 What are the management issues arising from these key themes?

↓

3 What are the management principles that could be applied?

↓

4 Suggest different approaches for addressing the management issues.

Sample notes extract

1. Key management themes
- Merger
- Opportunities
- Costs and efficiencies
- New market

2. Management issues arising
- Implementing the merger
- Workforce motivation
- Communicating a vision

3. Apply management principles
- Management functions
- Motivational theories (Mayo, Maslow, Herzberg)
- Leadership styles (autocratic, participative, consultative)

4. Possible approaches for dealing with management issues
- Formulating a business case for the merger

Using bullet points in your notes for Part A will allow you to include more details on the two sides of A4.

Dividing your Part A notes into sections gives them more structure and will help you when completing the set task activities.

When applying management principles always start by identifying the management functions that will be most relevant in addressing the management issues in the case study – for example, issues relating to poor performance could focus upon the monitoring and controlling functions of management.

Now try this

Identify how two management functions could be applied in the Bradbury and Bestle case study.

Consider functions such as planning and monitoring.

121

Part A: Analysing data

You need to spend some of your preparation time analysing the data that will be included in the set task information (Part A). Here are some data based upon the revision task information featuring Bradbury and Bestle.

Worked example

Business profiles – latest annual reports of the two companies

	Bradbury plc	Bestle plc
Gross profit	£559m	£225m
% annual increase in sales turnover	6%	9%
Market share	31%	11%
+/– change in market share	–2%	+5%
Locations	UK & Europe	UK & Far East
UK site	Coventry	Manchester

Sample notes extract

Business profiles – analysis

- Bradbury plc has generated £334 million more in gross profits than Bestle plc.
- Bradbury plc has a bigger market share than Bestle plc (+ 20 percentage points).
- Bradbury plc's market share has decreased year-on-year by 2 per cent. Bestle plc however has performed well with its annual sales turnover and market share increasing by 9 per cent and 5 per cent respectively.
- Bestle's presence in the Far East could add value to Bradbury's business model.

When analysing the data from the task information in Part A, look for any trends (increases or decreases) and identify the possible relationships between variables (direct or indirect relationships). In this example, the learner has analysed the data to identify clear differences in the characteristics of each business.

Worked example

Workforce composition of the two companies

Age band	Bradbury plc	Bestle Ltd
Under 25	150	175
24–35	200	150
36–50	400	140
51–59	350	80
60+	100	55
Males	480	180
Females	720	420
Average length of service	15 years	5 years

Sample notes extract

Workforce – analysis

Both companies employ a high proportion of women: Bradbury plc (60 per cent); Bestle plc (70 per cent). However, Bestle plc has a higher percentage of younger employees than Bradbury plc (55 per cent of Bestle plc's workforce are aged 18–35 years compared to over 63 per cent of Bradbury plc's workforce who are aged 36–59 years).

When you are given comparative data, a good way to analyse them is to work out percentages as the learner has demonstrated here.

Now try this

Identify any issues which arise when analysing data based upon the figures for only one year.

 Consider the risks involved when making a business decision.

Part A: Analysing management information

The set task information will also contain management information which you will need to analyse and prepare notes on. Here is some management information on Bradbury and Bestle as part of the revision task information, and a learner's analysis in note form.

Market analysis

Latest annual UK figures for chocolate confectionery show that the value of sales fell by 2.8% over the last year.

The volume of chocolate sales in kg fell by 5.8%.

Unit sales (number of packets) fell by 4%.

On-shelf chocolate prices rose by 2.5% as a result of increase in cocoa prices.

Overall grocery retail prices rose 0.5%.

UK consumers traded down by 2% on average across all groceries over the last year.

A new production process which allows fruit extracts to be mixed with other raw materials has resulted in new products being introduced in the last year by companies such as Bestle plc which performed above the market average. These new products commanded higher retail prices than the overall market average.

UK chocolate exports to China have grown by 18% in the last five years.

The government is under pressure from health organisations to introduce a sugar tax on confectionery.

Sample notes extract

PESTLE analysis

- **Political**: possibility of a sugar tax
- **Economic**: link between cocoa price increase, chocolate prices and consumer demand; increasing importance of Chinese market
- **Social**: Potential increase in the demand for premium-priced new chocolate products
- **Technological**: new production processes
- **Legal**: are there legal implications of the merger that need to be taken into account, e.g. employment legislation?
- **Environmental**: potential impact on corporate social responsibility?

A PESTLE analysis is an effective way of analysing the impact of market information and other factors in the external environment which will **impact** on the two firms involved in the merger.

Completing a PESTLE analysis using the Part A information will help you formulate a business strategy which takes account of the specific factors in the external business environment that could impact on the proposed merger.

🔗 **Links** Revise PESTLE analysis on page 19.

This is a good answer because it uses the information provided in the market analysis plus the outcome of the PESTLE analysis to draw together the points which will provide a rationale and a business case for the merger.

Sample notes extract

Impact on Bradbury plc and Bestle plc

- Competitive pressures between producers in the chocolate industry are likely to increase following a 2.8% fall in the value of market sales.
- Increases in the on-shelf price of chocolate may partly account for the fall in consumer demand.
- Producers who can introduce new chocolate products to the market may be able to benefit by pricing these products higher than average market price.
- China is a potential growth market.

Now try this

Analyse how the merger of the two companies could reduce competitive pressures in the market.

Plan your response to this task. Think about the number of competitors in the market.

Part A: Identifying management principles

In your notes, you will need to apply your knowledge of management principles – functions, theories and leadership styles – to the management issues you have identified in the task information. Here you will see how management principles can be applied to Bradbury and Bestle from the revision task information.

In each of the examples, notice how each point is directly referenced to a specific aspect of the case study in the task information and provides evidence of how management functions can be applied in a practical setting.

You could also identify at this stage the key **leadership** functions that will need to be exhibited when implementing the merger such as **inspiring** the workers, **influencing** stakeholders and **energising** the management teams in both companies.

Links Revise management functions on page 93, leadership styles on page 96, Maslow and Herzberg on page 105 and Taylor and Mayo on page 106.

Sample notes extract

Management functions

Management actions required to complete the merger will need to be:

- **planned** – merger timelines and actions
- **organised** – management responsibilities identified
- **coordinated** – keep all interested parties informed and up to date
- **controlled** – ensure that actions are completed on time and within budget
- **monitored** – review targets in the merger plan
- **delegated** – allocate tasks to individual managers.

Risks and change

If you propose any changes, identify the risks which will need to be managed.

Sample notes extract

Management theories

The merger has already resulted in union representatives raising concerns about the merger which may impact on motivation.

- **Mayo** – managers need to take account of the influence of work groups within the work place when meeting with the unions.
- **Maslow** – the merger may impact upon 'safety needs' of the workforce (a lower order need in the hierarchy).
- **Herzberg** – the perceived 'threat' of the merger is a hygiene factor which can contribute to poor 'psychological health'.

Sample notes extract

Leadership style

The merger is likely to require a range of leadership and management styles:

- **Consultative** – meeting with union representatives
- **Action-centred leadership** – provide a vision for the merger, a sense of purpose to the team and support individuals affected by the merger
- **Situational leadership** – adapt leadership style as circumstances change, e.g. what if the union calls a strike against the merger?

Now try this

Give one other leadership style that may be appropriate when implementing a business merger.

 Consider leadership characteristics.

Part B: Completing the set task

When completing the set task (Part B) in the supervised external assessment, you will apply your knowledge of the principles of management and refer to the set task information (case study) and your preparatory notes (from Part A) to produce two business documents. Here are the two activities relating to the revision task (from pages 119 and 121).

Task

ACTIVITY 1

Refer to the performance indicators and workforce data in the set task information to prepare a report for the editor of *The Business Journal* highlighting:

- the HR issues which may arise as a result of the merger
- your recommendations for addressing these issues.

ACTIVITY 2

Prepare a maximum of six slides with speaker notes for a presentation to the editorial team of *The Business Journal* in which you:

- identify the benefits and potential business risks of the merger
- recommend a set of management actions which could maximise the benefits and reduce the potential business risks of the merger.

Before starting the Part B activities it's a good idea to make a note of the main points you want to include, such as those outlined here. You can use these points as a 'checklist' when you are completing the Part B activities so that you cover all the points you have thought of.

Sample notes extract

Business report – HR issues

- Workforce motivation and the impact on:
  - productivity
  - staff turnover
- Potential reductions in the workforce
- Potential relocation of some staff
- Redundancies
- Mistrust in management
- Restructuring of teams
- Change in business culture
- Managing change

Sample notes extract

Business report – my recommendations

- Identifying the business case for merger – 'telling'
- The Vision – 'selling'
- Opportunities for staff
- Consultation
- Communication channels
- Financial motivators (redundancy packages)
- Non-financial motivators (new job roles; new skills)

Sample notes extract

Presentation – potential benefits

- Lower costs – efficiencies in production
- New products
- New market opportunities
- Reduced competition
- Higher sales growth

Sample notes extract

Presentation – potential risks

- Low staff morale
- Skill shortages
- Higher short-term costs
- Lower productivity

Now try this

Add one additional bullet point to the HR issues, your recommendations and the potential benefits and risks of the merger.

Remember you can use the notes you have prepared in Part A to help you.

Part B: Formal report

In Activity 1 of the revision task on page 125, you are required to produce a report for the editor of *The Business Journal*. This is a formal business document written in a format which meets certain standard business conventions. This page provides a format which you could use to present your report. The report must be produced on a computer.

What the report is about

> This should be short and to the point

Title of report

- A concise description of the content of the report
- Who the report is for
- Who wrote the report
- Date submitted
- The status of the report: is it for 'information' only or is it for 'discussion', or does a 'decision' have to be made?

The purpose of the report

> Be concise and accurate; use an impersonal tone (avoid the first person such as 'In this report I will...')

Introduction

- Background
- Purpose of the report – in this case, with reference to the proposed merger between Bradbury plc and Bestle plc

How the work was carried out

> The specific content must be wholly relevant to what is being asked for in the activity.

Analysis and managment issues

- How the report writer approached the task
- Your analysis of the HR data relating to Bradbury plc and Bestle plc and the management information relating to the confectionery industry; identifying the management issues

What the findings were

> Conclusions are rarely certain. Start your conclusions with 'It appears that...' or 'This suggests...' and use words such as 'may', 'might' or 'could'.

Conclusions and recommendations

- How your analysis of the data and management information links to your conclusions and recommendations regarding your proposed management actions

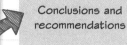

Bradbury plc and Bestle plc are in talks to merge their operations to secure efficiencies and open up new markets. The newly merged company would develop new products for international markets to withstand the current market pressures brought about by falling UK sales.

The merger will result in significant management challenges in terms of workforce planning and motivation; for example, a reduction in the workforce and workplace re-location, which could impact upon productivity and labour turnover. The merger will need to be planned with management establishing a clear vision and rationale for it backed up by clear targets and milestones which will need to be communicated to the workforce.

Management will engage constructively with workforce representatives and will introduce a number of financial and non-financial measures to ease the transition to a new merged business.

This is a useful summary of the main points. It highlights the business case, identifies the main issues management will have to face and provides an overview of how this will be done by providing some examples of the actions which will need to be taken.

When writing the content of the report:

1. Look for patterns of information.
2. Inform the reader what the summary is about.
3. Use examples of positives, negatives and any outstanding issues.
4. Use words like 'next', 'before', 'after', 'to sum up', 'most important', 'for example', 'as a result'.

Now try this

Write the title and introduction sections of the report to the editor of *The Business Journal*.

Think of the issues that the editor would want addressed when considering the merger.

Part B: Presentation

In Activity 2 of the revision task on page 125, you are required to prepare a visual presentation to the editorial team of *The Business Journal*. In the external assessment, this will involve producing a maximum of six slides with speaker notes. This page provides a format which you could use. You should prepare your slides and notes using presentation software.

Identify what the topic is about and what you will be covering in the presentation

> **SLIDE 1**
> Background to the merger

Slide 1 'sets the scene' and identifies the points you are going to raise in the presentation.

> **SLIDE 2**
> Business profiles of Bradbury plc and Bestle plc

- Organise the slides in a logical sequence, e.g. slide 3 will include growth areas in the market and is followed by slide 4 which will identify how the merger could exploit the growth areas
- Establish a theme or topic for each slide
- Avoid large blocks of text
- Use bullet points for key points
- Maximum of six/seven bullet points per slide
- Use simple graphics

> **SLIDE 3**
> Market analysis

Slides 2–5 and your speaker notes will provide the details which back up your presentation.

> **SLIDE 4**
> Benefits of the merger

> **SLIDE 5**
> Management issues

- Three or four main conclusions
- Finish with a question for the audience to capture their attention

> **SLIDE 6**
> Summary and conclusions

Slide 6 usually covers:
1 impact on business performance
2 management issues
3 proposed management actions
4 business risks.

Sample response extract

Slide 1

> **MERGER PROPOSAL**
> - Background to the merger proposal
> - Business profiles
> - Market analysis
> - Potential benefits
> - Potential HR risks
> - Recommended HR actions to minimise the risks
> - Proposed structure of the new business

> **Slide 1 speaker notes**
> - Introduce self
> - Business profiles to cover financial data, market share and workforce compositions
> - Market analysis to include trends and consumer demand
> - Potential benefits to look at efficiencies, new product development and new market opportunities
> - Potential HR risks to cover both financial and non-financial risks

Now try this

Prepare slide 2 of the above presentation for *The Business Journal* with speaker notes.

 It is useful to prepare a draft of each slide on a piece of paper before you start to enter text into the software.

Business ideas

Businesses must keep generating ideas to ensure success. On this page, you will revise the factors that start-up and developing businesses take into account when making and justifying business decisions.

Start-ups

Start-ups need to show potential investors there is a market for their product.

These are the factors the start-up will use to convince investors of the viability of the new business:

- Is there a gap in the market?
- Are there competitors?
- What are the current market trends?
- What is the likely demand for the product?
- How much will it cost to produce?
- Will the business make a profit?

Business decision making

The key to success in your external assessment will be to ensure that you are able to use your knowledge of the different environments in which businesses operate – internal and external – in order to put forward logically consistent arguments which support (justify) your business decisions.

Developing businesses

A developing business needs to generate new ideas; otherwise its products may become outdated and customers will switch to competitors' products. When making decisions, the business should take into account three main factors.

 Changes in economic climate – external influences which may impact upon business decisions and performance.

 Market trends – influenced by both sellers and buyers.

Sellers influence the market by:	Buyers influence the market by:
- Developing innovative products - Advertising - Creating a brand image - Creating new distribution channels - Joining together with other sellers to control the supply or influence the price of a product	- The pattern of their expenditure - Providing feedback to sellers

 Impact of competition may lead to diversification. Where there is market competition, the consumer has a choice of which product to purchase from which supplier. They can base their choice on:

 Now try this

Outline the reasons why a business may decide to produce more than one type of product.

Think about the different ranges of goods businesses offer to their customers. You will also need to consider the product life cycle and changes in fashion.

Purpose and structure

Businesses exist to provide goods and services to consumers. You need to revise the way they do this in terms of aims and objectives, products and services, ownership, structure and location.

Purpose

When researching a business, you should consider:

- its core aims and objectives – what the business wants to achieve and the targets it sets itself
- the products and services it offers.

Many businesses capture their core purpose in a mission statement. For independent retail distributor Nisa Retail this is: 'Passionate about independent retailing; committed to creating benefits for members.'

Ownership

The ownership of a business is closely associated with its size:

Sole trader – one owner	Limited capital	e.g. hairdresser
Partnership – more than one owner	Additional partners contribute more capital and range of skills	e.g. solicitors
Private or public limited company – owned by shareholders	Shareholders bring more capital and enjoy limited liability	e.g. large manufacturer

A **franchise** is a business arrangement that allows the franchiser to produce and distribute goods and services using the brand name of an established business. A business can also grow by merging with another business or being taken over by a competitor.

Business structures

1 Business functions can be grouped together and managed in different layers to form a management hierarchy. The fewer the layers, the flatter the structure.

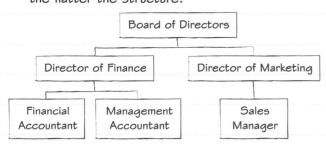

2 The matrix structure is based on project teams made up of specialists from each of the functional areas.

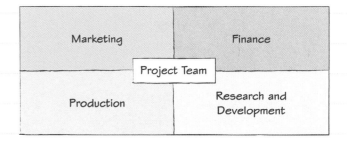

Location

A small business is likely to be located in one place serving a local market. As it grows, it may open branches nationally. The largest businesses are multinationals that operate in many different countries.

Approaching a case study

You need to be able to evaluate a business by weighing up how far it is achieving its purpose and to justify whether it is worth investing in the business by assessing its potential for generating profit and further growth.

Now try this

What would be the advantages to a business of changing from a hierarchical structure to a flatter structure?

Consider aspects such as internal communications, impact on management costs and the relationship between managers and their staff.

Data sources

Making the right decisions will result in a business's products and services meeting the needs of consumers in the target market. Decision making is based on information. On this page, you will revise data collection, storage and use.

Sources of business information

Primary research is first-hand research	+	Secondary research is second-hand research – sometimes called desk research	=	Business information

Information in business

Information is central to the decision-making process:

 Businesses need information to make decisions.

 This requires the collection of data, i.e. raw facts and figures.

 When data are processed, they become information.

Decision-making process

1 Analysing the data

2 Identifying relationships between data sets

3 Evaluating the data

4 Predicting consequences

5 Providing alternatives

6 Justifying solutions

Data storage

A business's data need to be stored securely:

- to protect people's personal details
- to comply with 'data protection principles' set out in the Data Protection Act 1998
- to prevent competitors gaining access to sensitive information.

Businesses must act ethically to ensure that data are used fairly and for the purposes intended. Sensitive information such as cultural background must also be handled with care.

Justifying your solutions

In the external assessment you will be expected to consider different data sets in order to justify your solutions to a specific business issue.

Now try this

Your manager has asked you to analyse the performance of the company's sales agents over a three-year period. The North Region has two sales reps and the South Region has three sales reps. In Year 1 the total sales in the North region were £150 000, in Year 2, £162 000 and in Year 3 £179 820. The figures for the South Region were £330 000 (Year 1), £349 800 (Year 2) and £356 796 (Year 3). Prepare a table to record your findings and a set of bullet points to summarise your conclusions.

 You might want to look at trends in sales in each region and compare the performance of the sales force in each region.

Business models 1

Business models help a business to analyse its current position, make decisions regarding its future direction and put in place strategies to enable it to meet its long-term objectives. On this page, you will revise how business models can aid decision making and how Porter's Five Forces model can be used to analyse competitive forces in a market.

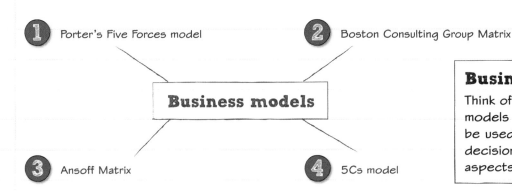

Business model toolkit

Think of the different business models as a **toolkit** that can be used to make business decisions regarding different aspects of business strategy.

Developing a business strategy

Your external assessment will require you to analyse and evaluate business data and information in order to justify your recommendations or solutions to a business situation. One approach is to think of how the business models can be used as part of a **process** when developing a business strategy.

| Potential business idea, e.g. new product or service | ▶ | 1 Use Porter's Five Forces model to analyse the market for the product | ▶ | 2 Use Ansoff's Matrix to assess risks to the business's growth | ▶ | 3 Use the Boston Matrix to review current products | ▶ | 4 Use the 5Cs model to develop a marketing plan |

Porter's Five Forces model

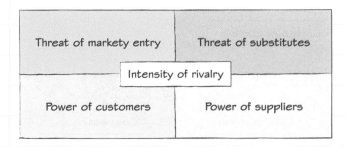

Porter's model can be used to analyse competition within an industry to determine the potential for future profits. The more powerful the forces, the lower the profit potential.

The model helps businesses to:

- better understand the competitive forces in their industry
- assess the attractiveness of entering a new industry and the opportunities it presents for business growth.

Now try this

Analyse the competitive forces in the following sectors using Porter's Five Forces model: (a) mobile phones; (b) car manufacturers; (c) food retailing; (d) fashion industry.

 Think about how the features you identify in your analysis can help identify business risks and the potential for profit.

131

Business models 2

On this page, you will revise three more models businesses can use to build their strategy.

Links Revise business models on page 131.

Boston Consulting Group Matrix

Many businesses produce more than one product which together make up the **product portfolio** or **product range**. The Boston Matrix evaluates each product in relation to its **market share** and its potential for **market growth**. It can be used to assess the contribution of the current product portfolio to business objectives and to determine future strategy for each product type.

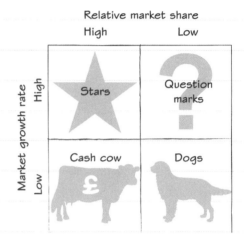

The Ansoff Matrix

The Ansoff Matrix identifies the four main growth strategies based upon new or existing products and new or existing markets. Different levels of risk are associated with each growth strategy.

The matrix helps a business to assess the risks associated with **business growth**.

	Existing products	New products
Existing markets	Market penetration	Product development
New markets	Market development	Diversification

The 5Cs model

A SWOT and PESTLE analysis can help the business to develop its marketing plan by using the 5Cs model.

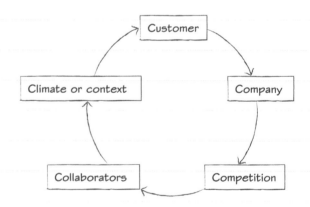

Now try this

The Delaware Corporation plc manufactures computing equipment. Describe how the company could apply the business models to determine its business strategy for the development of a new tablet computer.

Make sure your response makes reference to the data and information required when using each of the business models.

Representative values

Business data can often be complex and difficult for decision makers to interpret. On this and the next page, you will revise techniques to help you analyse data.

Representative values

First, you need to agree a representative value or average of the data set to help you understand what the data are telling you. There are three ways to calculate representative values:

- **Mean** = the value of all items in the data set divided by the number of items
- **Median** = the middle number in the data set
- **Mode** = the most frequent number appearing in the data set

If the data set is made up of even numbers take the mean of the two numbers in the centre in order to obtain the median value.

Calculating mean, median, mode

The Mobile Shop Ltd: Weekly value of sales of mobile phones.

Week 1	£100 000
Week 2	£105 000
Week 3	£98 000
Week 4	£110 000
Week 5	£115 000
Week 6	£95 000
Week 7	£98 000

- **Mean** = £721 000/7 = **£103 000**
- **Median** = £95 000, £98 000, £98 000, **£100,000**, £105 000, £110 000, £115 000
- **Mode** = £95 000, **£98 000, £98 000**, £100 000, £105 000, £110 000, £115 000

Interpreting representative values

Be careful to identify those values in the data set which contain 'outliers', i.e. those values which are well above or well below the other values in the data set and which could influence the average, and lead to you drawing the wrong conclusion.

Five steps to analyse data

Here are five basic steps to follow when analysing business data in the external assessment:
1 Define the problem.
2 Collect data.
3 Analyse the data.
4 Present the results.
5 Draw conclusions.

Terms used in data analysis

Here are some statistical terms that you can use when producing business documents in the external assessment.

Sample – a representative cross-section

Trend – the general direction in which a variable is moving

Probability – forecasting the likelihood of a particular event or outcome occurring

Terms used in data analysis

Dispersion – how variables are distributed around the average

Average – a representative value

Now try this

Input the following number of retail transactions by payment type into a spreadsheet and calculate the mean: cash 14; debit cards 47; credit cards 63; store cards 20.

What else could the company use this information for? Think about possible future marketing promotions and campaigns.

Analysing data

On this page, you will revise more techniques to help you analyse data.

🔗 **Links** Revise representative values on page 133.

Measures of dispersion

Representative values do not show how the values are distributed about the middle.

You can use **standard deviation** to measure how spread out numbers are from the average. The values are plotted on a **normal distribution curve**.

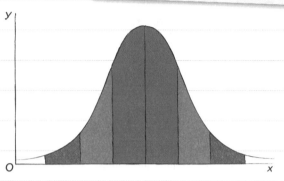

68% of values are in the red area.
95% of values are in the red + green areas.
99% of values are in the red + green + blue areas.

Uses of standard deviation

- **Buffer stock level**: By determining the average demand for stock the business can work out the standard deviation in its requirements each month and manage stock levels accordingly.

- **Control**: Standard deviation can be used to monitor costs, quality and people, e.g. the average number of customer service complaints in a hotel chain could be used to determine the standard deviation across the group.

Percentiles and quartiles

- **Percentiles**: A business scores 35 out of 50 in an independent consumer satisfaction survey, and wants to know how it compared with its competitors, i.e. percentage of competitors who scored higher or lower than 35 out of 50. If 58 per cent of the scores were below 35 out of 50, the business's score would be the 58th percentile.

- **Quartiles**: The **median** divides a set of ordered data into two parts with equal items on either side. The same data can also be divided into four parts, or **quartiles**.

Correlation coefficient

- A positive correlation occurs when an increase in one variable results in an increase in another variable (0 to +1).

- A negative correlation occurs when an increase in one variable leads to a decrease in another variable (−1 to 0).

Positive correlation

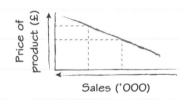

Negative correlation

Think about what the results are telling us about the business and whether they are similar to the results you would expect for a successful business.

Now try this

Comment on a business's performance using the following data:

Sales performance:	in lowest quartile of companies selling similar products
Sales of most profitable product:	−1 standard deviation from average industry performance
Customer satisfaction percentile score:	47%
'Hits' on website and online sales volume:	Correlation score of 0

Presenting data

Graphs provide pictorial views of business data. On this page, you will revise how to present your data using appropriate graphs.

Selecting graphs for your presentation

Spreadsheets automatically create graphs from inputted data. Different graphs can be used to present different aspects of the same data set, e.g. marketing data could be presented as:

- a **pie chart** to show market segmentation by age
- a **bar chart** to show average annual spending by region
- a **line graph** to show annual sales turnover by month.

1 Line graph – use for time series and frequency distribution, e.g. a business's profit levels over a specific period of time.

2 Pie chart – use for description of component and its relative value, e.g. contribution to total sales of each product in a product portfolio.

3 Bar chart – use for comparison of different items (by category), e.g. income per head of different countries.

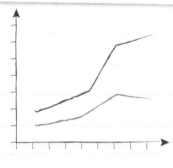

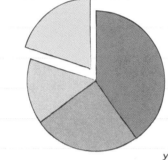

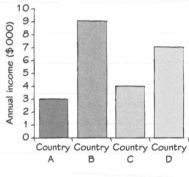

4 Histogram – use for comparison of different items (by a quantifiable variable), e.g. score on final exam per number of students.

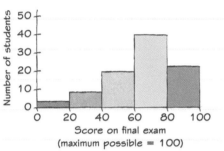

5 Scatter (XY) graph – use for analysis of relationships between two variables, e.g. income per head of different age groups.

y = income

x = age range 18–40 years

Creating graphs

1. Determine the variables.

2. Select appropriate data.

3. Determine if there are sufficient data.

4. Name the variables within the data set in specific cells.

5. Enter the data correctly.

6. Select the graph which most clearly identifies the relationship between the variables.

Interpreting graphs

You need to be able to describe what the graphs show, identify any relationships between different data sets and recommend actions that could be taken to address any issues you have identified.

🔗 **Links** You can revise how to design presentations and write business reports on pages 126 and 127.

Now try this

In 2010 profits of Emla plc were £350 000. Over the next five years profit levels were as follows: +10%, +3%, –2%, –6%, –1%. Input these data into a spreadsheet and choose either a line graph or bar graph to display the data.

Why is it better to use a line or bar graph to display this information?

Information and decision making

Software-generated business information is produced by a management information system (MIS) and can aid decision making by processing and analysing vast amounts of data relating to income, costs and performance.

Management information systems

A management information system (MIS) is a series of networked computers which allows managers access to real-time information on current performance and to use this alongside historical data to:

- determine business trends
- identify potential risks
- analyse data
- make operational, tactical and strategic decisions.

Decision making in business

- **Strategic decisions**: define the general direction of the business – 'the big picture'.
- **Tactical decisions**: those decisions which determine the specific actions required to take the strategy forward.
- **Operational decisions**: the day-to-day decisions involving the implementation of specific actions.

Information and decision making

Software-generated information contributes to the decision-making process in a number of areas:

1 **Accounting software**: fixed and variable costs of opening the new stores; costs of business finance; return on investment

2 **Customer relationship management**: potential demand and sales; potential impact of promotional activities

3 **Business planning**: market research, 'what if?' analysis, risk analysis

Information and project management

A business project comprises:

- a series of **interrelated tasks**
- a specific **planned outcome**
- a given **period of time.**

Project management involves three elements:

1 The **scope** of the project – the outcome
2 The **cost** of the project – the budget
3 The **time** involved – the completion date

All three elements of the project will impact upon the overall quality of final project outcome.

The project triangle

If the project involves building a new factory and the business decides to increase the size of the new factory (scope) it will require additional resources (cost) and the completion time will need to be extended (time). Software-generated management information will help the business to 'model' the impact of changes in each element of the 'project triangle'.

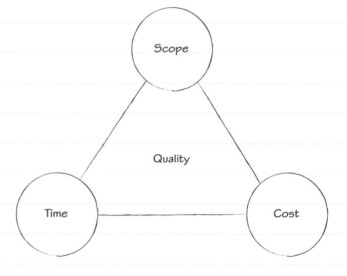

Now try this

Identify the management information required by senior and middle managers who are engaged in making decisions regarding a specific business objective.

 Consider the decisions which need to be made, for example, relating to the opening of a new factory site.

Project management and financial tools

Software-generated information is particularly useful in project management and when using financial tools. On this page, you will revise project management techniques and financial tools.

Project management

Project management tools are used to coordinate the various tasks which must be completed.

1 Networking – a visual representation in the form of a **flow chart** of the various stages involved in implementing a project.

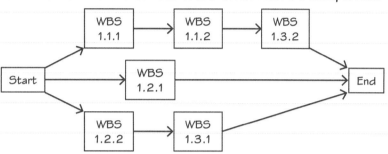

2 Critical path analysis – builds upon the networking principle and is used in large projects.

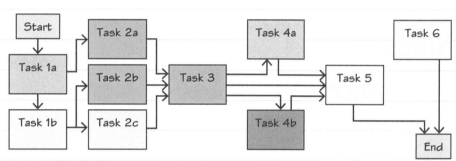

3 Gantt charts – used for scheduling project activities as well as monitoring and communicating the progress of programmed project activities.

	3 Dec	10 Dec	14 Jan	21 Jan	28 Jan	4 Feb	11 Feb	18 Feb
Visual Research								
Market Research								
Initial Drawings								
Moodboards								
Character Development								
C.D. Phase 2*								
Beta Scarf Competition								
MMU Bag Competition								
Threadless Competition								
Branding Ideas								
Network Behance & LinkedIn								
Newtwork Phase 2**								
Final Ideas								
Prep for hand-in deadline								

Financial tools

1 Investment appraisal is used to determine whether it is worthwhile investing in a project where cash flow income varies over the lifetime of the investment. One technique used to do this is to calculate the **discounted cash flow** which values a project by using a discount rate to convert future cash flows into current values.

2 **Internal rate of return (IRR)** is used to determine which projects are likely to return the greatest yield per £ of capital investment.

3 **Net present value** is the difference between the future cash flows and the amount of the investment.

Now try this

A business is deciding whether to invest in a new factory or to re-equip its current premises. It has calculated that the internal rate of return is 7.5 per cent on the new factory and 8.5 per cent if it re-equips. The current market rate of interest is 8 per cent. Is it worthwhile investing in either of the projects?

 Try to identify the opportunity costs of an investment decision.

Market research

Bringing a new product or service to market involves costs and risks. A business must research the target market to assess if the development costs will result in future profits. You will need to revise how primary and secondary research are used to justify marketing.

Types of research

Market research can identify the market share of the main suppliers in a particular market and their relative strength.

- Primary research finds out the opinions of consumers, e.g. surveys, interviews, observation, focus groups.
- Secondary research focuses on facts, e.g. published reports, back data, industry reports, government data, consumer reviews.

Market research alone will not identify if the development of a new product will generate long-term financial gains but it is the starting point for developing a marketing plan.

Costs and risks

Developing and marketing a new product involves **costs** and **risks**. The risks can be reduced if the business undertakes market research to identify potential sales of the product in the target market.

Costs	Risks
• Research and development • Market research • Investment in new equipment • Business loans	• Poor sales • Low sales turnover • Poor cash flow • Inability to cover costs • Competitors

 Links See page 10 to revise primary research, and pages 11–12 to revise secondary research.

Cost to the business

Market research involves employing people or specialist agencies to collect data, and may involve using the business's management information system to analyse the data and produce the necessary reports.

Costs of market research

When analysing case studies involving the costs of developing a new product remember to include the costs of market research. For example, you may have to justify the costs of employing a market research agency.

Key market research questions

A business seeking finance for the development of a new business idea will need to show potential investors they have undertaken in-depth market research.

Now try this

Choose an advertisement for a new or re-launched product from a television, social media or magazine marketing campaign. Describe the primary and secondary research the company will have needed to conduct before launching the product in the advert.

 Market research aims to identify if there is sufficient demand for the business's product or service to generate a profit.

Competitor analysis

When developing a new product or service, a business will carry out a competitor analysis to identify its potential competitors, their strengths and weaknesses. On this page, you will revise how businesses use the results of a competitor analysis to develop their strategy.

Effect on product or service

A business needs to have a clear understanding of who its main competitors are in its target market to ensure that it does not lose market share. Analysing its competitors will enable a business to formulate ways in which to establish a **competitive advantage**, e.g. a business might choose to reduce the price of the product or service or focus on developing the brand image of the product or service it offers.

Location

Market research and a competitor analysis can help businesses spot market opportunities in particular **locations** which currently have few competitors but a large potential market. The location of a business is increasingly becoming less important, in terms of accessing the market, since the **internet** presents opportunities for all businesses to sell their products nationally and internationally.

Pricing strategies

 Cost-based pricing, e.g. mark-up pricing
– a set percentage mark-up based on cost of product/service

 **Pricing strategies**

 Customer-based pricing, e.g.
- penetration pricing – set a low price when the product/service first enters the market
- price skimming – set a high price before new competitors enter the market
- loss leaders – price reductions as part of sales promotion campaign
- psychological pricing – charging £3.99 rather than £4 seems better value for the consumer

 Competitor-based pricing, e.g. the going rate –
market price in line with all competitors (businesses compete on other factors such as quality)

Market map

A **market map** is a tool used by businesses to identify a potential gap in the market with reference to price and quality. For example, the grocery market has attracted two new players, Lidl and Aldi, which recognised a potential gap in the market for discount priced grocery products of good quality. Use the market map opposite to position other major food retailers such as Waitrose, Tesco and M&S.

Now try this

Complete a market map which incorporates the following leading motor car manufacturers: Audi, BMW, Ford, Hyundai, Jaguar.

Consider the different car manufacturers and whether their brand is focused on value or quality.

Trends

One of the main challenges faced by a business is its ability to respond to changes in economic, market and social trends. This will help it to stay ahead of its competitors.

Economic trends

Economic trends influence the level of consumer demand within the economy as a whole.

Unemployment	High levels of unemployment reduce consumer demand
Changes in interest rates	A low rate of interest can stimulate consumer demand
Changes in taxation	A high rate of income tax can lower consumer demand
Rate of inflation	A low rate of inflation increases consumer demand
Changes in exchange rate	A fall in the value of the £ makes imports cheaper
Developments in technology	Advances in technology can reduce the price of products

All of these factors will influence the level of consumers' disposable income

Market trends

Market trends are determined by changes in the spending pattern of consumers on particular goods and services.

Age, gender and cultural diversity	The population profile of the target market will influence demand for different products and services
Changes in fashion and tastes	Markets are influenced by marketing, advertising promotions and branding
The product life cycle	All products have a life cycle and will eventually decline, to be replaced by other products

Businesses need to analyse these factors to determine if they need to change their current strategy

Social trends

Social trends concern people's views and opinions about key issues.

Public opinion	This includes aspects such as environmental concerns, fair trading and animal rights
Technology	Online reviews by consumers of products and services provide access to information on price, quality and customer service
Social media	Online campaigns can be started, aimed at highlighting and changing poor business practices
Changes in lifestyle	These include fundamental changes in consumer behaviour patterns such as the development of online shopping

Social trends are linked to how people perceive their own welfare and the well-being of others

---

Now try this

What economic, market and social trends have resulted in many businesses developing online shopping?

 Consider aspects such as costs, demand, competition and profits.

Marketing plan

Once the business has completed market research and competitor analysis, it is ready to create its marketing plan based on the four Ps.

The marketing plan

The marketing plan comprises a set of **actions** and related **targets** which clarifies how the goals identified in the business's **marketing strategy** will be achieved.

The four Ps and the marketing mix

Think of the four Ps as the ingredients of the marketing plan which must be combined together to get the best results – the marketing mix.

Place | Price | Product | Promotion | The marketing mix

Links Revise the four Ps on pages 21–26 (Unit 2).

Marketing mix in a marketing plan

| Define what the **product** has to offer to consumers in the target market | ▶ | Set an appropriate **price** informed by competitor analysis | ▶ | Identify the right **place** for the product to be sold | ▶ | Set up an effective **promotional** campaign | ▶ | Review the marketing plan to ensure that there are no conflicting messages |

Unique selling point (USP)

In a competitive market, the consumer will have a choice of similar products offered by different firms. A business must convince the consumer that its product has a special or unique characteristic that sets it apart. This **unique selling point** will give the business a **competitive advantage**. USPs provide an opportunity for higher prices for products. Once competitors offer similar features the USP is lost.

Target market and segmentation

Market research will identify the **target market**. **Market segmentation** enables companies to target **market segments** – a group of consumers with similar wants, needs or values, such as:

- geographical location
- buying power
- demographics (including age, gender, occupation, religion)
- lifestyles.

Links Revise market segmentation on page 5 and target market on page 9.

Now try this

Describe the USP of a tablet computer or smartphone.

 Consider aspects such as speed, design and usability.

The seven Ps

The traditional four Ps model of the marketing mix needs to be adapted when it is applied to businesses which deliver services. On this page, you will revise the extended marketing mix – the seven Ps – and how this forms part of the marketing plan.

 **Links** See also trends on page 140.

Service versus product

There are some important differences between marketing a service and a product. A service is a unique experience. Unlike a product, it is intangible and cannot be owned. It may not be stored, returned or resold.

A service must be consumed at the point of delivery.

The seven Ps

For businesses selling services **three new elements** are added to the traditional four Ps marketing mix:

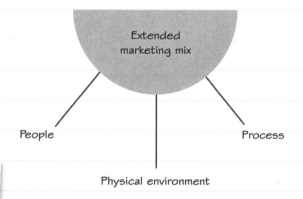

Extended marketing mix

People

Process

Physical environment

People

Employees are responsible for delivering the service and play a key role in developing and maintaining the **corporate image** – how consumers view the business – through their interaction with customers. To enable them to carry out their role effectively, employees require high levels of customer service skills and personal skills.

Physical environment

The business can use the physical environment in which it operates to establish a unique **corporate identity**, e.g. through its choice of:

- livery and logos
- colours, design and décor
- use of space, e.g. level of comfort, security.

Process

Customers using a service may have to go through processes, e.g. interacting with a hair stylist. Establishing **service standards** will ensure that the processes involved in delivering the service can be measured and monitored:

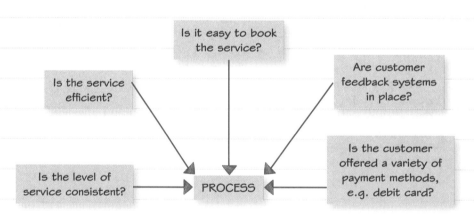

Is it easy to book the service?

Are customer feedback systems in place?

Is the service efficient?

Is the customer offered a variety of payment methods, e.g. debit card?

Is the level of service consistent?

PROCESS

Now try this

Describe how the owners of a new restaurant incorporate the different elements of the seven Ps model into their business plan.

 Remember that a business plan considers the business's mission, costs, finance, marketing and performance indicators.

Legislation 1

Laws govern the way in which a business can operate when it undertakes business activities. On this page and the next, you will revise the four main areas of legislation that apply to businesses.

1 Health and Safety at Work Act (1974)

Ensure the safety of people at work

Ensure safe entry and exit

Provide protective equipment and clothing

Appoint Health and Safety Officer

Employer's health and safety duties

Record and report accidents

Establish health and safety policies

Assess and prevent risks

Provide training

2 Employment legislation

This governs the employment and management of people in the workplace.

Legislation	Implications for business
Equality Act (2010)	• Employment practices including recruitment, pay and dismissal must not discriminate • Covers race, gender, disability, religious beliefs, sexual orientation • Notion of reasonable adjustment to accommodate needs of disabled workers
Employer's Liability (Compulsory Insurance) Act (1969)	Insure against liability for injury or disease to employees

3 Consumer legislation

This seeks to protect the consumer against personal injury or unfair business practices.

Legislation	Implications for business
Consumer Rights Act (2015)	• Includes the right for a consumer to get a full refund up to 30 days for a faulty product • Goods sold should be fit for the intended purpose • Covers digital content • No hidden fees or charges
Trade Descriptions Act (1968)	Must not give false information about a product
Consumer Credit Act (1974)	Must state rate of interest charged on credit agreements

Industry legislation

There are specific laws which apply to certain businesses and industries, e.g. The Food Safety Act covers the production, processing, storage and distribution and sale of food no matter how large or small the business.

Penalties

Depending upon the Act and the severity of the offence, a business may be fined and, in the most extreme cases, employers may be imprisoned.

Now try this

Identify the employment legislation that should be complied with at each stage of the recruitment process.

 The recruitment process starts from assessing the need for the job role through to confirming the job offer.

Legislation 2

On this page, you will revise the fourth main area of legislation – data protection – that affects how a business operates.

 Links See also legislation applying to businesses on page 143.

 Data protection

The Data Protection Act (1998) controls the use of personal information. Businesses must abide by strict rules when using and storing personal data.

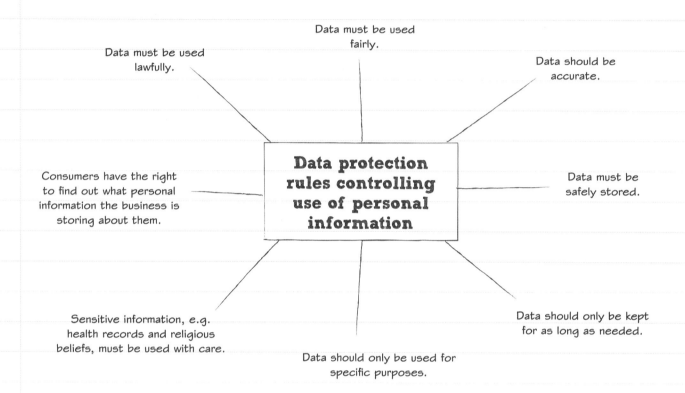

Data must be used fairly.

Data must be used lawfully.

Data should be accurate.

Consumers have the right to find out what personal information the business is storing about them.

Data protection rules controlling use of personal information

Data must be safely stored.

Sensitive information, e.g. health records and religious beliefs, must be used with care.

Data should only be kept for as long as needed.

Data should only be used for specific purposes.

Legal consequences

Breaking the law can have serious consequences for the corporate image of the business. Consumers do not look favourably on those businesses which break the law and may switch to competitors. This can result in a fall in market share, sales turnover and profits. In addition, existing and potential shareholders and investors may decide that the business is no longer a good long-term investment.

Business operations

An employer must ensure that personnel in key positions are aware of the legal implications of their decisions, e.g.

- staff in human resources must be aware of the Equality Act
- a customer services assistant must be aware of the implications of the Consumer Rights Act.

Remember: Employees act on behalf of the business.

Now try this

What are the risks to personal data held by a business which sells goods online?

 Consider the risks from the perspective of both the business and the consumer.

Quality issues

Businesses ensure the quality of their products, services and customer care in different ways depending on their resources, systems and processes. On this page, you will revise the seven main methods of quality control.

 **Links** Revise quality standards and control on pages 115–117.

Quality control and quality assurance

- **Quality control** involves the systematic testing or inspection of products either on an ad hoc or regular basis using statistical sampling techniques.
- **Quality assurance** aims to minimise the reasons for defects identified in the quality control.
- **Self-checking** or inspection is a less formalised system of checking for defects and may not involve specialist quality control staff.

Quality circles and benchmarks

- **Quality circles** are groups of employees who meet to discuss production problems which impact upon quality, identifying their causes and suggesting solutions to management.
- **Benchmarks** are standards of best practice against which a business can compare the quality of its own products and services. Some of these benchmarks are national quality standards or industry-specific quality standards.

ISO 9000

This is a certified quality kite mark awarded to a business whose management quality systems meet internationally recognised standards of excellence.

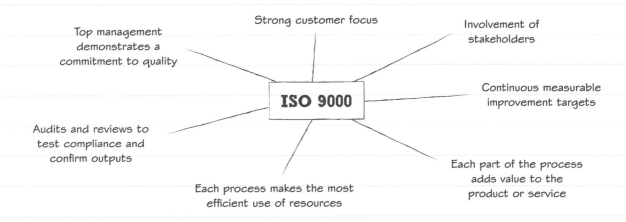

Top management demonstrates a commitment to quality

Strong customer focus

Involvement of stakeholders

ISO 9000

Continuous measurable improvement targets

Audits and reviews to test compliance and confirm outputs

Each part of the process adds value to the product or service

Each process makes the most efficient use of resources

Total quality management (TQM)

TQM is based upon the principle that the customer is at the heart of all business operations. The business aims to:
- produce quality work first time
- focus on the customer
- have a strategic approach to improvement
- improve continuously
- encourage mutual respect and teamwork.

Benefits of a quality system

For customer	For business
• Customers' expectations are met • Repeat purchases • Creates 'customer ambassadors'	Positive impact on: • market share • brand image • corporate culture • staff morale • cost control • profit margins

Now try this

Evaluate the argument that introducing a quality system only adds to business costs.

 Your evaluation should weigh up both sides of the argument and come to a reasoned conclusion.

Human resources

Businesses must ensure that employees make the maximum contribution towards the achievement of business objectives. On this page, you will revise how businesses manage their human resources effectively.

Efficiency

Business efficiency is a measure of how well the business organises its resources and is directly related to the quality of its workforce. This will be influenced by:

- how the business recruits its workforce
- how much the business pays its workforce
- how the business trains its workforce
- how the business organises its workforce.

How to get the best people

Businesses can increase their chances of getting the best people by:

- offering higher financial rewards
- offering additional benefits such as holiday pay
- introducing family-friendly working practices
- offering flexible working arrangements
- using an employment agency
- employing both full-time and part-time staff
- using an employment agency to assist with recruitment, particularly for hard-to-fill vacancies
- offering both full-time and part-time positions to attract more people.

The recruitment process

| 1 Evaluate need | 2 Job description | 3 Person specification | 4 Recruitment plan | 5 Shortlist | 6 Selection | 7 Appointment |

Training

The quality of labour can be improved by training. Below are the benefits and limitations of in-house and external training.

In-house		External	
Benefits	Limitations	Benefits	Limitations
👍 Directly related to needs of the business 👍 Inexpensive 👍 No travel costs	👎 Staff may be called away to deal with urgent work 👎 Trainers and resources not up to date 👎 No experience gained from meeting employees from other businesses	👍 No distraction from day-to-day work tasks 👍 Up-to-the-minute resources and trainers 👍 Delegates can benefit from each other's business experiences	👎 Training may not be perfect match for business 👎 Expensive 👎 Travel costs

Now try this

A business has calculated that labour productivity is below that of the industry benchmark. Suggest three actions that could be introduced by the human resources department to address this situation.

 Labour productivity is influenced by both the quality of labour and the quality of equipment they are using.

Physical resources

The physical resources of a business include all the tangible assets owned and used by a business. On this page, you will revise four types of physical resources required by a business.

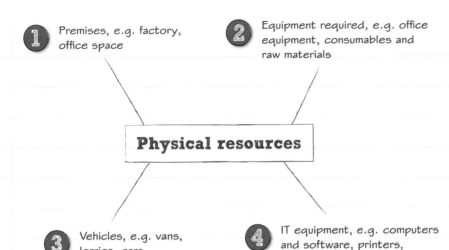

1 Premises, e.g. factory, office space

2 Equipment required, e.g. office equipment, consumables and raw materials

Physical resources

3 Vehicles, e.g. vans, lorries, cars

4 IT equipment, e.g. computers and software, printers, scanners, photocopiers

Add-on costs

Purchasing equipment usually involves significant expenditure. However, the business must also account for the add-on cost which will arise once the physical resources have been acquired. Failure to do so will result in cash flow problems which can result in the business being unable to pay its short-term liabilities.

Premises

Most business premises are either purchased outright or leased/rented. Businesses need to ensure that the premises are large enough to accommodate equipment and staff and take into account relevant legislation covering health and safety and equality issues.

Add-on costs include:

+ utility costs

+ property insurance

+ maintenance.

Equipment

The equipment will largely be dependent upon the type of business, e.g. a manufacturer is likely to require production equipment while a market research firm will require office equipment. The quality of the equipment will likely impact upon the quality of the product or service produced.

Add-on costs include:

+ replacement costs

+ servicing contracts.

Vehicles

The cost of vehicles is dependent upon type, make and specifications.

Add on costs include:

+ fuel costs

+ vehicle tax

+ road tax.

IT hardware and software

A business will be unable to operate without access to computers which will require up-to-date software in order to ensure that it meets the required specification to communicate with its customers and suppliers.

Add-on costs include:

+ maintenance and service contracts

+ broadband connection charges

+ software updating costs

+ technical support costs.

Now try this

Identify one additional 'add-on cost' for each of the physical resources identified on this page.

 Once the physical resource has been bought, what else might the company have to pay for either before or after use?

Purchasing decisions

A business can either use its own resources to purchase physical resources or use other methods to finance the resources it needs. On this page you will revise the finance options when purchasing physical resources and the factors to take into account when dealing with suppliers.

Purchase or rent premises

Option	Advantages	Disadvantages
Purchase	• Property is an asset of the business • Property may appreciate in value • The business is the legal owner of the property	• A significant deposit may be required • The property market may slump • Property maintenance costs
Rent	• Smaller deposit required • No depreciation costs • Major property maintenance may be the responsibility of the landlord	• May not be able to enlarge the premises • Cash flow difficulties if rent increases • No benefit if property prices increase

Purchase or lease

Most physical resources such as vehicles, equipment and IT hardware are either purchased outright or leased. **Leasing** involves paying a set sum each month for a specific period of time and then returning the equipment to the supplier at the end of the lease period.

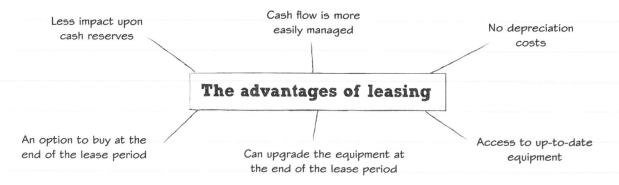

Less impact upon cash reserves — Cash flow is more easily managed — No depreciation costs — **The advantages of leasing** — An option to buy at the end of the lease period — Can upgrade the equipment at the end of the lease period — Access to up-to-date equipment

Securing value for money from suppliers

A business will also take into account a number of other factors when choosing its suppliers in order to secure **value for money**:

Good after-sales service — Availability of spare parts — Delivery schedules — Availability of online ordering — Packaging and returns policies — **Choosing the right supplier** — Delivery costs — Reputation — Special offers — Discounts for bulk or repeat orders — Technical support

---

Now try this

What are the advantages of trade credit for a business and its suppliers?

Think of cash flow and sales.

Financial resources

Financial resources are required by businesses to cover start-up and running costs.

Venture or start-up capital – required to start a business

Links Revise the different types of internal and external sources of finance on pages 64–66 (Unit 3).

Sources of business finance

Investment capital – used to finance the purchase of equipment or to finance business growth

Working capital or running costs – used in day-to-day running of a business

Uses of finance

Short-term (pay back in less than one year)	Medium-term (pay back in one to five years)	Long-term (pay back in more than five years)
• Trade credit – to purchase stock and raw materials • Bank overdraft – to deal with short-term cash flow problems • Invoice discounting/factoring – to improve cash flow	• Leasing – to provide capital equipment which may become obsolete or outdated over a relatively short period of time • Hire purchase – to purchase capital equipment, e.g. vehicles • Bank loan – to pay for machinery or equipment	• Commercial mortgage – to purchase business premises • Share capital – to finance long-term expansion and growth of the business

Other sources of finance

- **Angel investors:** wealthy individuals with a strong track-record in business who provide equity finance at the early stage of market entry.
- **Venture capitalists:** companies which specialise in providing equity finance for young and growing companies.
- **Government grants:** grants are available to support small businesses in certain regions, but these will not cover all of the start-up costs.

Questions to ask when seeking additional capital

1. Why does the business need finance?
2. What will be the impact on cash flow?
3. Can the business afford the repayments?
4. How long will it take the business to repay?
5. If the finance is for purchasing equipment, will this result in additional costs, such as costs of continuous updating?
6. What will be the impact of repayments on the net profit margin?
7. Does the business want to change its legal status?

Now try this

A young entrepreneur has developed a successful app which allows subscribers to order takeaway meals. She is now looking for premises to take the business on to the next stage of its development. Suggest the sources of finance which could support this strategy.

Business premises can either be classed as a non-current asset or as a business expense.

Sales forecast

Sales forecasting is the process of predicting what a business's future sales will be. On this page, you will revise how to create and analyse a sales forecast.

How to create a sales forecast

 Establish a unit of sale, e.g. one car.

 Break down the number of units into factors, e.g. a hotel could use the number of rooms occupied on average per week and the average revenue generated per booking per room.

 Estimate sales revenue =
unit of sale × revenue per sale.

Factors affecting sales forecasts

Forecasts are influenced by the **assumptions** that you make regarding those factors which influence sales revenue. In creating your sales forecast you must identify these assumptions, particularly if you are presenting a business proposal.

Your assumptions could include such factors as:

- current orders
- results from market research
- customer retention and turnover rates.

Analysing a sales forecast

Region	Jan	Feb	Mar	Apr	May	Jun	Jul	TOTAL
\multicolumn{9}{c}{Sales forecast extract for Copstone plc}
North	50 000	47 000	52 000	51 000	55 000	53 000	51 000	359 000
South	55 000	53 000	47 000	43 000	41 000	39 000	38 000	316 000
East	18 000	19 000	20 000	21 000	22 000	24 000	25 000	149 000
West	26 000	20 000	29 000	31 000	33 000	37 000	40 000	216 000
TOTAL	149 000	139 000	148 000	146 000	151 000	153 000	154 000	1 040 000

Why are sales in the South region declining month-on-month?

Why do sales in the West region fall by £6000 in February?

Why do total sales fall in February?

How does the total sales figure compare with the previous six months' sales figures?

Why are East region sales increasing month-on-month but always lower than other regions?

Forecasts and decision making

Analysing a sales forecast enables a business to raise key questions which can assist planning and future strategy:

- ✓ How do our prices impact on sales?
- ✓ Should we increase our advertising?
- ✓ How are sales influenced by the number of sales agents?
- ✓ What is the impact of new products on sales?
- ✓ Should we stop producing some of our products?
- ✓ What is the impact of our competitors on our sales?
- ✓ Should we withdraw from certain markets?
- ✓ Can we cover our costs?

Now try this

Try to think of some of the usual reasons that could account for the trends in Copstone plc's monthly sales forecasts.

 Internal and external factors may both influence sales forecasts.

Cash flow forecast

A cash flow forecast predicts how much money a business will receive and spend at any point in time. On this page, you will revise how to create and interpret a cash flow forecast.

 Links There's more on cash flow forecasts on page 69.

Interpreting a cash flow forecast

CASH INFLOW = movements of cash into the business (note that Copstone plc is planning to obtain a business loan of £20 000 in April)

CASH OUTFLOW = movements of cash out of the business (note that Copstone plc is planning to purchase equipment valued at £50 000 in April which will result in loan repayments of £600 per month from May)

Cash flow forecast Copstone plc

	Jan	Feb	Mar	Apr	May	Jun	Jul	TOTAL
CASH INFLOWS								
Sales	149 000	139 000	148 000	146 000	151 000	153 000	154 000	**1 040 000**
Business loan				20 000				**20 000**
Total inflows	**149 000**	**139 000**	**148 000**	**166 000**	**151 000**	**153 000**	**154 000**	**1 060 000**
CASH OUTFLOWS								
Labour costs	90 000	80 000	89 000	90 000	110 000	110 000	112 000	**681 000**
Marketing	10 000	10 000	10 000	10 000	10 000	10 000	10 000	**70 000**
Equipment	0	0	0	50 000	0	0	0	**50 000**
Stock	20 000	15 000	14 000	20 000	15 000	20 000	17 000	**121 000**
Loan repayments					600	600	600	**1800**
Total outflows	**120 000**	**105 000**	**113 000**	**170 000**	**135 600**	**140 600**	**139 600**	**923 800**
NET CASH FLOW	**29 000**	**34 000**	**35 000**	**-4000**	**15 400**	**12 400**	**14 400**	**136 200**
Opening balance	80 000	109 000	143 000	178 000	174 000	189 400	201 800	**1 075 200**
Closing balance	109 000	143 000	178 000	174 000	189 400	2 018 000	216 200	**1 075 200**

NET CASH INFLOW = Cash inflow – cash outflow

CLOSING BALANCE = balance in the bank at the end of the period

OPENING BALANCE = balance in the bank at the start of the period

Golden rules of forecasting

☑ Be realistic (and sometimes pessimistic).

☑ Capture all projected income (don't leave anything out).

☑ Factor in all costs (remember both fixed and variable costs).

☑ Plan for seasonality (shops may sell more goods at Christmas).

☑ Allow for contingencies (sometimes things go wrong).

Helpful hints

☑ Use a spreadsheet (automatically calculates inflows and outflows of cash).

☑ Break down costs into categories (fixed costs and variable costs).

☑ Remember that if sales fall then costs may fall (but not fixed costs).

☑ Generating new customers may require hiring additional staff.

☑ Additional stock may be required if sales increase.

☑ Business loans may have to be repaid by fixed monthly payments (will increase fixed costs).

Now try this

Copstone plc operates in an industry in which average labour costs are below 60 per cent of sales turnover. Comment on Copstone plc's planned labour costs with reference to its cash flow forecast.

 Industry benchmarks are used to identify the relative strength of a business compared to its competitors.

Break-even chart

Break-even analysis is used to determine when a business will be able to cover all costs and begin to make a profit. On this page, you will revise how to interpret break-even charts.

Break-even

Break-even analysis enables firms to analyse the consequences of changes in sales volume, prices and costs. Consider the following data which show the predicted costs and revenue of producing a product which sells at £10 per unit.

Output costs	Fixed costs (FC)	Variable costs (VC)	Total costs (TC)	Sales revenue (SR)	Profit/(Loss) (SR – TC)
	£	£	£	£	£
0	2000	0	2000	0	(2000)
100	2000	500	2500	1000	(1500)
200	2000	1000	3000	2000	(1000)
300	2000	1500	3500	3000	(500)
400	**2000**	**2000**	**4000**	**4000**	**NIL**
500	2000	2500	4500	5000	500
600	2000	3000	5000	6000	1000
700	2000	3500	5500	7000	1500

The business would have to sell 400 units at a price of £10 each before it reaches its break-even point.

Predicting consequences

A business is concerned about **profit margins** and **unit costs** because it can then calculate how much profit is being made, on average, from each individual product it sells.

From the data table above you could predict that it would cost £5000 to make 600 items so the cost per item would be:

$$\frac{£5000}{600} = £8.33.$$

So it is making a profit of £1.67 on each product sold (£10 – £8.33).

Justifying solutions

Businesses also calculate how much, **on average**, it costs to produce one unit of output, i.e. **unit cost**. In the above data table, if the sales target was set at £3000, i.e. 300 items sold, the total cost would be £3500 or, **on average**, £11.67 **per unit** (£3500 divided by 300). This would result in a loss of £1.67 per unit at a price of £10 per unit.

Therefore, sales revenue alone does not generate profit – sales targets must be based upon a review of fixed and variable costs.

Break-even point

The break-even point can be calculated by creating a break-even chart or by formula.

The formula for the break-even point is:

Fixed costs divided by the contribution per unit (selling price – variable cost)

 Revise how to create a break-even chart on page 71.

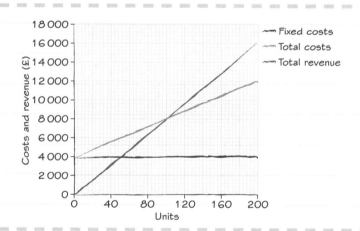

Now try this

Analyse what happens to unit costs as output increases.

 Think about the types of costs associated with break-even analysis.

152

Income statement 1

The income statement is an end-of-year summary of a business's trading activities. You need to revise what information is contained in an income statement.

 There's more on the statement of comprehensive income on page 73.

Gross profit is based on sales turnover and takes into account changes in the inventory level.

Income Statement for Maystar plc

	£	£	£
Sales revenue			15 400
Less Cost of sales:			
Opening stock (1 Jan)		5000	
Purchases (31 Dec)		4800	
		9800	
Less closing stock		4600	5 200
Gross profit			**10 200**
Less Operating costs			
Wages	3800		
Utilities	500		
Rates	810		
Insurance	150		
Stationery	35		
Interest on loan	100		
Advertising	100		
Transport	200		5695
Operating profit/net profit			**4505**
Less tax	901		
Operating profit after tax			3604
Retained profit			**1604**
Distributed profits			**2000**

Net profit takes into account business costs such as administration, advertising and transport.

Finance costs must be included in any calculation of net profit.

The top section of the income statement determines the gross profit.
gross profit = sales – cost of sales

This section of the income statement determines the net profit.
net profit = gross profit – overheads

The distributed profits are those profits that are given to shareholders as dividends.

 There is more about this on pages 77 and 78.

Profitability

The cash amounts of gross profit and net profit are not necessarily useful decision-making factors on their own. You can gain a better understanding (or **interpretation**) of business performance by expressing these values as a percentage of **sales**. These percentages are called **profit margins**.

 Gross profit margin = $\dfrac{\text{Gross profit}}{\text{sales}} \times 100\%$

 Net profit margin = $\dfrac{\text{Net profit}}{\text{sales}} \times 100\%$

For Maystar plc, the gross profit as a percentage of sales is $\dfrac{10\,200}{15\,400} \times 100\% = 66\%$

You can also say that Maystar plc generated **66p** in gross profit for every **£1** of sales income.

For Maystar plc, the gross profit as a percentage of sales is $\dfrac{4505}{15\,400} \times 100\% = 29\%$

You can also say that Maystar plc generated **29p** in net profit for every **£1** of sales income.

Now try this

Here is some information about a small manufacturing business.

Stock at 1 July £2410; Wages £8420; Transport £490; Utilities £590; Purchases £18 000; Stock at 30 June £2500; Sales £29 550; Rent and Rates £1160; Stationery £80

(a) Prepare an income statement based on this information.

(b) Calculate the gross and net profit margins for this business.

 Remember to take care when calculating the 'cost of sales' figure.

Income statement 2

Income statements are an essential decision-making tool for businesses. On this page, you will revise how to interpret an income statement.

🔗 **Links** There's more on the income statement on page 153.

Using the income statement

These are some of the ways business owners and investors can use the information in an income statement.

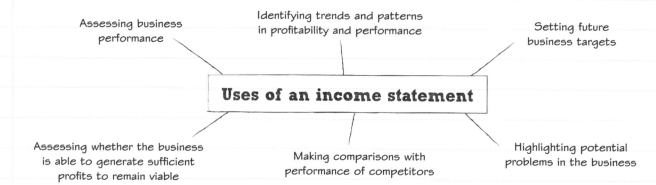

Assessing business performance

Identifying trends and patterns in profitability and performance

Setting future business targets

Uses of an income statement

Assessing whether the business is able to generate sufficient profits to remain viable

Making comparisons with performance of competitors

Highlighting potential problems in the business

Comparing businesses

Gross and net profit margins are useful when comparing the profitability of two different businesses. Net profit margins enable you to interpret the **efficiency** of an organisation since they take into account the level of overhead costs used to generate the profit. Therefore, net profit margins will increase if the business reduces its overhead costs.

 **Links** Look at page 153 to revise calculating profit margins.

Calculating net profit margin

	Company A	Company B
Sales (£)	100 000	75 000
Net profit (£)	75 000	60 000
Net profit margin (£)	0.75	0.80

Company A has a higher net profit, but Company B has a higher net profit **margin**. Company B generates more money per £1 of sales.

Other data

When interpreting the performance of a business don't just rely on the income statement. Use other **financial statements** such as the statement of financial position as well as **financial and non-financial performance ratios**.

Investment decisions

Shareholders and financial institutions such as banks use a range of financial information, including income statements, to make investment decisions.

 Links You can revise these topics on pages 155–158.

Now try this

Look at the data above for Company A and Company B and suggest the ways in which Company B could improve its profit margins.

 Remember that profit margins include both gross and net margins.

Statement of financial position 1

A statement of financial position (SOFP) provides a snapshot at a given moment in time of a business's assets (what it owns or is owed) and its liabilities (debts) which can be used to assess its financial viability. You need to revise what information is contained in a SOFP, often referred to as the balance sheet.

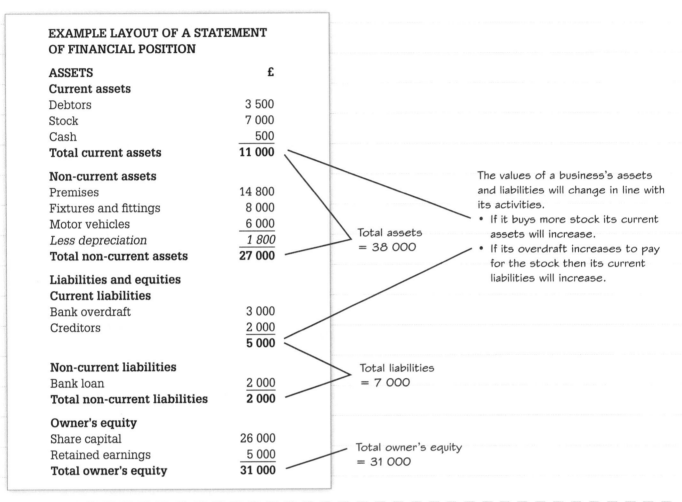

EXAMPLE LAYOUT OF A STATEMENT
OF FINANCIAL POSITION

ASSETS	£
Current assets	
Debtors	3 500
Stock	7 000
Cash	500
Total current assets	**11 000**
Non-current assets	
Premises	14 800
Fixtures and fittings	8 000
Motor vehicles	6 000
Less depreciation	*1 800*
Total non-current assets	**27 000**
Liabilities and equities	
Current liabilities	
Bank overdraft	3 000
Creditors	2 000
	5 000
Non-current liabilities	
Bank loan	2 000
Total non-current liabilities	**2 000**
Owner's equity	
Share capital	26 000
Retained earnings	5 000
Total owner's equity	**31 000**

Total assets
= 38 000

Total liabilities
= 7 000

Total owner's equity
= 31 000

The values of a business's assets and liabilities will change in line with its activities.
- If it buys more stock its current assets will increase.
- If its overdraft increases to pay for the stock then its current liabilities will increase.

The accounting equation

You can check the accuracy of a SOFP by using the **accounting equation**:

assets = capital (or owner's equity) + liabilities

In the example above:

£38 000 = £31 000 + £7 000

Performance ratios

Data in the SOFP can be used to calculate **performance ratios**.

 You can revise how on page 157.

Assessing a business's performance

The three main financial statements used to assess a business's **performance and viability** are:
- ✓ the SOFP
- ✓ the income statement
- ✓ cash flow forecast.

 Revise this on page 151.

Links Revise this on pages 153–154.

Now try this

Amend the above statement of financial position based on the following transactions: the business takes out an additional loan of £30 000 to purchase a company vehicle.

 Check that the SOFP still balances using the accounting equation.

Statement of financial position 2

Statements of financial position (SOFP) are an essential decision-making tool for businesses. On this page, you will revise how to interpret an SOFP, also known as a balance sheet.

 Links There's more on statements of financial position on pages 74–76.

Using the SOFP

These are some of the ways business owners and investors can use the information in a statement of financial position.

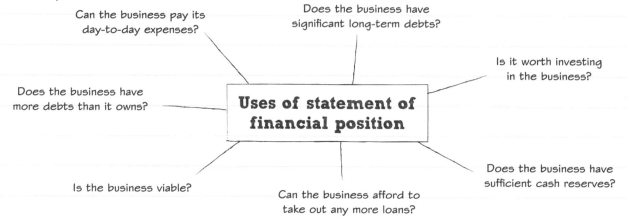

Can the business pay its day-to-day expenses?

Does the business have significant long-term debts?

Does the business have more debts than it owns?

Is it worth investing in the business?

Uses of statement of financial position

Is the business viable?

Can the business afford to take out any more loans?

Does the business have sufficient cash reserves?

Can the business pay its day-to-day expenses?

1   Calculate its **working capital**

working capital = current assets – current liabilities

If working capital is **negative**, the business will not have sufficient working capital to pay its debts in full.

2   Calculate **current ratio**

current ratio = current assets ÷ current liabilities

Check if the current ratio is less than 2:1 (current assets:current liabilities) – it could indicate cash flow problems. A current ratio of 2:1 means that the business has £2 of current assets to cover each £1 of its current liabilities.

3   Calculate **acid test ratio**

(current assets – stock) ÷ current liabilities

This excludes stock which is more difficult to convert into cash.

Can the business pay its debts?

1   Look at how much it owes and compare this with the current assets of the business.

2   Assess whether it has sufficient cash balances.

3   Look at how much it is owed.

4   Make an assessment of whether you think all the money it is owed will be repaid. Enquire as to the value of bad debts.

Is it worth investing in the business?

1   Look at how much the business owes, i.e. its debts (this will impact on future profits).

2   Look at depreciation costs (this may be a sign of out-of-date equipment).

3   Look at the figure for net profit or retained earnings.

4   Compare the net profit figure with the business's future profit projections in the business plan.

 Now try this

Assess the financial viability of the business whose statement of financial position is given on page 155.

Include calculations of both working capital, current ratio and the acid test ratio.

Calculating ratios

The owners of a business will want to know if it is viable and how well it is performing. On this page, you will revise the main calculations which enable the business to measure its liquidity, profitability and performance.

Liquidity ratios

The figures you need to calculate liquidity are found in the **statement of financial position** (balance sheet).

The two main types of liquidity ratios are:

1 The current ratio or working capital ratio
2 The acid test ratio or quick ratio

Calculating liquidity ratios

$$\text{current ratio} = \frac{\text{current assets}}{\text{current liabilities}}$$

$$\text{the acid test ratio} = \frac{(\text{current assets} - \text{stock})}{\text{current liabilities}}$$

For example, current assets £30 000, current liabilities £15 000, stock £10 000

$$\text{Current ratio} = \frac{30\ 000}{15\ 000} = 2{:}1$$

$$\text{Acid test ratio} = \frac{20\ 000}{15\ 000} = 1.3{:}1$$

Profitability ratios

The profitability ratios are referred to as:

1 gross profit margin
2 net profit margin.

The figures you need to calculate profit margins are found in the **income statement**.

A business will also want to measure the ratio of profits generated from the capital it has invested – **return on capital employed** (ROCE). Figures to calculate the ROCE are found in the statement of financial position.

Calculating profitability ratios

$$\text{gross profit margin} = \left(\frac{\text{gross profit}}{\text{sales revenue}}\right) \times 100$$

$$\text{net profit margin} = \left(\frac{\text{net profit}}{\text{sales revenue}}\right) \times 100$$

$$\text{ROCE} = \left(\frac{\text{net profit}}{\text{capital employed}}\right) \times 100$$

For example, if gross profit is £20 000; net profit £12 000; sales revenue is £80 000 and the capital employed is £200 000

Then:

$$\text{gross profit margin} = \frac{20\ 000}{80\ 000} \times 100 = 25\%$$

$$\text{net profit margin} = \frac{12\ 000}{80\ 000} \times 100 = 15\%$$

$$\text{ROCE} = \frac{12\ 000}{200\ 000} \times 100 = 6\%$$

Performance ratios

Performance measures relate to how well the business is using its resources. One important measure of performance is the ratio of the efficiency of the workforce which is referred to as **labour productivity**.

Another measure of performance is the **inventory turnover rate**. Figures to calculate the inventory turnover rate are found in the statement of financial position and the income statement.

Calculating performance ratios

$$\text{productivity} = \frac{\text{total output}}{\text{numbers of workers}}$$

For example, if 200 workers produce 100 000 tables:

$$\text{labour productivity} = \frac{100\ 000}{200} = 500 \text{ tables per worker}$$

Inventory turnover rate =

$$\frac{\text{value of average inventory}}{\text{cost of sales}} \times 365$$

$$= \frac{(\text{opening inventory} + \text{closing inventory}) \div 2}{\text{cost of sales}} \times 365$$

For example, opening inventory £24 000, closing inventory £30 000, cost of sales £175 000:

inventory turnover rate =

$$\frac{(24\ 000 + 30\ 000) \div 2}{175\ 000} \times 365 = 56.3 \text{ days}$$

Now try this

What figures do you need to extract from a business's financial statements to calculate its main liquidity, profitability and performance ratios?

It's a good idea to include financial ratios in your business plan.

Interpreting ratios

On this page, you will revise how a business can interpret liquidity, profitability and performance ratios and the actions needed to improve each of the ratios.

Interpreting liquidity ratios

Liquidity ratios measure the ability of a business to use its assets to meet its short-term financial obligations. Liquidity is vital to the survival of the business, although too high a level of liquidity may mean the business is not using its cash productively. The higher the current ratio, the more liquid the business is considered to be, i.e. it has sufficient short-term current assets to pay its short-term debts; the acid test ratio does not take into account illiquid inventory (stocks) so is a more accurate measure of liquidity.

How to improve liquidity ratios

✓ Improve cash flow, ensure effective stock control systems are in place, pay suppliers on time and avoid loans that over-stretch the business.

Some analysts believe a current ratio of 2:1 is ideal, i.e. the business can 'cover' each £1 of liabilities with £2 of assets. Some businesses need to carry more inventories, e.g. a manufacturing business will have a high current ratio because it needs to hold stocks of raw materials whereas a supermarket will have a low current ratio because it will only hold fast-moving inventories of finished goods and its sales will be for cash rather than credit.

Interpreting profitability ratios

Profitability ratios measure the amount of profit generated from each £ of gross profit and each £ of net profit.

- **Profit margins** measure how much profit is generated by the sale of one unit of output. Improved profit margins mean the business is making more profit from each sale.
- **Rate of return on capital employed** (ROCE) – the business will want ROCE to be greater than the rate it pays for its borrowed funds.

How to improve profitability ratios

✓ **Gross profit margin**: reduce the cost of sales, i.e. take measures to reduce the cost of goods which will be resold; increase sales revenue.

✓ **Net profit margin**: take steps to reduce business expenses including labour, energy and raw material costs.

✓ **ROCE**: increase the net profit of the business; increase gross profit and reduce expenses (this in turn will have the benefit of increasing both gross and net profit margins).

Interpreting performance ratios

Performance measures relate to how well the business is using its resources.

- If **labour productivity** improves it means each worker is producing, on average, more units of output in a given period of time.
- A short **inventory turnover** period is generally preferred because holding inventories involves inventory holding costs as well as no sales revenue being generated from the stock.

How to improve performance ratios

✓ **Labour productivity**: improve training of the workforce; reduce the size of the workforce and increase investment in capital equipment.

✓ **Inventory turnover**: improve inventory control systems; increase sales. Carrying too little stock can result in a loss of sales; price increases in supplies can increase the costs of purchasing stock; take account of seasonal fluctuations in sales.

Now try this

Identify three other performance indicators which could be used to measure business performance.

 Think of aspects such as quality, customers and market share.

Threats and 'what if?'

Businesses need to identify and evaluate the likely impact of risks to their operations. You need to revise the decision-making tools used to assess threats.

Links You might want to revise SWOT and PESTLE on page 19.

SWOT analysis

This gives the business the information it needs to OPTIMISE its strengths, IMPROVE its weaknesses, EXPLOIT the opportunities and MINIMISE the threats.

Positive factors	Negative factors
Strengths	**Weaknesses**
Strong brand	Low market share
Large market share	High staff turnover
Strong financial reserves	Poor reputation for quality
Trained workforce	Outdated equipment
Opportunities	**Threats**
A competitor is in financial difficulties	Negative publicity
	Shortages in skilled labour
New developing markets	Increased competition
Developments in technology	Loss of a major contract

PESTLE analysis

This identifies and assesses factors in the external environment. A business must make an assessment of the possible impact of all of these factors on its long-term objectives. It must strive to maximise the business benefits of any changes in these factors and analyse the potential damaging impact on the business so it can respond accordingly.

PESTLE factors

Political, Economic, Social, Technological, Legal, Environmental.

'What if?' scenarios

These help the business to evaluate how well placed it is to respond to changes in its environment. For example:

What if there is an increase in taxation on business profits?	• Look at ways to increase sales turnover. • Look at ways to reduce operating costs. • Consider relocating to another country.
What if the business can't recruit skilled labour?	• Begin an in-house training programme. • Look to increase wages for new recruits. • Advertise vacancies in other countries.
What if the government starts to offer financial incentives to exporters?	• Undertake market research to identify new market opportunities overseas. • Establish a new marketing plan.
What if a competitor gets into financial difficulty?	• Analyse the reasons for the financial difficulties. • Analyse the potential benefits of a business take-over. • Evaluate the costs of a take-over.

 Now try this

Identify **three** possible responses that a business could take if a major new competitor entered its main market.

Think of the responses in terms of offensive or defensive strategies.

Contingency plans

A business must have a plan of action to deal with any major event that could have a significant impact on its costs, revenue, reputation or operations. On this page, you will revise the risks faced by a business and how contingency plans can manage these risks.

Business risks

Most business risks will impact directly or indirectly on the two main aspects of running a business – generating sales income and keeping costs under control. When establishing a contingency plan, a business will try to evaluate the impact of the risk on both of these areas.

Risk analysis

Contingency planning involves identifying, analysing and evaluating **business risks**.

Business risks can be classified in a number of ways but you need to consider them in the following three areas:

1　Financial risks

2　Legal risks

3　Reputational risks

Examples of business risks

1 Financial risks	**Example** A major fire results in the destruction of one of the business's major production facilities.
2 Legal risks	**Example** A customer is injured by a product supplied by the business.
3 Reputational risks	**Example** The business is investigated by the press for poor working conditions in its overseas factory.

The business must have a contingency plan in place so that the impact on its costs and revenue streams can be evaluated and minimised.

The contingency plan

The contingency plan will deal with uninsured business risks. It will involve:

1　evaluating business risks

2　identifying staff who will take the lead

3　compiling a list of business support services including legal services

4　keeping an up-to-date list of suppliers

5　ensuring data security systems are in place for personal data (HR and customers)

6　establishing a business continuity plan in the event of total shutdown

7　preparing a communications plan.

Risk retention and risk transfer

The contingency plan will identify a business's plans for dealing with any major event. This could involve **retaining the risk** and using its own financial reserves to address any loss of income or increase in costs. Or the business could decide to **transfer the risk** to an **insurance company**. Should the business decide to retain some of the risks then it must ensure that it has sufficient financial reserves to meet any contingencies which may arise. These reserves would not be available to use for other purposes.

Now try this

Assess the risks and insurance requirements of a business start-up.

 Some business insurances are compulsory.

Had a look ☐ Nearly there ☐ Nailed it! ☐

Using IT skills

For the external assessment, you will need to revise how to prepare, present and interpret complex data in an appropriate format using your IT skills.

Document required in the supervised assessment	Software	IT skills	Good practice points
REPORT	Word processing and spreadsheet	Layout and design Numbering Bullets Tables Insert images and shapes Screenshots Review	• Follow the conventions of a normal business report • Divide the report into sections • Number each section • Include diagrams and graphs where appropriate • Explain the purpose of the graphs or diagrams you include • End the report with a conclusion or recommendations
EXECUTIVE SUMMARY	Word processing	Layout and design Review Numbering Bullets	• Keep it short and to the point • Short opening sentence to set the scene • Number each of the points • Refer to the data
PRESENTATION	Presentation software	Layout and design Formatting Formulae Duplicate Replicate Comment boxes Graphs and layout	• Don't put too many points on each slide • Don't let the graphics 'overpower' the key points and the overall message you're trying to get across • Keep colours to a minimum

Quality of business documents

Remember, however good your IT skills are, the quality of your business documents will be assessed on the accuracy and relevance of the analysis and evaluation of the data and information which form the basis of your business case.

Importance of data and information

Your business documents should be 'data rich'. Spreadsheets can help analyse these data. Remember the two golden rules:

1 Data must be entered accurately.
2 The formulae entered in cells must be correct.

Now try this

Using the IT skills identified in the above table, create a six-month sales forecast for a hotel. Use the data in the sales forecast to create one appropriate type of graph of your choice based upon the data in the sales forecast.

Think about sales per month and the percentage of total sales generated in different months.

Your Unit 7 external assessment

For this unit you will be assessed through completion of a set task, made up of two activities. The activities will be based upon a case study or a business scenario contained in a taskbook which you will receive at the start of the assessment period. You will not be expected to do any preparatory work on the set task prior to the assessment.

Marks allocated

The set task is divided into two activities worth a total of 70 marks: Activity 1 is allocated 52 marks and Activity 2 is allocated 18 marks.

Manage your time!

You have three hours to complete both activities. You should aim to spend just under 2 hours 15 minutes on Activity 1 and about 45 minutes on Activity 2. Remember to allow time to read through your work before you hand it in.

Your set task

The set task activities will ask you to make decisions and suggest recommendations to address a specific aspect of the business scenario. You will be expected to apply your understanding of how business decisions are made and use your knowledge to help you produce:

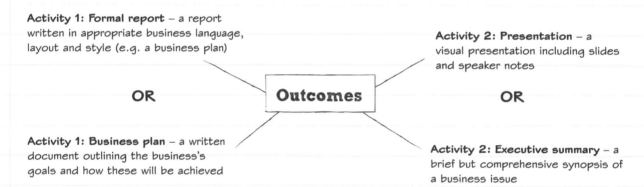

Activity 1: Formal report – a report written in appropriate business language, layout and style (e.g. a business plan)

OR

Activity 1: Business plan – a written document outlining the business's goals and how these will be achieved

Outcomes

Activity 2: Presentation – a visual presentation including slides and speaker notes

OR

Activity 2: Executive summary – a brief but comprehensive synopsis of a business issue

The documents must be produced using word-processing, spreadsheet or presentation software. The taskbook will tell you which documents you will need to submit.

The task brief

Over the next few pages, you'll work on a revision task similar in style to one you might be given in order to help you understand how to approach the external assessment. Here is the revision task brief.

The local council has received a grant from the government to support new businesses. A committee of councillors will consider each application.

You are on work placement in the Regeneration and Community Engagement Division. You have been asked by your supervisor to read through a business plan submitted by the owners of 'Eastern Fusion' and then make recommendations to the committee in a formal report format. You will also be required to prepare some presentation slides.

Now try this

Using the above task brief, identify the documents which you would expect to be submitted by the owners of the Eastern Fusion restaurant in its application for financial support from the Council.

 Some of these documents will be provided to you as part of the revision task information.

162

Making business decisions

Making the right business decisions involves going through six different stages – see the flow chart below. You will complete each stage in relation to the two activities in the Eastern Fusion restaurant revision task to enable you to reach a decision.

 Links Look back at the revision task brief on page 162. The task activities are on page 164.

1 Prepare	Identify the issue/problem/opportunity	This will set the context for the decision
2 Gather	Gather the information together	Select the information required to make the decision
3 Analyse	Analyse the situation	What different interpretations of the data might be possible?
4 Develop	Develop a set of possible options	What alternative courses of action may be appropriate?
5 Evaluate	Evaluate the different alternatives available	Evaluate for feasibility, acceptability and desirability
6 Select	Select the preferred option	Make the decision and provide a rationale

Decision-making skills

You will be required to use a range of different skills throughout the decision-making process. Over the next few pages, you will work through each of the skills required to make business decisions.

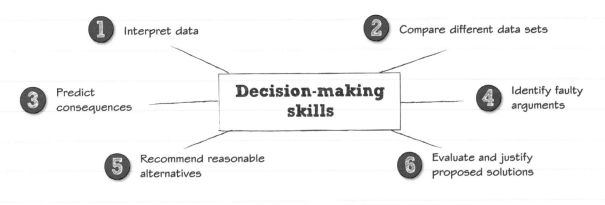

1 Interpret data

2 Compare different data sets

3 Predict consequences

Decision-making skills

4 Identify faulty arguments

5 Recommend reasonable alternatives

6 Evaluate and justify proposed solutions

 Now try this

Draw up a table and complete an assessment of your own strengths and the areas you need to improve mapped against each of these skills.

Think about what you need to do to improve your skills in each area.

Background information

As part of your set task, you will be given some background information, including a set of documents, to inform completion of the two activities. Over the next few pages you will look at a set of documents relating to the revision task brief from page 162 prepared by the owners of the Eastern Fusion snack bar. They are applying for a grant from the local council to finance a new restaurant.

Here are the two revision activities relating to the revision task brief from page 162. Keep referring back to the two activities you have been set when analysing all background information.

NOT WRITE IN THIS AREA

Activity 1

Using the information provided, decide whether you consider the application for financial support should be approved and present a set of recommendations to councillors in the style of a formal report. Your report should include:

- rationale supported by data
- consideration of business risks.

Activity 2

Summarise the viability of Eastern Fusion's business proposal in a way that will convince councillors.

Prepare a maximum of four presentation slides with brief speaker notes.

Background information

You will be given background information in the external assessment which will provide details about the business context. Here is some information about Eastern Fusion.

Background Information

Prema and John have submitted an application for a business grant from the Council. They started a sandwich snack bar four years ago, Eastern Fusion, and are applying for a Council grant of £20 000 which they will use as a deposit to purchase a vacant property adjacent to their snack bar to open a new restaurant. They plan to take out a mortgage to finance the purchase of the property.

Extracting data

You need to extract relevant data from the information you are given. This will help you set the **context** for making your business decisions.

Sample notes extract

1. Owners have business experience
2. Applying for £20 000 grant
3. Plan to open a restaurant
4. Will also take out a mortgage on commercial premises

These four points are a useful summary extracted from the task information.

Supporting documentation

The owners of Eastern Fusion have provided the following supporting documents. These are included in the background information.

1 The summary income statement (statement of profit or loss) for their current business

2 The latest statement of financial position (balance sheet) for their current business

3 A cash flow forecast for their new business

4 Market research data

You can use financial statements and market research data to determine:

- ✓ business performance
- ✓ profitability
- ✓ liquidity
- ✓ viability of the business proposition
- ✓ business risks.

Links Revise financial statements on pages 153–156 and market research on page 138.

Now try this

Explain why business decisions need to take into account both quantitative and qualitative information.

Consider the relationship between information and business risks.

Interpretation of data

The interpretation of data forms part of gathering together the information which you will use to reach your decision. Here are some data provided as part of the Eastern Fusion background information.

Summary Income Statement for the Eastern Fusion Snack Bar for the year ending 31 December

	£
Sales revenue	80 000
Cost of sales	30 000
Gross profit	**50 000**
Less Operating expenses	36 000
Net profit for the year	**14 000**

Performance ratios

You can provide a greater in-depth analysis of financial data by **calculating performance ratios** based on the data.

You can show the relationship between sales and profit by calculating the **profit margins** which could be compared with industry benchmarks.

 **Links** Revise income statements on pages 153 and 154.

The snack bar generated both a gross and net profit of £50 000 and £14 000 respectively for the year ending 31 December.

The gross profit margin of the Eastern Fusion snack bar was 62.5% with a net profit margin after tax of 17.5%.

Operating costs are £36 000 although there are no details provided regarding how these costs are broken down.

Although it is important for a business to make a profit this doesn't tell the whole story about its performance or business risks.

Calculating profit margins, as this student has done, provides a more reliable indicator of profitability than simply identifying the gross and net profit figures.

This is a good point because a break-down of these expenses will provide information about the efficiency of the business.

Identifying additional information and risks

- Are there any trends which can be derived from the data?

- It is also useful at this stage to identify the potential business risks which may arise. You will be able to use this when completing Activity 1 which requires you to consider business risks.

- One initial risk factor is the additional business costs which would be generated as a result of the mortgage.

Trends in profitability could be derived from an analysis of previous years' income statements.

You could consider how this risk might be addressed, e.g. would it be better for Prema and John to consider renting the new premises rather than purchasing outright?

Now try this

Identify other information Prema and John could provide to back up the information in their income statement.

The information in the income statement includes both revenue and costs.

Comparing information and data

In Activity 1, you will need to analyse the financial position of a business. This will allow you to consider its performance, viability and any potential risks. You can do this by comparing data and information from different sources. This page looks at a different set of financial data drawn from an analysis of the statement of financial position.

Summary Statement of Financial Position for Eastern Fusion Snack Bar at 31 December	£	£
ASSETS		
Current assets	10 000	
Non-current assets	28 000	
Total assets	**38 000**	
EQUITY		
Owner's equity	3 000	
Profit for the year	14 000	
		17 000
LIABILITIES		
Current liabilities	5 000	
Non-current liabilities	16 000	
Total liabilities		21 000
TOTAL EQUITY AND LIABILITIES		38 000

🔗 **Links** Revise statement of financial position on pages 155 and 156.

Analysing data

Begin your analysis of the data by performing some calculations which will allow you to draw preliminary conclusions.

Sample response extract

Total assets of £38 000 and total liabilities of £21 000 giving a net worth of £17 000 is relatively healthy (given that it's a snack bar).

Working capital is £5000 (current assets – current liabilities).

Working capital is £5000 and the current ratio is 10 000 : 5000 = 2:1 although this does not take into account the impact of stock valuation.

Non-current liabilities are relatively high at £16 000 which could signify a long-term loan.

 You could also calculate the ROCE from the data in the SOFP.

🔗 **Links** Revise ROCE on page 157.

This learner raises a good point at this stage because it identifies an understanding of different types of liabilities and the implications for the business.

Sample response extract

Business risks

A non-current liability will not be repaid within one year so the £16 000 non-current liabilities is a risk given that the owners of Eastern Fusion want to take out an additional non-current liability (a mortgage).

If the £5000 in working capital was tied up in stock this could create cash flow problems.

This shows an understanding of the importance of business liquidity.

Remember

👍 It's useful to show that you can use financial terminology in an appropriate context.

👍 Comparing the information in one data set (the SOFP) with data from another source (the income statement) will help you to identify potential business risks.

👎 Don't make generalisations which may lead you to the wrong conclusion. Would this business be a low risk if its profits had fallen by 25 per cent over the last three years?

Now try this

Identify other information Prema and John could include to support the information in their statement of financial position.

 Consider the make-up of assets and liabilities and how their different elements impact upon the ability to raise business finance.

Predicting consequences

Making business decisions involves evaluating risks. You can do this by trying to predict events which may occur in the internal or external business environment and their impact on a business. In the Eastern Fusion revision task the cash flow statement will provide the basis for predicting probable consequences.

Summary one-year cash flow forecast for the proposed new restaurant £'000

	J	F	M	A	M	J	J	A	S	O	N	D
Cash inflows	10	15	20	32	33	35	36	42	35	30	35	42
Cash outflows	12	16	16	20	20	20	22	26	22	18	24	26
Net cash flow	–2	–1	4	12	12	13	14	16	13	18	11	16

Financial assumptions within the cash flow forecast

Prema and John have included the following explanatory note with their cash flow forecast:

'The restaurant will have space for 40 diners; will open seven evenings a week, 5.00 pm until midnight; average spend per customer of £25; planned target maximum occupancy 60 diners per evening.'

 Links Revise cash flow on page 151.

Predicting consequences from the cash flow forecast

How realistic are the owners' financial assumptions which underpin their cash flow forecast?

'What if?' analysis of financial data can be conducted using a spreadsheet.

- ✓ WHAT IF the average spend per customer is only £20?
- ✓ WHAT IF the occupancy rate is 50 diners per evening?
- ✓ WHAT IF they have to pay higher wages in order to recruit staff?
- ✓ WHAT IF the cost of utilities increases?
- ✓ WHAT IF the price of supplies increases?

Sample notes extract

Analysis of Eastern Fusion's application for the grant from the council

Positives	Negatives
Business experience	Insufficient detail in financial statements
Profitable current business	
Working capital of £5000	Over-optimistic cash flow forecast
Assets of £38 000	Non-current liabilities of £16 000
Net worth of £17 000	No performance trends
Net profit margin of 17.5%	No industry benchmarks provided

 When you read through the case study, make short notes to refer to when you are writing up your tasks.

 Ensure that you record the results of your analysis. In this example, the learner has clearly presented the positives and negatives, which will make it easy to refer to when they come to assess and evaluate business risks.

Now try this

Identify the risks associated with each of the negative points identified from the analysis of the Eastern Fusion revision task data.

 It's good practice to evaluate business risks as high, medium or low.

Identifying faulty arguments

A faulty argument is one which is based upon an inaccurate, weak or flawed rationale. On this page, the business case presented in Eastern Fusion's application for a business grant is subject to a critical evaluation.

Background information

Below is additional information provided by Prema and John in support of their business proposal.

> We have presented a strong cash flow forecast which shows that the new business will generate high profit levels. Our family and friends have commented favourably on the new menu which is indicative of future high sales turnover. Our current business has a healthy working capital and we have already run a profitable business which generated a high profit level of £14 000.

Faulty arguments in a business proposal

Faulty arguments are usually associated with:

 lack of understanding of financial data

 over-ambitious performance targets

 weak market research

4 lack of understanding of the target market.

When weighing up whether a business case is faulty, make sure you clearly identify each argument. In this example, the learner has worked methodically through the business proposal commenting on the faulty arguments in turn.

Sample response extract

The strong cash flow argument

This is a faulty argument because a strong cash flow forecast will not necessarily mean high profits if a high proportion of projected sales are on credit and may result in late payments or debt default.

The working capital argument

This is a faulty argument because the working capital is only £5000 and does not take account of stock valuation which could impact upon liquidity and the ability of the business to pay its short-term liabilities.

The projected sales argument

This is a faulty argument because market research based solely on family and friends may not be sufficiently independent or robust.

The net profit argument

This is a faulty argument because the net profit figure is only for one year; it could be that this figure represents a fall on the previous year's profits which confirms a trend of falling net profit over time.

Now try this

Explain how John and Prema could improve their arguments regarding projected sales targets and the level of net profits.

 The more detail they include the more robust their arguments will be.

Recommending alternatives

When reaching a business decision, it is good practice to show that you have considered reasonable alternatives which could still meet the objectives of the business proposal. This page looks at the alternatives related to Eastern Fusion.

Background information

Here's another extract from Eastern Fusion's business proposal.

> Prema's uncle owns a successful restaurant business in a nearby town. His restaurant is currently being refurbished.
>
> Prema and John's restaurant is based in the town centre which has grown in size due to the increase in office space built to accommodate the influx of corporate head offices being located in the town.

Try to set out your alternatives with a clear rationale and business case identified for each option. In these examples, the learner has ensured alternatives are reasonable by relating them to the needs of the business, making them realistic, relatively low risk, creative, cost effective and supported by a business case.

It would be useful for you to recommend to Prema and John that they prepare a detailed business plan in support of their application.

Sample response extract

Legal status of the business – option 1

Currently Prema and John are in partnership and are personally responsible for all business debts.

Reasonable alternative

Consider the possibility of forming a limited company.

Business case

👍 With a limited company their liability for business debts would be limited to the amount they have invested.

Finance of the business – option 3

Prema and John are planning to purchase new equipment and furniture for their new restaurant.

Reasonable alternatives

Explore the possibility of leasing expensive kitchen equipment; ask Prema's uncle if he will donate any kitchen equipment; consider renting business premises rather than purchasing with a mortgage.

Business case

👍 Initial start-up capital costs would be reduced.

Control of the business – option 2

Currently Prema and John are in control of all business decisions.

Reasonable alternative

Consider bringing on board Prema's uncle as an additional investor or partner.

Business case

👍 Additional funds secured

👍 Access to expertise

👍 Reduced risk of business failure

Routes to market – option 4

Prema and John are proposing to open a new restaurant.

Reasonable alternatives

Open up a 'pop-up' mobile restaurant; consider expanding current business by securing contracts to provide lunches for office workers in corporate head offices.

Business case

👍 Can test the market

👍 Use existing business experience to develop the market

> You could use one or two of these reasonable options in your report.

Now try this

Explain the business case for franchising.

 Look at reasonable alternatives in terms of business risks and potential returns.

Formal report

In Activity 1 of the revision task on page 164, you are required to prepare a business report to be read by local councillors. This page provides a format which you could use to present a formal report. The report must be word processed.

1 Title of the report
- Concise and to the point
- Who the report is for; name of the person who wrote the report; date

- A concise description of the content of the report
- The status of the report: is it for 'information' only or is it for 'discussion' or does a 'decision' have to be made?

2 Introduction
- The purpose of the report
- List the 3 or 4 main sections that will be covered

- Background
- Purpose of the report
- Key questions or issues to be addressed
- Approach taken

3 Numbered sections of the report
- Analysis of the data and information in each section
- Sources and research used

- How the report writer approached the task
- Key findings

4 Conclusions and recommendations
- Summarise the main findings in the report
- List a set of recommendations which relate to each of the main sections in the report

- The results of the analysis
- Any gaps or shortcomings in the data which may affect the findings
- Link back to the purpose of the report and the key questions identified in the Introduction to the report

Now try this

Write the title and the introduction of the report to the council on Eastern Fusion's business proposal.

Think of the questions that the council would want answered when considering applications for financial support.

Business plan

In the external assessment, the set task may require you to prepare a business plan in Activity 1. This page provides a framework which you could use.

Business plan for Eastern Fusion

You have proposed that Prema and John prepare a detailed business plan. The following is a suggested format of what should be included in their business plan.

Templates

You can find a range of possible templates for business plans on the internet by searching 'business plan templates'.

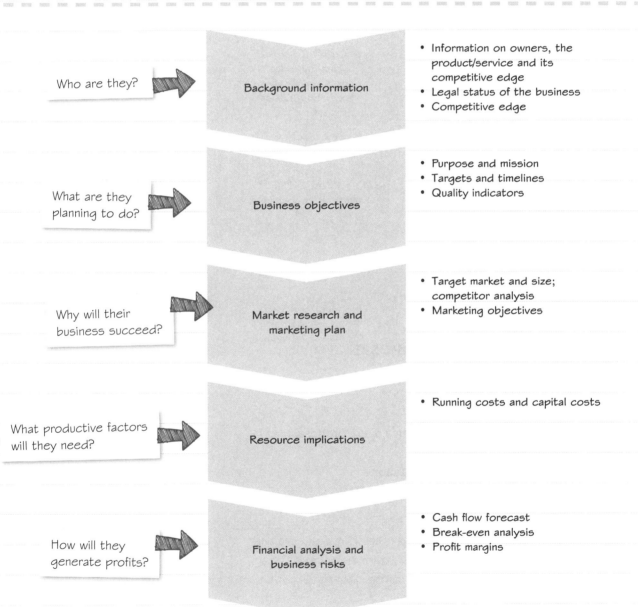

Who are they? → Background information
- Information on owners, the product/service and its competitive edge
- Legal status of the business
- Competitive edge

What are they planning to do? → Business objectives
- Purpose and mission
- Targets and timelines
- Quality indicators

Why will their business succeed? → Market research and marketing plan
- Target market and size; competitor analysis
- Marketing objectives

What productive factors will they need? → Resource implications
- Running costs and capital costs

How will they generate profits? → Financial analysis and business risks
- Cash flow forecast
- Break-even analysis
- Profit margins

Refer to the diagram above for points to consider in the 'Background information' section of your business plan.

Now try this

Write a set of bullet points to highlight the data you would refer to in the 'Background information' section of Eastern Fusion's business plan.

Business plans should be 'data rich' so that potential investors can identify the opportunities on offer.

Business presentation

In Activity 2 of the revision task on page 164, you are required to prepare a visual presentation to local councillors. In the external assessment this will involve producing four slides with speaker notes. This page provides a format which you could use. You should prepare your slides and notes using presentation software.

What the topic is about and what you will be covering in the presentation.

INTRODUCTION
Background to the business proposal
Plan of the presentation

Don't write out the full presentation. Use bullet points.

- Establish a theme or topic for each slide avoiding large blocks of text.
- Use maximum of six or seven bullet points per slide.
- Use simple graphics.
- Include three or four main conclusions.

SLIDES 2 AND 3
Financial data
Strengths and weaknesses
Presenting issues

Use the speaker notes to provide some of the detail which backs up the presentation and to point out some of the issues.

Finish with a question to capture the attention of the audience.

FINAL SLIDE
Summary and conclusions

Use the speaker notes to explain why these are the important conclusions.

1 BUSINESS PROPOSAL

- New town centre restaurant
- £20 000 grant required
- Analysis of the financial data
- Evaluation of strengths and issues of the proposal
- Conclusions
- Recommendations for consideration

A well-constructed slide 1:
👍 Clearly laid out
👍 Easy to read
👍 Does not contain any distracting graphics
👍 Only covers six bullet points
👍 Presents an overview of what will be covered in the presentation
👍 States the amount of grant required
👍 Supplemented by a set of speaker notes which are directly related to the points made in the slide

Speaker notes

- Proposal submitted by Prema and John, owners of Eastern Fusion
- Currently own a snack bar which they have operated for four years
- New restaurant will be located in vacant premises adjacent to the snack bar
- Documentation submitted
- Presentation coverage – financial analysis, risks, alternative strategies and recommendations

Prepare slide 2 on Eastern Fusion's financial data with accompanying speaker notes.

 Refer to the good points of slide 1.

Executive summary

In Activity 2, you may be required to produce an executive summary. This page provides a format which you could use to present your summary. This document must be produced on a computer.

Create a mind map; Look for patterns of information.

1
Identify the main points

For each section highlight the main points and statements.

Inform the reader what the summary is about.

2
Begin the summary with an introductory sentence

Who? What? When? Where? Why?

Use examples of positives, negatives and any outstanding issues.

3
Include details only where necessary

Identify any relationships in the information being summarised.

Use words like 'next', 'before', 'after', 'to sum up', 'most important', 'for example', 'as a result'.

4
Use transition words to connect sentences

Using transition words will help to reduce the amount of detail in the summary.

Check that you have covered all the main points.

5
Proof-read for presentation, spelling and grammar

Edit the summary to reduce unnecessary words or phrases.

Sample response extract

The proposal requires a grant of £20 000 to support the opening of a new restaurant located in vacant premises adjacent to a current snack bar which has been operated by the applicants for the past four years.

The most recent income statement identifies a net profit of £14 000 with a 17.5% net profit margin. The SOFP shows a net worth of £17 000 and working capital of £5000. Financial statements presented by the applicants were only for one year.

The cash flow forecast for the business proposal is over-ambitious and based upon limited market research. Evidence of risk analysis is limited.

When writing an executive summary, begin by outlining the current situation and what is proposed. In this sample extract the learner identifies the amount of business finance requested, what the grant would be used for, along with an overview of the background of the business owners. It is essential to refer to business data, risk and the market in your summary. Here the learner refers to calculations using data extracted from the financial statements, and has made comments about the cash flow forecast, market research and risk analysis.

Now try this

Complete the summary above using a maximum of 100 words.

 Think about reasonable alternatives and summarise your decision on the proposal.

Answers

Unit 2: Developing a Marketing Campaign

1. Purposes of marketing

It depends on the type of business and the stage that the business has reached. New businesses might start by either anticipating or recognising demand. Established businesses might focus on satisfying existing demand.

2. Marketing aims and objectives 1

Innovation is all about being at the cutting edge of new product development. It is about thinking ahead and anticipating what the market might want or need in the future. It is also about pushing the boundaries of technology. Being an innovative business gives the company a chance to stay ahead of the competition and secure sales with its new products before the competitors catch up with it.

3. Marketing aims and objectives 2

Diversification might be one option. The business could open a petrol station on the site or offer car servicing and repairs.

4. Mass and niche markets

Pubs, independent restaurants and smaller chains all compete in the niche market for premium burgers.

5. Market segmentation

Sandi needs to research the town centre and categorise the different types of people (particularly at lunchtimes). She is likely to consider occupation, income, buying habits and age. There may also be ethnic, cultural and religious factors to consider.

6. Branding

The USP of the brand is what recognisably sets the brand apart from its competitors in the minds of the customers. For example, for decades Fairy Liquid's USP has been the fact that it remains a concentrated washing up liquid compared to many of its competitors. The USP suggests that the product will last longer than the competitors' products and that this justifies the comparative premium price. At the same time, Fairy Liquid has always maintained that it will not dry or harm the skin, particularly the hands, something that many other manufacturers cannot claim as a USP.

7. Internal influences on marketing

Breakfast slot $\frac{300\,000}{1000} = 300$; $\frac{£500}{300} = £1.66$ per thousand

Early peak slot $\frac{750\,000}{1000} = 750$; $\frac{£4000}{£750} = £5.33$ per thousand

Late peak slot $\frac{900\,000}{1000} = 900$; $\frac{£7500}{900} = £8.33$ per thousand

8. External influences on marketing

She would have to be aware that ethical questions might be asked about her decision to manufacture in Bangladesh. She would need to be sure about the working conditions, the workers' pay and the business practices of the factory owners. There are other factors such as economic, technological and environmental to consider.

9. Identifying what customers want

She needs to work out which designs are the most popular and why. She should carry out market research and ask her regular customers which types of designs they prefer.

10. Primary research

Carrie has a limited budget so it needs to be cost-effective. A survey or questionnaire should identify what customers want and they could then send out email offers featuring the most popular designs.

11. Internal secondary research

It would have sales records and details of interactions with customers. It would also have delivery addresses, phone numbers and email addresses. All of these could be used to carry out market research or for a marketing campaign.

12. External secondary research

The company needs to look at services that are being supplied by competitors to customers similar to its own. It should profile its customer segments and research these groups. It should also survey its existing customers and ask them if they would be interested in other services.

13. Validity and reliability

Rohan needs to decide what he wants the research to look at. What questions need an answer? He should then ask the agencies how they would find that out, how long it would take and what the cost would be. He can then make a considered choice with all the information.

14. Quantitative and qualitative data

Research methods one and three are quantitative as they produce statistical data only. The second research method is qualitative as it involves collecting opinions and views from the people being interviewed.

15. Appropriate market research

The three key reasons are:
- customer needs are not understood from the outset;
- the wrong market research methodologies are being used;
- the data that are collected do not provide the information needed in a format that can be understood and used as a basis for future decision making.

16. Interpreting and analysing data

(a) The sample is far too small. It has no chance of representing the 1 million people. It is both invalid and unreliable.
(b) The example suggests using old data. The older the data, the less reliable they become. They might be valid, but they are unreliable.
(c) It is unlikely that the French and UK markets are the same. It is not valid and very unreliable.

17. Product life cycle

1   A business could identify the stage by looking at the sales figures and comparing them over a period of time.
2   Many businesses have products at various stages of the life cycle. Often they will introduce a replacement for a product near the end of its life cycle and sell both alongside one another.

18. Suitability of marketing aims and objectives

The three aims and objectives are:
- saving the indigenous Dartmoor pony
- maintaining the presence of these ponies on Dartmoor
- protecting our heritage.

19. Situational analysis

The business could:
- buy or make a deal with a competitor with leading technology
- invest in better recruitment and training
- diversify by developing a new range of products
- look for more reliable suppliers or demand better quality standards
- consider moving factory to a cheaper location.

20. Use of research data

The main competitors are Marks & Spencer and Next, Peacocks, H&M, Gap and the discount retailers B&M and TK Maxx.

21. Marketing mix

- Delicate products need protective packaging. Good examples are biscuits, Easter eggs and electrical goods.
- Customers need to be protected from products that could endanger them. Household cleaning products such as bleach is a good example. Cutlery and other kitchen products with sharp edges are also good examples.
- Most products need packaging to display their branding. Some packaging is deliberately designed to look different by using unusual shapes (Toblerone) or bright colours (Weetabix).
- Instructions and contents are included on all food and drink products as well as products such as toothpaste.

22. Pricing strategies

1   Customers will have an idea about the price they are prepared to pay for a product or service, based on the benefits that it will bring them and comparisons with similar products or services. Beyond a certain point they will be reluctant to purchase, regardless of the benefits.
2   Theoretically, a fall in price should see a rise in demand. A fall in price may simply lead to sales stabilising in a competitive market, where the competitors are already offering similar products or services at that lower price.

23. Promoting the product 1

Social media, magazines targeted at the same age groups, poster sites at transport hubs, instore advertising and promotion.

24. Promoting the product 2

Products and services that are either expensive or require a long-term commitment are most likely to benefit from personal selling. Good examples include: car sales, home buying, electrical and technology products, home improvements, holidays and restaurants (where waiting staff try to sell the most profitable products to the customers).

25. Promoting the product 3

'Engage with their customers' means communicating or interacting with customers.
'Generate sales leads' means using social media to find potential customers that can be contacted by the business.

26. Place and distribution

1   A direct distribution system involves a business, possibly a manufacturer, delivering products and services directly to the end user without the use of any intermediaries. Indirect distribution involves having at least one intermediary or partner in the supply chain between the manufacturer and the end user.

2   Technology businesses sell direct through their own websites to end users, but also have a sophisticated distribution chain which incorporates distributors, wholesalers and retailers. Book publishers and record companies sell direct through their own websites, have national and sometimes regional distributors, and their products are available in a wide variety of bricks-and-mortar and online retailers or re-sellers.

27. Extended marketing mix

The seven Ps are
- product: the physical features of the product, its purpose and use
- price: the price or price range for consumers and for other businesses
- place: how the product is distributed, and where or how it can be found or purchased
- promotion: deals and offers related to the product
- process: the procedures and mechanisms used to deliver customer service
- physical environment: where customer service takes place
- people: individuals that represent the business or product, and how they interact with customers.

28. Marketing messages

The marketing message needs to get across what the club is about and make use of the name – '365live music every night'.
The club needs to target the under-30s and offer live music to suit their tastes from different genres each night. Entry pricing should be low as most sales will be made at the bar and any food sold. Promotions should focus on posters and social media, good opportunity to use Instagram and other platforms. Place is covered by the location of the club; it should be convenient for most people being in the centre of the city.

29. Media and budgets

Social media is ideal as it gives the club the chance to directly engage with its customers. It can have an ongoing conversation and interaction with them. It can share 'live' stories and news, and advertise promotions at no cost to them.

30. Timelines and evaluation

It depends on many other factors. Raw figures suggest that the two things are linked. What you do not know is:
- whether prices have increased
- whether a competitor has closed down
- whether the business is offering a new product or service
- whether the economy is performing well and customers are more prepared to spend.

31. Appropriate marketing campaigns 1

Ben & Jerry's states that it has three key brand values:
- Its product mission focuses on the quality of the ice cream.
- Its economic mission focuses on managing the business in such a way as to ensure sustainable financial growth.
- Its social mission focuses on ensuring that the business uses innovative ways to make the world a better place.

All three link with the cleaner, greener freezer. By using Fairtrade ingredients, Ben & Jerry's can ensure the quality of its product and has a deal which promotes environmentally sound farming practices for the local communities.

32. Appropriate marketing campaigns 2

- A new competitor emerges during the campaign.
- A better or cheaper version of the product or service becomes available.
- New legislation means changes to the product, the advertising or costs.
- Demand drops due to economic problems.

33. Legal and ethical campaigns

The company may have received adverse publicity in the press and social media. If the social media campaign went viral, the resulting publicity could have badly damaged the brand. Some consumers may have called for a boycott, and the company could have been reported to the Advertising Standards Authority. To prevent this possible backlash and in the hope that it could limit the potential damage to its brand and reputation, the company may have decided to acknowledge its error of judgement by stopping the advertising campaign and apologising to consumers. This would go some way to restoring its reputation and also show customers that it listens to their views.

34. Your Unit 2 external assessment

Volvic Spring Water – focuses upon the purity of the product; healthy living – outdoors and youthful; freshness; contribution to physical and cognitive functions; up-market focus.
Irn-Bru – strong Scottish focus; sells the drink indirectly through 'seaside postcard' adverts; cheeky and rude; down-market focus.

35. Preparing for assessment

Skill	My strengths	What I need to improve	Actions
Research skills	I can use the internet to find relevant material.	I find it difficult to sort out the main points from all of my research notes.	Divide the material into manageable chunks and allocate to different sections of the task; review the smaller chunks and be ruthless with the material not required.
Analytical and evaluation skills	I can weigh up good and ineffective advertising (evaluation).	I find it difficult to analyse data and numbers, especially percentages.	Practise working out percentages from my research notes.
Time management skills	I complete written tasks on time.	I don't leave enough time to read through my work.	Practise writing a piece of work in a set period of time.
Presentation skills	I am creative and have high level presentation skills using computer software.	I spend too much time on the graphics and not enough time on the details of the task.	Review my past presentations and see how they could be improved.
Communications	I can present my ideas using good grammar; my spelling is a strong point.	I don't use enough marketing terminology in my written work.	Compile a glossary of marketing terms and see where they could have been included in my previous written work.

36. Part A: Preparing your support material

- How businesses in the industry have applied different elements of the marketing mix (and the extended marketing mix)
- The influence of the product life cycle on marketing and promotional activities in the industry
- How businesses in the industry use pricing strategies to achieve their marketing objectives (loss-leaders; skimming; penetration pricing; cost-plus pricing)

37. Part A: Research skills

Research questions	Information required	Source
Size of the soft drinks market	• Sales volume • Sales value	Trade associations (British Soft Drinks Association website: BSDA)
Composition of soft drinks market	• Proportion of market share taken by products • Demographic composition	BSDA
Competitor analysis in the soft drinks market	• Market leader(s): by % share, product and value • Barriers to entry	Company websites Trade journals BSDA
Market trends	• Increases/decreases in value • New products and growth areas • Impact of external factors e.g. government legislation and regulation	National consumer surveys Marketing journals e.g. *Marketing Week* Specialist websites e.g. www.just-drinks.com
Case studies of soft drinks companies	• Examples of innovative marketing strategies, e.g. use of social media • Establishing the marketing message; USP • Application of the marketing mix and the extended marketing mix	Company websites e.g. www.coca-cola.co.uk Company annual reports Newspapers Social media e.g. Facebook, Twitter, YouTube TV

38. Part A: Using your research

Impact of healthy lifestyles on the demand for food and drink

39. Part A: Analysing market research data

- High start-up costs
- Licences
- Health and safety legislation

40. Part A: Applying marketing principles

Market segmentation in the soft drinks market is dominated by four main areas – bottled water, still fruit juices, energy drinks and carbonated drinks.

The demographic profile of the target consumer for a premium priced healthy soft drink is likely to be a well-educated younger person with an active lifestyle in a higher income bracket who is most likely to be employed in a professional capacity.

41. Part B: Using additional information

ACTIVITY 1:

Aims and objectives: Financial and non-financial targets

Research data: Energy drinks market (in relation to soft drinks market); growth trends; main brands; target demographic of main brand.

Rationale: Growth area (energy drinks); increasing importance of healthy living; current energy drinks may be perceived as focusing on young active males; gap in the market for an energy drink aimed at young active females; note social responsibility aspect of the new drink.

ACTIVITY 2:

Determine marketing budget; map marketing activities against each marketing objective; allocate budget between each of the marketing activities; establish targets and milestones for each marketing activity.

42. Part B: Synthesising your ideas

Market size: Soft drinks market is valued at £15.7 billion in sales per year.

Growth: 5.3 per cent growth per annum in the energy drinks market

Demographics: Current demographic profile for energy drinks are teenage males with a fast-paced lifestyle; young mothers (growing demographic); potential gap in the market for energy drink aimed at young and active females.

43. Part B: Developing your campaign

Financial target: To achieve a sales turnover of £100 000 in the first year.

Non-financial target: To achieve a 'shelf presence' in two of the top five UK supermarkets within 3 years.

44. Part B: Costing the campaign

15 per cent of the total marketing budget (£60 000) is equal to £9000. With such a limited budget you would need to be creative in how you get the biggest impact so you need to think of ways which will generate an impact for a relatively small investment. Examples of internet marketing activities include:

- setting up a Facebook, Twitter or Pinterest account (all free)
- linking with the media department of a local college or university to see if students could be involved in making a short promotional film or designing a website
- online coupons or voucher offers
- free product to review online (via social media) plus access to email addresses to establish a customer database
- affiliate programme
- customised product websites
- web hosting
- managed website
- pay-per-click.

45. Part B: Presenting the campaign

- To establish our brand image on social media by getting 5000 Facebook followers within three months of the launch of the marketing campaign
- To increase the number of visitors to the company's website by 30 per cent within six months of the launch of the marketing campaign
- To sell an average of 1000 bottles per week by the end of Year 1.

Unit 3: Personal and Business Finance

46. Functions of money

Unit of account, means of exchange, store of value and legal tender

47. Role of money

Financial commitments could include a first car, holidays/travel, the first house, marriage, children, savings for future large purchases, etc.

48. Planning expenditure

The lender may give Ruksana some time to get a new job, but there will be fees or charges to pay. If she cannot recommence instalments then the car will be repossessed. It will have an impact on her credit rating. She will have had legal action taken against her and she will have got into debt.

49. Ways to pay 1

- Credit cards are physical or digital cards. They allow the use of a credit account. Online, the card number is entered. An authentication box requires the user to enter part of their password.
- Debit cards are physical or digital cards. They allow access to a debit account.
- Prepaid cards have a fixed maximum amount, the user has already transferred funds to the card.
- Gift cards represent a stored value of money. These are usually issued by either the merchant or by a bank.
- A loyalty card identifies the buyer when they make a transaction; the merchant can give rewards for repeat purchases.

50. Ways to pay 2

(a) These are used for regular payments such as salaries, pensions, state benefits and tax credits.

(b) These tend to be used to make large numbers of small value payments, such as bills, expenses, supplier payments and online transfers.

(c) This is a same-day payment method for high value transactions, such as property purchases.

51. Current accounts

1   The best current accounts are:
    (a) Packaged, premium account
    (b) Standard account
    (c) Basic account
    (d) Student account

2   You should not keep the same bank account throughout life because:
    - Your income will change as you progress throughout your life and some banks stipulate a minimum deposit amount per month to access certain accounts.
    - There's the opportunity to take up promotional offers from banks by switching accounts.
    - The items you buy will change as you grow older and you may require a higher overdraft amount at times.
    - Some benefits attached to bank accounts, for example, insurances and breakdown cover, are more relevant once you own houses, cars and other significant assets.

52. Borrowing

Gary needs to pay the capital of £900. In addition he needs to pay $9 \times £23.88$. He also has to pay $3 \times £15$ for defaulting on his payments three times.

£900 + £214.92 + £45 = £1159.92

53. Savings

Nigel paid £4014 for his shares. Nigel received 9p of dividends per share: $0.09 \times 1800 = £162$. The current value of his shares is £4950.

£162 + £4950 = £5012

£5012 – £4014 = £1098

Nigel would also have to pay a transaction fee to sell his shares.

54. Insurance

(a) travel; (b) car; (c) house; (d) contents

55. Financial institutions 1

- Customers can access their accounts at all times regardless of whether branches are open.
- Customers can use the automated systems which means that fewer staff are needed, in turn this means that the institution can use the savings to offer incentives for customers.
- Online customers are easier to handle and cost the business less to attract.
- The institution can design systems quickly to deal with problems or to provide additional services for customers.

56. Financial institutions 2

Alice could withdraw cash from either a current or savings account. She could also obtain a short-term loan from a payday loan company, or pawn an asset. The cheapest option is to use her own money (she might lose a small amount of interest if she withdraws money from a deposit account). Interest fees on the short-term loan could be expensive. She would also pay interest on the cash obtained from pawning her asset, which she may lose if she doesn't repay her debt to the pawnbroker.

57. Customer communication

- When the customer wants to either deposit or take out large sums of cash or deposit coins.
- Instances when the customer needs advice about financial products or services.
- When they need to sign documents or authorise payments.

58. Consumer protection

She has a 14-day cooling-off period where she can change her mind and cancel her agreement. It does however mean that she will either have to cancel her TV order or find another way of paying for it.

59. Consumer advice

- Citizens Advice – they are free, impartial and with good access. Advisers are volunteers and may not be financial professionals.
- Independent financial advisers (IFAs) – offer guidance on a range of financial products, protection from the FCA, but may suggest products that offer the IFA the best reward.
- Price comparison sites – free, accessed anytime, but may not have all the options that are available.
- The Money Advice Service – this is free, impartial with a wide range of advice and guidance. Service is only available online or phone.
- Debt counsellors – this is free and offers a wide range of guidance. They are regulated by the FCA.

60. Accounting

An accountant will look at various financial records and results of the business. This will include the gross and net profit, sales revenue, how well the business collects debts, its expenditure and its general costs.

61. Income

Capital income examples are (a), (b) and (f)

Revenue income examples are (c), (d) and (e)

62. Capital expenditure

Capital expenditure examples are (b), (c) and (f)

63. Revenue expenditure

Revenue expenditure examples are (a), (d) and (e)

64. Internal finance

The business intends to reinvest the retained profit. It may be developing new products or services or have made the decision to save the money to buy a major asset. Alternatively, it might have forecasted a poor financial period ahead and have chosen to retain the funds to see it over this period.

65. External finance 1

A fixed-interest rate loan means that the rate of interest is agreed at the beginning of the loan and remains the same throughout the duration of the loan.

A variable-interest rate loan has an interest rate that changes according to the base rate of interest. So it can go up or down.

A fixed-interest rate loan is more predictable and may be slightly more expensive if interest rates drop. A variable-rate loan may be cheaper but it could increase significantly if the interest rate rises.

66. External finance 2

Pavel could sell his own invoices to a third party (debt factoring). The factor agency will pay him the amount he is owed by his debtors (less a fee), allowing him to pay his creditors. He could also extend the time he has to pay his creditors by agreeing trade credit with them. He could also consider invoice discounting, whereby he borrows against the value of outstanding invoices for a fee.

67. Cash inflows

The only cash inflow mentioned is the cash sales of £25 000.

68. Cash outflows

Adejola sold the five chairs at £40 each, which is a total of £200 and the table for £95. This gives a total of £295. This was the only money that Adejola had received from the customer by the end of September. The customer still owed Adejola £210 on the second deal but this was not due until October.

69. Cash flow forecasts

His monthly inflow is £1200 + £1500 = £2700

Multiply this by 12 for the annual cash inflow of £32 400.

70. Costs and sales

$12\,000 \times £12.45 = £149\,400$

71. Break-even analysis

(a) A profit of £20 000 is made when sales have achieved 8000, as total costs are £44 000 and total revenue is £64 000.

(b) The margin of safety is 5000 units (as the break even point is at 3000 units). The margin of safety in total revenue is £41 000, compared to the break-even point of £24 000.

72. Using break-even

The business could:
- raise the selling price
- try to bring down fixed costs
- try to grow the market allowing them to sell more – meaning they spread the fixed costs further
- try to renegotiate with suppliers to get the variable costs down.

73. Statement of comprehensive income

$\dfrac{£22\,000}{12} = £1833$ per month

May to end of November = 7 months

$£1833 \times 7 = £12\,831$

Therefore, the prepayment was:

£22 000 – £12 831 = £9169

74. Statement of financial position 1

The list from most liquid to least liquid is:
- cash in safe
- bank balance
- debtors (assuming that the payments are due or due very soon)
- stock.

75. Statement of financial position 2

Despite not knowing whether they are current or non-current, you can still see that Erdem has net assets of £30 000. In other words, the business has a net value of at least £30 000. Erdem has been able to build up the assets of his business so that it exceeds its liabilities in the first 12 months. Effectively the £30 000 can be seen as his capital.

76. Statement of financial position 3

£12 750 – £250 = £12 500

$$\frac{£12\,500}{5} = £2500$$

You would therefore depreciate the asset by £2500 per year using the straight-line method.

77. Gross profit and mark-up

1   $\frac{\text{gross profit}}{\text{revenue}} \times 100 = \text{gross profit margin}$

Revenue is £500 000 − £50 000 = £450 000

Gross profit £450 000 − £100 000 = £350 000

$$\frac{£350\,000}{£450\,000} \times 100 = 77.7\,(78\%)$$

2   $\frac{\text{gross profit}}{\text{cost of sales}} \times 100 = \text{mark up}$

$$\frac{£12\,000}{(£96\,000 - £12\,000)} \times 100 = 14.28\,(14.3)\% = \text{mark up}$$

78. Profit margin and ROCE

1   $\frac{\text{profit}}{\text{capital employed}} \times 100 = \text{ROCE}$

Note that Rav actually invested £96 000 - £13 000 = £83 000 in his business, therefore:

$$\frac{£92\,000}{£83\,000} \times 100 = 110.8$$

2   $\frac{\text{profit}}{\text{revenue}} \times 100 = \text{net profit margin formula}$

$$\frac{£92\,000}{£226\,000} \times 100 = 40.7\%$$

79. Liquidity

(a) $\frac{\text{current assets}}{\text{current liabilities}} = \text{current ratio}$

(NB. Unsold stock is considered a current asset)

$$\frac{£77\,000}{£56\,000} = 1.37{:}1$$

This is less than the recommended 1.5:1 but sufficient to cover their short-term debt.

(b) $\frac{(\text{Current assets} - \text{inventory})}{\text{Current liabilities}} = \text{Liquid capital ratio}$

$$\frac{(£77\,000 - £22\,000)}{£56\,000} = 0.98{:}1$$

This shows that the business has insufficient assets to cover its short-term debt. This is a concern. The business will struggle to pay its short-term debts unless it can sell some of its stock.

80. Efficiency

$$\left(\frac{\text{Average inventory}}{\text{cost of sales}}\right) \times 365 = \text{inventory turnover}$$

$$\left(\frac{£3200}{£76\,450}\right) \times 365 = 15.2\ \text{days}$$

Fran turns her stock around every 15 days or so. In order to stay in stock she should visit the cash and carry supplier twice a month (just over two weeks between each visit).

81. Limitations of ratios

Ratios are number based, so there is no information about quality, customer service, employee motivation, etc. Ratios consider past figures and not future ones; this means that assumptions need to be made. They are useful when comparing performance over a period of time, but newer businesses do not have a history to consider. Financial figures can be massaged in the sense that it is possible to delay payments to creditors to show higher cash balances or to change invoice dates to show sales in different months.

82. Your Unit 3 external assessment

Questions which ask you to 'describe two factors' require you to include more detail when answering the question so that you show you understand the factors, whereas 'identify' questions only require you to recall facts.

83. Preparing for assessment

This is an extract from a sample revision schedule:

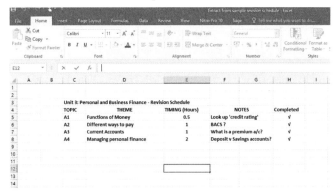

84. 'Give' or 'Identify' questions

Possible responses: owner's capital, retained profit, sale of business asset, bank loan, hire purchase.

85. 'Describe' or 'Outline' questions

A debenture is a form of IOU issued by a company to raise business finance. Debentures carry a fixed rate of interest, are paid before dividends are distributed and, unlike ordinary shares, do not carry voting rights.

86. 'Explain' questions

A person with a current account can arrange an 'overdraft facility' which allows them to exceed the amount of funds in their current account up to a set limit. It is the equivalent of a 'contingency fund' and when it is used requires the account holder to pay a rate of interest which can vary over time. A bank loan is a set amount of money which is repaid in regular instalments over a specific period of time with a fixed rate of interest.

87. 'Discuss' questions

The purpose of travel insurance is to compensate the policyholder and other family members in the event of financial loss or unforeseen circumstances. These financial losses and unforeseen circumstances are the risks which are insured in the insurance contract. For example, if family illness prevents the family from going on holiday, the insurance policy will compensate the policyholder who will receive a sum of money equivalent to the cost of the holiday. If flights are delayed compensation will also be payable and if, while on holiday, one of the family has an accident then the policy will cover medical expenses. It should be noted however that if none of the insured risks arise, then the insurance premiums will not be returned to the policyholder and therefore insurance costs should be taken into account when calculating the total cost of the holiday.

88. 'Calculate' questions

Liquid capital ratio $= \dfrac{\text{current assets} - \text{inventory}}{\text{current liabilities}}$

$= \dfrac{20\,000 - 10\,000}{5000}$

$= 2$

89. 'Analyse' questions

Trade receivables is money owed to the business by customers and therefore has a direct influence on the sales turnover which, in turn, impacts upon profit levels. Many businesses provide credit facilities to their customers so that they do not have to pay for their goods upon receipt and will be allowed a set period of time within which to settled their debts. This can be advantageous to the seller because it may result in additional sales, increased sales turnover and higher profit levels in the future. However controls need to be put in place to ensure that buyers who are provided with credit facilities have a good credit history of paying their bills on time and not defaulting on their debts. If credit controls are poor and businesses do not pay their invoices on time then cash flow could be affected. This in turn could impact upon the availability of working capital. If irrecoverable debts (bad debts) arise and customers default this will impact upon profit levels since the cost of sales will not be matched by sales revenue. The business's statement of financial position will also be adversely affected since the impact of irrecoverable debts is to reduce the value of the business's current assets.

90. 'Assess' questions

The aim of business planning is to ensure that the resources available to a business are utilised as efficiently as possible in order to achieve its business objectives which are likely to centre upon sales turnover, market growth and profitability. Since the business operates in an environment of risk it uses a number of business models and planning tools to inform its decisions and break-even analysis is part of this 'toolbox', using an analysis of its fixed and variable costs to determine the level of output, sales and price at which it will break even (not make a loss or profit). It follows that sales above the break-even point will generate profit. Break-even analysis is therefore important in the planning process because it enables a business to identify the impact of different levels of costs, output and price on the break-even point. This can result in a business putting in place cost control measures which will influence the break-even point since higher fixed costs, for example, will lead to a higher break-even point. Using break-even analysis will also enable a business to set targets for the sales and marketing function and can be incorporated into a formal business plan to be presented to potential investors.

The main limitations of break-even analysis centre upon the assumptions made regarding costs, output and price. For example, variable costs are unlikely to stay the same at different output levels because a business may be able to negotiate discounts for bulk purchases which will impact upon its costs. This same principle applies to a business's own product which it may offer at a discount price when the product is first launched as well as discounts for bulk purchases when it is established in the market. Planning is further complicated if a business produces more than one product.

However, despite these limitations of break-even analysis it does focus business decision makers to calculate business costs as accurately as possible and to perform relatively straightforward calculations which provide quick estimates and helpful insights into different scenarios.

91. 'Evaluate' questions

Measuring business performance provides business owners, managers and decision makers with the necessary information to assess how far they have achieved their strategic objectives and operational targets. Measuring business performance can also be used to compare a business's performance against industry benchmarks and can be the stimulus for introducing efficiency measures to reduce unit costs and increase productivity. Both of these will influence the potential for long-term profitability and increased shareholder value. Business performance is also a key factor in the investment decisions made by potential providers of capital.

Ratios for profitability, liquidity and efficiency are all used to measure different elements of business performance. Profit margins for example can be used to identify the profit generated from selling one unit of output whereas the current ratio identifies a business's ability to meet its short-term liabilities which is an important measure of a business's liability.

However, despite the positive contribution of ratios to the assessment of business performance, they do have their limitations. For example for those firms who operate different divisions in different industries it may be difficult to find a set of industry-average ratios. The impact of inflation over time can distort ratio analysis because it will impact on the real-value of profits over time. Different accounting practices can also impact on ratio analysis. For example the value of a business's inventory, used in the calculation of inventory turnover, will be influenced by the method used to calculate the value of the inventory (FIFO, LIFO). It is also likely that different ratios for different measures of profitability, liquidity and efficiency may result in both 'good' and 'poor' ratios making it difficult to draw an overall judgement on a business's performance.

Overall, ratios are a good starting point in assessing the performance of a business over time and in comparison to its business rivals and overall industry benchmarks. In addition, since much of the data used in ratio analysis are drawn from a business's financial statements, ratios are a good way of analysing and interpreting the information in a business's statement of comprehensive income, its statement of financial position.

Unit 6: Principles of Management

92. Management and leadership

A manager is responsible for supervising or directing employees and other resources. A manager will also put action plans in place for their team and set them targets to meet and then monitor whether or not they were met. They will conduct appraisals and agree rewards and bonuses.
A leader may also do this, but they will have a vision and a driving personality that aims to create dynamic teams and accomplish goals. Their aim is to inspire and succeed. They can create or change the culture within their team and are usually the driving force behind the immediate working environment. They can improve the success of their team by being inspirational and delivering motivational speeches. This can in turn empower their employees to become more creative and independent when it comes to dealing with problems in the workplace.

93. Management functions

It would probably be planning. The process of creating a plan is a fundamental skill because it will tell the manager the resources that are needed, when they will be needed and how they should be used.

94. Leadership functions

Leaders are able to change the course of an organisation. They are able to overcome resistance to change. Investors can recognise the importance of good leadership. They know that a good leader can make a success out of what may seem to be a hopeless situation. A poor leader, on the other hand, can quickly turn success into failure.

95. Business culture

Business culture is about creating a system of shared values and beliefs about what is important. It also identifies appropriate behaviours and how relationships inside the organisation and external to it are handled. The values and cultures are unique to each organisation. They do need to be widely shared and they need to reflect the daily practice of the organisation. Although there is no single best culture to adopt it needs to reflect the business's purpose and strategy. These are the main advantages to adopting a particular business culture:

- Uniform working environment for all colleagues makes it easier for staff to work in different areas or outlets of the same company.
- A particular culture might suit the demographics of your workforce better such as Google having an informal culture in their organisation allowing their employees to be more creative.
- Some business cultures are expected in certain industries, for example, accountancy firms usually have a formal culture and the customers would be wary if they didn't.

96. Management and leadership styles 1

The local manager and employees have a much better understanding of the local market and customer needs. They will also be able to make decisions and respond to customer problems without delaying decisions as a result of having to refer to senior management. The local branches would have to work within certain parameters and have limited freedom in order to ensure customer satisfaction and sort out problems as they arise.

97. Management and leadership styles 2

They can all be seen as ways of multiskilling the workforce. Each of them broadens out the job that the individual was originally employed to carry out. Each time the employee is given an opportunity they will pick up new skills, experience and abilities that can be used by the organisation. In this way the employee benefits from a more varied and rewarding job while the organisation benefits from a workforce with enhanced skills and abilities, as well as job satisfaction.

98. Management and leadership styles 3

Coaching is making an effort to provide formal or informal training and support to employees. It means guiding them through a learning process that aims to help them develop their career potential. Coaching allows a more personalised and effective means of training. The usual benefits of coaching are as follows:

- Direct and specific training tailored for the job.
- The employees feel settled more quickly in the role.
- Fewer mistakes being made by the new employee as they have access to experienced colleagues from the outset.
- The employee's confidence in their own abilities being gained more quickly.

99. Leadership skills

The main problem is that once employees know how she does this they will be suspicious of positive feedback, knowing that they are about to get some negative feedback. As a result, they may not focus on the positive but be waiting for the negative.

100. Human resources

HR would have to compete with other organisations to attract the best employees. It would have to offer better pay or working conditions. As unemployment falls, those with skills find work quicker than those without skills. For employers this would mean having to take on unskilled or semi-skilled workers and then training them to fulfil more complicated roles at work.

101. Human resource planning 1

The organisation should consider what it is it wants to accomplish by testing and then find the right test. It wants to be able to improve its hiring process and increase the chance of matching the right person with the right job. A good aptitude test will highlight talents, strengths and limitations.

102. Human resource planning 2

(a) For businesses that have unpredictable demands, zero-hours contracts are ideal if extra employees need to be brought in at short notice. It is also seen as a way of keeping valuable employees that might want to go from full-time to part-time work.

(b) It gives employees flexibility to choose to work or not, particularly if they have other commitments such as education or care responsibilities.

103. Human resource planning 3

$$\frac{120\,000}{8} = 15\,000 \text{ bricks laid per employee per month}$$

What this means is that 15 000 is the average. It does not take into account the fact that one bricklayer may be laying 17 000 and another 13 000. In order to work this out more accurately each worker would have to be observed over the course of a few days to work out their average output.

104. Human resource planning 4

1 The total number of potential working hours is 235 hours per person per year (47 weeks × 5 days). For 38 employees the total annual working hours are:
235 × 38 = 8930
Therefore:
$$\frac{612}{8930} \times 100 = 6.85\%$$

2 Suggested responses might include: minor illnesses, e.g. coughs, colds, flu, sickness, diarrhoea; headaches and migraines; back pain, neck pain and other musculoskeletal problems; toothache; heart, blood pressure; stress, anxiety, depression; serious mental health problems; respiratory conditions, e.g. asthma, pneumonia; gastrointestinal problems; pregnancy and other female-related health issues; accidents and infectious diseases; caring duties, e.g. child/elderly/disabled relative; issues within the work environment, e.g. bullying, lack of motivation. (Source of illness categories: Office for National Statistics, 'Full Report: Sickness in the Labour Market, February 2014', 25.2.2014)

105. Maslow and Herzberg

- By varying work within a team, to broaden skill sets and ensure variety where possible.
- By giving them the ability to control their own work.
- By ensuring that they are receiving competitive pay.

106. Taylor and Mayo

The main thing is to consider the fact that not everyone can work to the same pace. Some may be more expert or have greater dexterity. Some are fast and others take their time but still get the job done. Some will look for opportunities to vary the way they do their work to make it less boring. Humans also need a break and they may be interrupted. Money does not always motivate employees. Below is a list of other ways to motivate employees:

- Better terms in their contract of employment
- A greater number of annual leave days
- The prospect of promotion
- Being given more responsibility
- Being involved with the day-to-day operations in the business.
- Meeting their social and emotional needs

107. Motivating employees

It locks the employee into a long-term relationship with the bank. They will lose their preferential rates if they leave the bank. They would have to renegotiate their loan or mortgage. Their choices of alternative employer may be limited to those that offer similar benefits or incentives.

108. Skills requirements

It could use a combination of techniques including recruitment, upskilling, reskilling, training, outsourcing and changing job roles.

109. Training

On-the-job training takes place in the working environment. Off-the-job training involves work release to a training provider. Skills acquired with on-the-job training:

- Direct and specific advice for that job role
- Specific product/service knowledge
- Usual working practices within that business culture

Skills acquired with off-the-job training:

- An unbiased approach to dealing with commonplace issues in that job role
- Alternative knowledge about products and services being offered generally within the industry
- An opportunity to see how other businesses adapt their working environment to get the best possible outcomes for the product or service

110. Performance appraisal

- It should give the employee enough time to prepare.
- It should have a suitable private location.
- Previous targets and appraisals should be discussed.
- A summary and a set of outcomes should be agreed.
- An action plan should be drawn up.
- Explore the possibility of gaining more qualifications to assist the employee in their role.
- The employee should have the opportunity to give feedback on the way they are managed.

111. Types of appraisal

Self-assessment would work well as the first stage of a face-to-face system, but on its own it is not supportive enough. Ratings scales are very subjective and if there is a problem between the manager and the employee then this would be a very unfair appraisal system to use.

A 360° appraisal seems to offer many advantages. It encourages honesty and openness, as it is a two-way appraisal system.

112. Impact of appraisals

There are many advantages, which include:

- They provide a record of employee performance.
- They provide a structured conversation about performance.
- They allow the manager to provide feedback and discuss goals and whether they have been accomplished.
- They provide an opportunity for managers to clarify expectations.
- They provide a structure to plan ahead and develop employee goals.
- They motivate employees if there is a link between performance and remuneration.

113. Managing change

They know that the increased competition will affect their business. There are a limited number of buyers in the area and some will choose to buy from the new competitors. In order to compete the existing businesses will probably have to drop their prices. The fear will be that this change will mean that some of the existing businesses will be forced to close as they will be unable to compete.

114. Stakeholders and change

They will begin by looking at individuals and groups that may be directly or indirectly affected by their actions. They will then begin to categorise them and determine how much influence they have. They will also try to work out what their current attitude is toward the business.

115. Quality standards

Job satisfaction brings a more dedicated and motivated workforce that is more productive. It also aids employee retention, which means that employee turnover is reduced. All of these issues make the business more productive and more profitable.

116. Quality culture

Advantages

- It should provide the business with a shortcut, providing it can find out sufficient information about how the competitor operates.
- It should be able to learn from the mistakes that the competitor has made.
- It should be aware of quality issues that the competitor suffers from and try to avoid these.

Disadvantages

- It may find it difficult to replicate systems and procedures.
- It may find that its products and services are actually very different.
- It may find that the systems used are not relevant, affordable or desirable.

117. Quality management

Because it relies on the suppliers to hold stock for it and the suppliers need to be very fast at responding to orders for stock to keep the manufacturing process running smoothly. It also needs to make sure that its quality control is kept to a consistently high standard.

118. Benefits of quality management

If the business is in any way interested in total quality management then it will be looking for quality, reliability, good customer service, excellent communications and a partnership approach as well as a reasonable price.

119. Your Unit 6 external assessment

- Be clear on what you are being asked to present.
- Read carefully through the case study material.
- Manage your time between the set tasks.
- Check that you have covered all the points you are required to cover in the activity.

120. Part A: Approaching the case study

- Herzberg – motivation-hygiene theory: motivation factors – can bring about positive satisfaction (responsibility, recognition, achievement); hygiene factors 'dissatisfiers' – prevent dissatisfaction (salary, working conditions)
- Maslow – Hierarchy of Needs: from lower order (security/safety) to highest order of need (self-actualisation); notion of progression through each level
- Mayo: importance of work groups and status within work groups; influence of informal (unofficial work groups)

121. Part A: Preparing your notes

- Planning: establish a clear 'management message' and vision which will be communicated at each stage of the merger process; establish clear SMART targets and milestones; identify personnel responsibilities and reporting arrangements; identify potential risks to implementation
- Monitoring: establish accountability and responsibility among key managers with clear reporting lines (who?); monitoring timescales reporting procedures for each specific target (what?); monitoring timescales and review dates (when?)

122. Part A: Analysing data

Cannot identify trends; cannot identify if there have been any significant changes in one of the variables which make up the data set

123. Part A: Analysing management information

Competition involves independent businesses trying to attract consumers to purchase their goods in preference to their business rivals. Businesses compete on the basis of influences such as price and quality. Competitive pressure in the market is reduced when a merger takes place because there is one less business rival in the market. The resulting larger firm may have greater opportunities to reduce unit costs (as a result of purchasing economies and other efficiency savings) and therefore more power to influence market price by passing on efficiency savings to the consumer in the form of lower prices.

124. Part A: Identifying management principles

Transformational leadership – sets clear goals; high expectations; inspires; gets people to look beyond their own self-interest

125. Part B: Completing the set task

- Human resources – increase in workplace stress
- Recommendation – bring in external consultant to work with work groups
- Potential benefit – increase in long-term job security for the workforce
- Risks – key personnel may leave as a result of the uncertainty of the outcome of the merger

126. Part B: Formal report

Title of report	Review of the proposed merger of Bradbury plc and Bestle plc
Author	A Business Student
To	The Editor, *The Business Journal*
Date	3 July 2017
Status	Information

1. Introduction
   1.1 The purpose of this Report is to:
      (i) Provide a commentary to the proposed merger of Bradbury plc and Bestle plc
      (ii) Consider the potential benefits and risks of the proposed merger
      (iii) Present a set of recommendations regarding:
         (a) business risks of the proposed merger
         (b) the structure of the merged business.

127. Part B: Presentation

BUSINESS PROFILES

BRADBURY PLC
- Gross Profit £559m
- Market share 31%
- +/- Market share -2%
- Workforce 1,200
- Gender profile 60% female
- Av. Length of service 15yrs
- Age profile 36-59yrs

BESTLE PLC
- Gross Profit £225m
- Market share 11%
- +/- Market share +5%
- Workforce 600
- Gender profile 70% female
- Av. Length of service 5yrs
- Age profile 18-35yrs

ALWAYS LEARNING   PEARSON

Speaker notes
- Bradbury plc is the bigger company (gross profit; market share and workforce)

- Bradbury plc's market share is falling (–2%) compared to that of Bestle plc (+5%)
- Bradbury plc's workforce is older and has a longer average length of service than that of Bestle plc (potential impact of the merger on the workforce in each company may be different, e.g. older workers may find the impact of the merger more challenging to deal with)

Unit 7: Business Decision Making

128. Business ideas
- To promote market growth
- To reduce business risk
- To complement other products in the product range

129. Purpose and structure
- Shorter chain of command
- Business may become more responsive to changes in consumer demand
- Lower management costs
- Senior managers have a better understanding of operational workplace issues
- Develops team spirit
- Managers have greater freedom to make decisions
- Managers may become more motivated

130. Data sources

	Year-on-year increase in sales growth over 3 years	% growth in sales over 3 years	Average sales per sales rep	% growth in average sales per sales rep
North region	+£29 820	+19.88%	Year 1: £75 000 Year 2: £81 000 Year 3: £89 910	Year 1–Year 2: +8% Year 2–Year 3: +11%
South region	+£26 796	+8.12%	Year 1: £110 000 Year 2: £116 600 Year 3: £118 932	Year 1–Year 2: +6% Year 2–Year 3: +2%

Conclusions:
- appears to be greater growth potential in the North region than the South region since % growth in sales over the three-year period has increased year-on-year in the North while in the South it has increased at a slower rate
- may need to undertake a market analysis in the South (increase in competitive pressures? mature market?)
- increase number of sales representatives in the North region to exploit market growth
- review sales targets for sales reps in the South region.

131. Business models 1

Product	Barriers to entry	Degree of rivalry	Bargaining powers of suppliers	Bargaining power of customers	Number of substitutes
Mobile phones	Medium/High	High	Low	High	Low
Car manufacturers	High	High	Low/Medium	Medium/High	Low/Medium
Food retailing	Low/Medium	High	Low	High	High
Fashion industry	Low	High	Low	High	High

132. Business models 2

The Delaware Corporation could use the Ansoff Matrix to consider its growth strategy moving forward. The new tablet computer could generate growth in sales of the new product in the existing market (product development); opportunities could also exist to target consumers in the existing market (market penetration). Resources to support the development and marketing of the new product could be generated by ceasing production of 'dogs' (Boston Consulting Group Matrix) with the aim of making the tablet computer a 'star' with high market share and the potential for future market growth until such time as it matures and becomes a 'cash cow'. The company will need to give careful consideration to its marketing strategy and could use the 5Cs marketing model to construct a well-defined marketing strategy based upon a determination of the needs of the customer, conducting a company SWOT analysis, reviewing competitive pressures on the market, identifying the possibility of partnering suppliers or distributors and undertaking a PESTLE analysis to determine if there are any factors which will limit the company's operations.

133. Representative values

The mean is calculated as $14 + 47 + 63 + 20 = \dfrac{144}{4} = 36$.

The sales manager would find it useful to know the total value of sales generated by each payment method and the average sales value per transaction using the different payment methods. This information could be used to inform the company's marketing strategy. For example, the business might adapt its promotional offers to suit the preferred payment method from the customers to the business. The way people pay for their goods can give an insight into their demographics and make it easier to predict their spending habits. This allows the business to tailor its promotions accordingly.

134. Analysing data

Lowest quartile:–1 Standard deviation: the business sales performance is below the industry average
Customer satisfaction percentile score of 47%: the company's customer satisfaction rating is higher than 47% of all other similar companies (or below that for 53% of similar companies).
Correlation score of 0: this means that there is no correlation between the number of people visiting the company's website and the number of sales generated from the website.

135. Presenting data

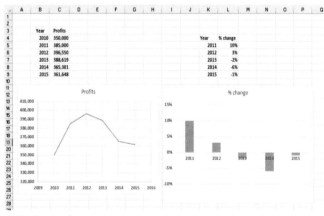

- Easier to view
- Shows trends
- Easy to quantify using the y axis

136. Information and decision making

- Senior managers: decide the location of the new factory and consider the costs and its contribution to the business's long-term strategic objectives. They will require a detailed financial analysis and comparative data on different locations.

- Middle managers: once the decision has been taken on the location of the factory, middle managers will decide the resources required to operate the factory in their respective functional areas based upon their allocated budget. They will require information on resource costs, supplier lists and the various finance options available.

137. Project management and financial tools

The opportunity cost of the investment decision is the foregone alternatives. In this case, if the business re-equips the existing factory the opportunity cost it forgoes will be the new factory as well as all the other things it could have purchased with the money. Since the business would achieve a rate of interest of 8 per cent if the investment funds were placed into an interest-bearing account, it would be unwise to invest in the new factory since the internal rate of return (IRR) of 7.5 per cent is below the current market rate of interest. However, re-equipping the existing factory would generate an IRR of 8.5 per cent which is above the current market interest rate. The business would therefore be advised to invest in re-equipping the existing factory premises.

138. Market research

It will be required to carry out primary research that relates specifically to its product such as questionnaires, surveys, focus groups, product testing, etc.
It will also rely on secondary research relating mainly to the targeted consumer group and the competition such as online reviews, product sales information, etc.

139. Competitor analysis

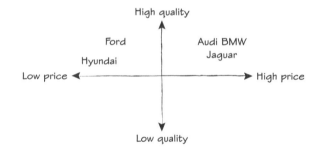

140. Trends

Economic trends: High street stores are expensive to operate; on-line shopping channels may provide opportunities for cost savings and additional sales revenue.
Market trends: Consumers are demanding 24/7 access to retail outlets to place their orders.
Social trends: Consumers have access to computers and mobile technology which allows them access to the internet.

141. Marketing plan

Apple iPhone 6s: screen size; 3D touch; 4K video; 12MP photos

142. The seven Ps

- Product: vegetarian/ethnic/number of items on the menu
- Price: value meals/specialist creations
- Place: high street/out-of-town shopping centre/in-store
- Promotion: vouchers/price reductions for dining early in the evening
- Physical environment: cleanliness/design
- Process: online bookings/ease of ordering
- People: well-trained and qualified staff/specialist staff in key positions (receptionist/restaurant manager/bar manager)

143. Legislation 1

- Identify the purpose of the job: be clear that the job will not result in a member of the workforce being displaced because it could result in a claim of constructive dismissal.

- Prepare a job and person profile: ensure that the person specification does not discriminate on the grounds of gender, ethnicity or other aspects covered by the Equality Act.
- Finding candidates: make sure that the current workforce is aware of the vacancy; otherwise there is a risk that members of the workforce will consider they are not being treated fairly or equally.
- Managing the application process: ensure that the shortlisting process is based upon the person specification; otherwise unsuccessful applicants could make a claim against the business on the grounds of unequal treatment.
- Selecting candidates: retain any interview notes in the event that an unsuccessful candidate claims unfair treatment.
- Making an appointment: ensure that the successful applicant meets the needs of the person specification as closely as possible; otherwise there is a risk of discrimination claims.
- Induction: include health and safety policies; otherwise there is a risk that an employee could claim for personal injury in the event of an accident in the workplace.

144. Legislation 2
- Security risks (hacking)
- Technical risks (system may break down)
- Legal risks (business may not adhere to the requirements of Data Protection legislation)

145. Quality issues
- Negative elements: Impact on costs: staff training costs; employment costs of specialist staff (quality controllers); process costs (management information systems and analysis); management time (additional time spent in meetings and monitoring activities); accreditation costs (fees to maintain quality kite marks)
- Positive elements: Fewer defective goods; less waste of raw materials; greater productivity; improved customer loyalty and retention; positive impact on business culture; increased sales and sales turnover; higher profit margins

On balance the benefits of quality systems outweigh the costs although, as with all costs, quality systems should be subject to the same level of cost control and scrutiny as other areas of the business.

146. Human resources
- Conduct a skills audit to identify any skills gaps in the workforce.
- Review staff training opportunities.
- Introduce a new wage structure based upon productivity targets.

147. Physical resources
- Premises: security costs
- Equipment: warranties
- Vehicles: servicing costs
- IT: training costs

148. Purchasing decisions
Trade credit enables the business to acquire goods now and pay for them later which assists cash flow.
Suppliers offer trade credit in order to generate additional sales.

149. Financial resources
- Commercial mortgage: this would create a non-current asset on the statement of financial position; the mortgage payments would be a business expense to be set against any gross profits.
- Overdraft or business loan: these could provide funds to make a deposit on rented business premises; this would be a business expense to be set against any gross profit but would not increase the assets of the business.
- Angel investors or venture capitalists: this may result in the owner having to give up some equity in the business which will impact upon their share of any distributed profits.

150. Sales forecast
Sales promotions; seasonal demand; introduction of a new product; withdrawal of a product or service; planned new contract; end of an existing contract

151. Cash flow forecast
Copstone plc's planned labour costs for the period January–July are £681 000 with planned sales of £1 040 000. This means that labour costs are 65 per cent of planned sales against the industry average of 60 per cent. This could mean that the business is at a competitive disadvantage compared to its competitors who are generating a proportionately greater volume of sales turnover from their workforce. Copstone plc should review workforce numbers and wage rates to identify potential reductions in labour costs; review its marketing strategy to identify new markets; look to secure efficiencies in its purchasing operations which could result in lower costs that could be passed on to the consumer in the form of lower prices (which may influence the level of demand and sales turnover).

152. Break-even chart
Unit costs (the cost, on average, of producing one unit of output) fall as output increases since fixed costs are being spread over a larger number of units.

153. Income statement 1
(a)

	£	£
Sales		**29 550**
Less cost of sales		
Opening stock	2410	
Purchases	18 000	
Less closing stock	2500	17 910
Gross profit		**11 640**
Less operating costs		
Wages	8420	
Transport	490	
Utilities	590	
Rent and rates	1160	
Stationery	80	10 740
Operating/net profit		**900**

(b) Gross profit margin = 39.4%
Net profit margin = 3.0%

154. Income statement 2
Increase sales revenue; reduce cost of sales; reduce operating costs

155. Statement of financial position 1
The £30 000 loan will be identified as a non-current liability on the statement of financial position which will be balanced by the increase in the value of non-current assets on the SOFP as a result of purchasing a new company vehicle.

156. Statement of financial position 2
Total assets of £38 000 against total liabilities of £7000 shows that the business is viable.
Breaking this down into short-term current assets and liabilities the working capital to pay short-term obligations is £6000 (current assets – current liabilities). Additionally the current ratio is 2.2:1 (current assets ÷ current liabilities) which shows that current liabilities can be 'covered' 2.2 times which is generally considered to make the business viable in the short term. However, it should be noted that the figure for current assets includes £7000 of stock (inventory) which is less liquid and, in addition, the value of debtors (trade receivables) currently stands at £3500 some of which may convert into irrecoverable debts (bad debts). The level of cash stands at £500 which is a cause for concern particularly when set against the high proportion of stock within the overall total of current assets. The business is profitable with the SOFP showing retained profit of £5000.

157. Calculating ratios

Gross profit, net profit, sales turnover, assets, liabilities, inventory, capital, cost of sales, productivity, labour rates

158. Interpreting ratios

- Number of defective goods per thousand produced
- Number of customer complaints per hundred purchases
- Value of bad debts as a percentage of sales turnover

159. Threats and 'what if?'

- Price cutting (offensive)
- Promotional activities (offensive)
- Efficiency savings and cost control (defensive)

160. Contingency plans

Consider business risks in three categories – legal, reputational and financial.
Then consider how to transfer some of these risks to an insurance company:

- Legal: employers' liability insurance (in the event of injury to an employee); motor insurance policies (in the event of an accident involving a third party)
- Reputational: public and product liability insurances (in the event of injury to an individual or damage to their property caused by the actions of the business (or its employees) or the product it sells)

- Financial: business interruption insurance (in the event of events such as fire and flood damage)

161. Using IT skills

Month	Total Sales
January	£200,000
February	£250,000
March	£175,000
April	£215,000
May	£220,000
June	£300,000

162. Your Unit 7 external assessment

- Business plan
- Latest audited income statement
- Statement of financial position for current business
- Cash flow forecast for new business
- Forecast income statement for new business

163. Making business decisions

Example response:

Skill	My strengths	What I need to improve	Actions
Ability to interpret data	I can input data into spreadsheet software and construct charts.	I find it difficult to use data to calculate financial ratios.	Practise performing calculations for profitability, efficiency and liquidity.
Ability to compare different data sets	I can interpret graphs to identify trends based upon more than one data set.	I don't understand inventory turnover.	Read through inventory turnover notes and practise calculations.
Ability to predict consequences	I can understand how changes in costs and revenue can impact upon a business's income statement.	I don't know how to interpret a statement of financial position (SOFP).	Revise SOFP, and link with calculations of performance ratios.
Ability to identify faulty arguments	I can identify faulty arguments which are linked to revenue.	I need to understand how different types of costs can impact upon the business.	Revise break-even analysis and prepare break-even charts using different cost data.
Ability to provide reasonable alternatives	I can provide alternatives relating to proposed marketing and human resources strategies of a business.	I need to be able to apply business models when identifying alternatives.	Practise applying the Ansoff Matrix and the Boston Consulting Group Matrix to different business scenarios. Use flow charts or mind maps to identify alternatives.
Ability to evaluate and justify proposed solutions	Can weigh up different business solutions to a problem.	Find it difficult to justify a solution to a problem.	Read through case study notes to see how justifications to business solutions can be structured.

164. Background information

Business decisions involve taking risks and in order to reduce the impact of these risks a business needs as much information as possible. This can include analysing hard data on aspects such as costs and revenue (quantitative information) but should also take account of information that is not based upon hard data (qualitative information) but is more concerned with making subjective judgements relating to trends and predictions.

165. Interpretation of data

Trends in profits over time; profitability ratios; profitability performance against business targets; analysis of cost structure including commentary on how costs are controlled within the business; explanations of any increases in costs; industry benchmarks

166. Comparing information and data

Identify value of current and non-current assets; how depreciation has been calculated; identify current and non-current liabilities; commentary on non-current assets (liabilities payable over more than one year) identifying the nature of any long-term loans and the financial commitments involved (payment structure; length of loan); liquidity ratios relating to working capital; ROCE

167. Predicting consequences

- Insufficient details included in the financial statements: unable to identify ratios for the profitability and liquidity of the business
- Over-optimistic cash flow forecast: may result in over-optimistic profit targets and other financial targets
- Non-current liabilities of £16 000: represents a long-term financial commitment; if it is a business loan it becomes the equivalent of a fixed cost which must be paid whatever the level of sales turnover
- No performance trends: unable to identify if the business's performance is an upwards or downwards trajectory
- No industry benchmarks provided: can't compare the business's performance with other similar businesses in the sector

168. Identifying faulty arguments

- Sales forecast argument: should be realistic and be based on an analysis of robust market research data, e.g. analysis of local demographic trends; local competitor analysis; independent market research produced by specialist market research company
- Net profit argument: provide details of net profit over a three-year period to identify trend in net profit over time; compare net profit with industry average; compare net profit with business targets; use performance ratios to identify gross and net profit margins

169. Recommending alternatives

A recognised brand has already been created; a strong marketing strategy; established corporate image and identity; training provided; quality standards in place; purchasing economies; equipment provided

170. Formal report

Preparing a business report:

Title of Report	Review of Grant Application
Author	A Business Student
To	Local Councillors
Date	3 July 20X8
Status	Information

1. Introduction
    1.1 The purpose of this Report is:
        (i) To present the case prepared by the owners of the Eastern Fusion snack bar for a £20 000 grant to finance the opening of a new restaurant
        (ii) To present an analysis of the information provided in the application
        (iii) To evaluate the business proposal
        (iv) To propose a decision.

171. Business plan

Application for a business grant
Applicants: Ms Prema Patel and Mr John Foster
Business plan

1. BACKGROUND INFORMATION
    1.1 This Business Plan provides details of the business case for a new restaurant to be opened in the town centre in vacant commercial premises adjacent to the 'Eastern Fusion' snack bar which is owned by Ms Prema Patel and Mr John Foster.
    1.2 The new restaurant would build upon the market presence which has already been established by the existing business and would offer a menu based upon the notion of 'fusion food' which blends together different aspects of foods from around the world.
    1.3 The new restaurant will build upon the business experience of the owners and offers an excellent opportunity for investors to participate in an innovative business venture.
    1.4 The initial funds to commence the first phase of the development of the business will be to secure a grant of £20 000 from the local Council which will be used as the deposit to purchase business premises.

172. Business presentation

FINANCIAL DATA

DOCUMENTS PRESENTED	MOST RECENT PERFORMANCE (CURRENT BUSINESS)
Income statement for current business	
Statement of Financial Position for current business	Gross profit £50,000
	Net profit £14,000
	Working capital £5,000
Cash Flow Forecast for proposed new business	Owner's equity £3,000
	Total assets £38,000
	Total liabilities £21,000

Speaker notes:
- Gross profit = revenue – cost of sales
        = £80,000 – £30,000
        = £50,000
- Net profit = Gross profit – operating expenses
        = £50,000 – £36,000
        = £14,000
- Working capital = £5,000 (note: includes stock – are there potential cash flow problems?)
- Non-current liabilities are relatively high (£16,000) – long-term loan?

173. Executive summary

It is difficult to present a sound rationale for supporting this application although there are other alternatives that could be considered including franchising, bringing on board additional investors, renting rather than purchasing business premises, reviewing the legal status of the business or expanding the services offered by the Eastern Fusion snack bar. On balance, it is suggested that a smaller grant is made available to the applicants that would enable them to expand their current business in order to determine the size of the potential market, test out new products, establish a market presence and re-evaluate the potential profitability moving forward. (100 words)